THE AIRCRAFT TREASURES OF
SILVER HILL

An edition printed especially for the
Contributing Members of The Smithsonian
National Associate Program

THE AIRCRAFT TREASURES OF

Books by Walter J. Boyne

FLYING: AN INTRODUCTION TO FLIGHT

AIRPLANES AND AVIATION CAREERS

MESSERSCHMITT ME 262: AN ARROW TO THE FUTURE

BOEING B-52: A DOCUMENTARY HISTORY

THE JET AGE: FORTY YEARS OF JET AVIATION,
    Edited with Donald S. Lopez

SILVER HILL

The Behind-the-Scenes Workshop of the
National Air and Space Museum

Walter J. Boyne

DIRECTOR
NATIONAL AIR AND SPACE MUSEUM
SMITHSONIAN INSTITUTION

Rawson Associates

New York

Library of Congress Cataloging in Publication Data

Boyne, Walter J., 1929–
    The aircraft treasures of Silver Hill.

    1. National Air and Space Museum.   I. Title.
TL506.U6W3727   1982   629.133′074′015251   82-12268
ISBN 0-89256-216-1

Published simultaneously in Canada by McClelland and Stewart Ltd.
Manufactured by Kingsport Press, Kingsport, Tennessee

Designed by Jacques Chazaud

Second printing March 1983

Contents

v

Foreword

The staff of the Garber Facility and the facility itself are among the most valuable assets of the National Air and Space Museum (NASM). The facility stands as an example of the way such an operation should be run, but it was not always this way. Within the last decade Silver Hill was the object of a great deal of well-deserved criticism, primarily for the lack of protection and care afforded to its priceless collection.

In 1975, the Director of NASM, Michael Collins, gave Walter Boyne, then Curator of Aeronautics, the additional positions of Move Operations Officer and Chief of the Preservation, Restoration and Storage Division (Silver Hill).

As move operations officer he was responsible for the movement and placing into position of all the major artifacts (aircraft, spacecraft, engines, etc.) to be exhibited in NASM at its opening. As the chief of Silver Hill, he was responsible for its reorganization and for the proper protection of the collection.

The success of both missions is clearly evident. On July 1, 1976, NASM opened, ahead of schedule, with all artifacts in place. In February 1977 all aircraft at Silver Hill were inside and the first two buildings of the Silver Hill Museum opened to the public.

There are really three stories at Silver Hill—the place, the people, and the planes. Walt Boyne, with his firsthand knowledge of the past seven years and the use of many interviews and other research, has melded these three stories into a fascinating book. In doing so, he has created a book that will not only be an invaluable enhancement to a visit to the Garber Facility but an excellent substitute for those unable to visit.

Donald S. Lopez
Chairman
Department of Aeronautics

March 1, 1982

Introduction

The Paul E. Garber Preservation, Restoration and Storage Facility, formerly and more widely known as "Silver Hill," is the subject of a thousand legends, myths, and good hard true stories. In telling of it, however, there are three basic areas that must be covered, three areas so integrally linked they become as one.

The first is of the facility itself, a sprawling 21 acres of streets and Butler buildings, unprepossessing on the outside but filled with the most fascinating collection of air- and spacecraft in existence, and manned by the most gifted restoration artists in the world. The second is the relationship of the namesake, Paul E. Garber, to the facility and to the National Air and Space Museum. Paul is a delightful man with a marvelous combination of puckish wit, tenacity, and endless knowledge of aviation; the fact that he is eighty-two does not intrude upon him or his constantly widening circle of friends and admirers. Finally, there is the story of the collection itself, individual bits of aviation history of absorbing interest. Some were triumphs, some were failures, some were simply part of an industrial rite of passage; but each represents an entrancing drama of human endeavor, and Paul Garber knows the plot of each.

In telling the first story, it is necessary to go into some detail of the past history, for the facility wasn't always so well regarded, and there was once fierce and justifiable criticism from both press and public. Fortunately, the people who manned the facility in those dark days were resilient; they fought the good fight, keeping the collection in as good a condition as possible without either resources or direction, and learning the skills they would need when resources finally became available.

The second story is less complicated and more fun. Paul Garber is a charming mite of a man, a living legend, sixty-plus years at the Smithsonian, still going strong, and in many ways almost totally responsible for the fact that there is a National Air and Space Museum (NASM) at all.

The hardest part about the third bit of the story, the history of the collection, is in choosing what to include and what to leave out. There are no dull aircraft at Silver Hill; each one is replete with history, personalities, and the aura of the time in which it was created. In the process of detailing the romance of the many aircraft we'll be talking about, I'll try to integrate the stories of people, planes, and situations to provide an insight into the richness and essential humanity of the collection. Some of the aircraft are famous, some are obscure. But all deserve notice.

A word about Paul Garber, personally. He is a man of infinite charm, who seems to move through a world of anecdotal events as he works ceaselessly to benefit the collection. He worked alone for many years, actually in opposition to the major trend of the Smithsonian, which tended to regard aircraft as technically interesting, perhaps, but certainly not artistically and not at all intellectually significant. Paul overcame the measured indifference, the skepticism, the lack of funding by going out and obtaining the treasures of his time, the *Spirit of St. Louis*, the *Winnie Mae*, and even such lesser-known curiosities as the Akerman Tailless and the Herrick Convertaplane. He ratholed these treasures, stolidly accepting the fact that there was no adequate storage nor prospect of any, convinced that it was better to have these jewels protected whatever the conditions than to let them go the way of most aircraft of his time—to the junk dealer and then to the smelter. He was quite right, and the collection endures as a wonderful testimony to his courage.

He would never admit to it—perhaps he never really thinks of it—but it would be less than human if he didn't occasionally recall those contemporaries of long ago, the academicians, the collectors of rare grasses or arachnids, who snubbed him as they ground out forgotten pamphlets on forgotten subjects, and who are themselves now forgotten and would gape in dumbfounded amazement at Paul's current reputation.

Paul is physically tiny, but his leonine features and modulated voice are wonderfully impressive. Past eighty now, he still puts in a hard fifty-hour work week at the office, plus indefatigably touring the country to speak, and answering hundreds of letters with his voluminous, often hand-typed replies. He lectures very well, managing to capture the imagination of his audience, lifting them to wonder with him at the magic of flight, and still conveys above all the good humor of a man who thoroughly enjoys life. He has the timing, and sometimes the delivery, of a stand-up comedian, weaving in irony and drama, indignation and amusement, and once in a while, the least little bit of smoke. But he is entitled to do so; he's seen the aviation industry grow from the single Wright Military Flyer demonstrated at Fort Myer, Virginia, in 1909, to its present state, and he has been known and loved by most of the major participants in the process.

He is still very gutsy and feisty, ready to take up arms for his causes, ready to hit the deck each morning to earn his daily bread, for the good Lord knows that collecting unwanted airplanes for the government is no way to get wealthy. While blessed with a lovely wife

"Buttons," whose acquisition was one of his major triumphs, Paul in his later years has had to cope with some unfortunate health problems among his children. He has faced these squarely, and his courage in doing so is only one more of his remarkable attributes.

Just for the record, Paul was born in Atlantic City, New Jersey, on August 31, 1899, and didn't become totally committed to aircraft until 1909, when he saw Orville Wright piloting the Military Flyer at Fort Myer. That airplane, incidentally, the very first military airplane in the world, now hangs in its original condition in the Early Flight Gallery of the National Air and Space Museum.

Legend has it that Paul made some tentative hops in a small hang glider–type aircraft he constructed from barrel staves in 1915, and this won him a place in an organization of flyers who soloed before December 17, 1916, the "Early Birds." He gained flight experience during World War I, then served with the Post Office Department Air Mail Service in 1918–19.

He joined the Smithsonian Institution on June 1, 1920, as a "Preparator"—a person who lovingly makes models, repairs artifacts, and contributes to the preparation of exhibits for the public.

In many respects, Preparator Paul was the tail that wagged the dog of the Smithsonian, for it was he who tended the almost random collection of aircraft, and it was he who had the temerity to suggest while Lindbergh was still en route that the Smithsonian acquire the *Spirit of St. Louis*. The acquisition of the silver Ryan monoplane was, of course, coincident with the "Lindbergh boom" in aviation, and Paul labored on, borne by a new and welcome current of interest.

He interrupted his work at the Smithsonian to enter the Navy during World War II, where he invented a target kite used for gunnery practice; he retired with the rank of Commander in the Naval Reserve. Then he returned to what would become the National Air Museum only in 1946. Paul was appointed Head Curator in 1952. During most of his tenure, funds were short to nonexistent, personnel were either lacking or of less than sterling quality, and the cares of the Smithsonian were firmly devoted to matters other than aviation. He labored on, gaining fame as a writer, educator, and speaker, and continued to expand the collection, knowing that some day he would achieve the necessary backing to make the Museum on the Mall a reality.

In the sometimes curious fashion of the Smithsonian, the reins of management and administration were shifted from Paul to others so that he could concentrate on his historical pursuits. It was unfortunate, for the correspondence of the time shows that Paul was as capable and aggressive an administrator as he was a historian. But for too long a period, the direction of the Museum was left in the hands of well-meaning individuals who, at best, and most charitably, could be called ineffective. They were totally unable to obtain the necessary backing and funding to sustain the collection, and, in fact, often made bad use of the limited resources available. As a result, they forfeited the respect of senior Smithsonian management, and the nascent Air Museum simply stagnated, its growing collection sinking into disrepair. It was not until later, when the Smithsonian could select a director in whom it had confidence, that the situation would change.

Paul, somewhat piqued at being out of the management mainstream, but a good soldier (sorry, Paul—sailor), nonetheless went on with his important work of expanding and documenting the collection. He retired in 1971, with only fifty-one years of service, but was asked to stay on as Historian Emeritus, a position that gave him free rein in pursuing his main historical interests while still permitting the Museum to call on his tremendous knowledge.

Paul has received many honors—the Gold Medal for Exceptional Service from the Smithsonian, the Frank G. Brewer Trophy, the Tissandier Diplome from the Fédération Aeronautique Internationale, and two honorary doctorates, one in engineering from the University of Ohio and one in aero science from Salem College, West Virginia. There are three other honors that please him more. The first of these was that the old Silver Hill facility was renamed for him. The second was the completion of the National Air and Space Museum downtown, where so much of his life's work obtaining the national collection of aircraft is so well displayed. The third was his continuing romance with his wife Buttons, herself the daughter of a great collector, the famed "Mother Tusch" whose home in Berkeley, California, became a mecca for the great and near great of flying during the late 1920s and 1930s, and whose collection is now a part of the National Air and Space Museum. For all of this, and more, Paul is grateful and happy.

Part One

THE
FACILITY

1
"Pyramid of Dreams"

The streets leading to the Garber Facility are lined with typical Maryland working-class red brick single-story shops, a bleak and dreary mélange of pizza parlors, sandwich shops, instant-printers, and unisex hair salons. They are all evenly decorated with discarded Colonel Sander's buckets, beer bottles, half pints of E&J Gallo brandy—the usual carefree detritus of a declining suburban shopping area. It looks down at the heels but busy, and surprisingly, even safe.

The Paul E. Garber Preservation, Restoration and Storage Facility, a.k.a. Silver Hill, is a complex of Butler buildings indistinguishable from the large fire station next door except for the lack of Bingo signs. The only real key to the special character of the place is the Polaris missile mounted in the parking lot, behind the 8-foot-high security fence.

Getting in is easy if you have made an appointment, and often not too difficult even if you have not, for the guards are friendly, aware that they are sitting on top of a treasure trove of aircraft and missiles, and more importantly, that they represent one of the very few government installations that could operate at a profit. Silver Hill is fascinating—and efficient.

The guard's office is in Building 24, where a miniature museum honoring Paul Garber sets the tone for the rest of the area. There are twenty-eight buildings in all, spread over 21 acres. They house the most incredible collection of aircraft, spacecraft, missiles, guns, uniforms, engines, and miscellaneous other air memorabilia in the world. Oddly enough, when you learn their stories, you'll find out that there is not a single machine in the establishment. Instead, there are multiple pyramids of dreams. Each one represents a dramatic point in time and history that reflects the skills, drama, hard work, and love of the people who created it. There are myriad stories, some epic dramas, some soap operas, but all the very basis of man's inveterate fascination with flight.

The Garber Facility is a classic fairy tale of the triumph of right over wrong, of ingenuity over sloth, and of human interest over government bureaucracy. Within its walls work some of the finest craftsmen and craftswomen in the United States, experts who can create any part of an air- or spacecraft ancient or modern, and do it with a fidelity that surpasses belief. The Garber Facility is the mecca of airplane buffs, antiquers, experimental aircraft builders, historians, patent attorneys, and the casual lover of fine workmanship.

It began, thirty years ago, as a forested swamp in the Maryland countryside, replete with dense fir thickets, wild dogs, copperheads, bees, poison ivy, and a lot of bugs. It went through twenty-five years of ignominy, neglect, and public decrial before beginning a renaissance that has made it one of the most attractive museums in the world for aviation aficionados. The first twenty-five years were the results of low budgets and bureaucratic indifference, forces that Paul Garber could fight against but not overcome; the last five are the

7

result of an outpouring of talent and love from the people who work there—and a little government money. Very little, given the normal scale of government projects, but enough.

The Garber Facility (we'll alternate "Silver Hill" and "Garber" throughout, just for variety) houses approximately 150 of the Museum's total collection of about 280 aircraft. The numbers are approximate because the collection varies almost from month to month, particularly at Silver Hill. In addition, there is a wide variety of spacecraft, and a whole host of miscellaneous related equipment. These precious relics are stored in large warehouse-type buildings, of which five are open to the public for tours.

Also open is the immaculate workshop "Building 10," where shabby shards of plywood and metal are returned to their original pristine condition. It is first and foremost a support facility for the justly famous Museum on the Mall downtown, creating the exhibits and restoring the artifacts that have made NASM the most visited museum in the world. Silver Hill is a warehouse museum, without frills, with aircraft tucked in side by side and overhead to make maximum use of space, and devoid of exhibit paraphernalia, audiovisual equipment, and so on.

Within the facility are biplane fighters from World War I, the fabric of the Spad XIII still bearing the black cross patches where German bullets passed through. There are tiny experimental aircraft like the 17-foot-wingspan Martin K-III Kitten, which besides having the first retractable landing gear in the United States is, believe it or not, the direct ancestor of Howard Hughes's enormous flying boat. There is an all-black Stinson Reliant, the Bonanza of its day, conventional enough looking except for the hook trailing from its aft fuselage, a hook used to effect the first human aerial pick-up, a wartime snatch-and-grab operation. There is a stubby German rocket fighter, a winged egg that was ten times more hazardous to the pilots who flew it then to the enemy, but nonetheless capable of speeds in excess of 600 mph in 1941. There is a flying saucer, a real one, no joke; and there is the *Enola Gay*, the real one, also no joke, but a very moving example of the hardware of history. The list goes

on and on, and in the third part of the book we will look closely at many of them.

The very first aviation material received by the Smithsonian Institution is housed here: a collection of gorgeous Chinese kites given by the Imperial Chinese government for the American Centennial celebration of 1876. They hang in glass cabinets, still bright and colorful, a slender and fragile foundation for the world's greatest assembly of winged vehicles. They are a source of great pride to visitors from the People's Republic of China, who have come to regard the National Air and Space Museum as their special place on the Mall, and who like very much to come to Silver Hill.

After the Chinese kites were acquired, there was not much aviation activity at the Smithsonian until its third secretary, Samuel P. Langley, began the aviation experiments that would lead him to significant triumphs and utter humiliation, but were of cardinal importance in attracting national attention to flight as a legitimate science. (There had been previous Smithsonian experience with flight. During the Civil War, Thaddeus Lowe demonstrated the possibilities of tethered balloon observation and the use of air-to-ground telegraphy on the Mall near the Smithsonian Building.)

With World War I, aviation activity quickened at the Smithsonian and representative aircraft of the era were put on display in a little steel Quonset-type hut on the Mall. (There would be no official National Air Museum until 1946.) The Quonset, called "the tin shed," proved to be the place where American military aviation research got started. In 1917, work began there that led in unbroken sequence to both McCook and Langley fields, and subsequently to Wright-Patterson and Edwards Air Force bases.

A fair number of aircraft were obtained during World War I, but interest lapsed, and the limitations of space and money prevented significant enlargement of the collection until 1927, when Charles A. Lindbergh made his New York to Paris flight on May 20–21. A tiny, soft-spoken, but immensely determined young man named Paul Edward Garber was thrilled with the news of Lindbergh's perilous takeoff from Roosevelt Field. He had the temerity to go to the august, non-aviation-minded fourth secretary of the Smithsonian, Dr. Charles Greely Abbot, and suggest that they wire ahead to Paris and ask that the plane be donated to the venerable Institution on the Mall.

Abbot almost threw Garber out of his office—not too difficult a task, as Garber weighed only about 110 pounds at the time—for like most people of that era, he rather expected Lindbergh not to make it. Garber's intensity appealed to him, however, and the wire was sent, and its offer accepted by Charles Lindbergh.

After the successful completion of the United States, Central America, and South America goodwill tours that Lindbergh undertook upon his return, he delivered the plane to Garber, personally, in Washington. It was hauled through the city streets and then reverently hung in the red brick Arts and Industries Building for forty-seven years before being moved to its present location in NASM. There, despite moon rocks, Apollos, Skylabs, and X-15s, it is still the most popular single exhibit.

The *Spirit* established Garber as a major figure in the eyes of the Smithsonian, and enabled him to go on to other important acquisitions, including the Curtiss NC-4, the first aircraft to cross the Atlantic, and Wiley Post's globe-girdling *Winnie Mae.* These and all of the others that were to follow came as a result of Garber's persistent acquisitiveness. He was working virtually alone and in tacit opposition to the general Smithsonian trend, where a rare bivalve is still prized over a rare biplane.

But Paul, and ultimately Silver Hill, obtained help from a totally unexpected quarter after World War II started. General of the Air Forces Henry H. "Hap" Arnold had determined to collect one each of all Allied and Axis aircraft to form the basis for a national air museum. It was not really intended that the Smithsonian Institution should be the caretaker of this collection, and in the end the holdings were divided to form the basis for the stirring Air Force Museum at Wright-Patterson Air Force Base as well as the present NASM collection. Arnold was not able to fulfill his desire to collect one of each, but hundreds of aircraft were set aside that would have oth-

erwise joined their brothers in salvage-yard smelting pots.

Many of the Allied (primarily U.S.) aircraft selected for the collection were standard service types, while most of the Axis aircraft had been brought over during or just after the war for test purposes, or to serve as trophies in war-bond drives. When at long last the decision was made to create a National Air Museum in 1946, the bulk of these aircraft had been taken to a huge inactive Douglas DC-4 factory operated by the Dodge Automobile Company, in Park Ridge, Chicago. It was an ideal location, the site of the future O'Hare International Airport, and within the factory's cavernous walls the aircraft were maintained in relative security, protected from the elements.

All went well until the advent of the Korean War in 1950, and a decision on the part of the Air Force to reactivate the factory for the production of Fairchild C-119s. A classic French seven-door farce ensued, in which the Smithsonian was required to move its collection to successively smaller areas around the airport, completely consuming its resources in a madcap shifting of boxes and aircraft from one spot to another. Much damage to the artifacts occurred during the moves—damage that would someday take thousands of man-hours to correct.

Eventually it became apparent that the Smithsonian would have to find another site. The Air Force was reluctantly convinced that it would be cheaper to box and ship the collection to Washington rather than to continue dealing with its peregrinations in Chicago.

The continual attempt to satisfy the Air Force yet protect the collection had taken its toll of Garber, as well as of the small contingent of workers actually stationed in Chicago. There was no room at the Smithsonian proper for the aircraft; the ones already on display were jammed against the ceiling of the Arts and Industries Building or placed cheek by jowl in the adjacent tin shed. The alternative—seeing the precious collection of fighters, bombers, and experimental aircraft bulldozed off the field and turned into scrap—was unthinkable. There was a terrible precedent for this sort of atrocity: the carefully chosen

Air Force Museum collection from World War I up to World War II suffered just that fate when Pearl Harbor came. Today, with the hundreds of affluent warbird collectors, it wouldn't be a problem. But in those days, the aircraft were just so much scrap wood and metal to the general public.

Catastrophe loomed. Then, after a series of frantic phone calls, Garber found out that there was a miserable tract of federal land located about 7 miles away from the Mall that no one had claimed because it was little more than a densely forested swamp. There were no buildings, no streets, no utilities, nothing but space. It was called Silver Hill, in Suitland, Maryland, and it would have to do.

The Air Force had the good grace to provide additional resources to pack and box the material at Park Ridge. There began a three-year period during which aircraft were disassembled, placed on skids, and shipped to Maryland. It must have been a cost-plus contract, because the skids were enormous sections of oak, and the big packing boxes offered wonderful protection for shipment.

Some of the larger aircraft were simply disassembled and placed on flatcars. Unfortunately, the pressures of time, space, and money resulted in a few decisions that are bitterly regretted today. Sometimes these large aircraft, like the Japanese Betty bomber, were simply cut up, with only parts being sent to Silver Hill. Such machines were irreplaceable, but in the early 1950s the huge interest in World War II aircraft had not yet materialized, and there was no general awareness of just how rare the planes were nor how desirable they would become.

For a completely ad hoc operation, things went very well. Garber had secured the area, and then proceeded to charm the Corps of Engineers from nearby Fort Belvoir Engineer Training Center to come out and clear enough space for the incoming collection. (It was not the last time Fort Belvoir soldiers would help; in 1975 and 1976, crews from the Center brought trucks and forklifts to transport many of the aircraft from Silver Hill to the NASM for installation.)

The movement of the collection took far longer than had been anticipated. While the process was going on, a few roads were built and a few "temporary" buildings acquired. The crew at Silver Hill became very skilled at stacking, and as the aircraft were brought in boxes they were levered into place compactly so that as many as possible were placed under shelter. Unfortunately, there were far more planes than the buildings could accommodate; many had to be simply dumped in their black boxes, or without any protection at all, to endure the hot Maryland summer sun and the dank winter snow.

A nightmare period of complacency and indifference on the part of the federal government and National Air Museum management followed, which relegated Silver Hill and its magnificent collection to the status of a national disgrace. The aircraft, many of them irreplaceable at any cost, were just allowed to molder away, with corrosion unarrested and even the simplest maintenance left undone.

The aviation press soon began to note the abysmal condition of the collection. As part of a genuine campaign to get funds released for the long-promised Museum on the Mall, aviation writers learned that they could make a fast fee for a story on "The Shame of Silver Hill" or "Scandal at the Smithsonian," and a quick trip to the facility with a camera provided hard evidence to back them up. The trees grew swiftly there, some finding their way up through the wings of parked aircraft. The black boxes which had served so well during shipment turned out to be humidity chambers instead of long-term storage; the aircraft were actually worse off in them than if they had been sprayed with oil and stored outside.

The small staff that had been acquired to service the facility labored against the onslaughts of time and weather, but the odds were against them. A curious poverty mentality emerged, one of self-denial and an almost anchorite conception of duty under adversity. The workers at Silver Hill simply did not expect to get any money, respect, promotion, or even attention. They were devoted to doing the best job they could under the circumstances, but the task was mammoth, the resources nil, and they did not even have a benign management to back them up.

If circumstances required them to move an

The Boeing B-17D, "*Swoose*," parked within the old Dodge aircraft plant at Park Ridge, Illinois. The disused plant was a perfect place to store aircraft. They could be flown in, prepared, and towed inside for safe, secure storage. Then came the Korean War, and with it a supposed requirement to bring the plant back into operation. As a result, the Smithsonian's aircraft began a game of musical storage that ultimately resulted in Silver Hill.

From relatively good indoor storage space at Park Ridge, the Smithsonian Institution was required to move its aircraft and stores to ever smaller areas on the perimeter of the old storage building. The aircraft were whole, and even armed, as in this shot of a Kawasaki Ki-45 Nick, taken in May 1953 by Dave Menard, whose photos have helped historians all across America for years.

The aircraft were brought from Park Ridge and elsewhere and dumped into the forest primeval of Silver Hill. Here a Vought XFB-U1 Crusader, Douglas Skyrocket, North American F-86, and Douglas C-54—the *Sacred Cow*, President Roosevelt's aircraft—as well as assorted boxes, molder under the swift-growing trees.

The aircraft from Park Ridge had been packed well for shipment, not long-term storage. Shown here is the type of skid that components were shipped on—perfectly adequate for transit, but naturally inclined to rot under years of outdoor exposure. The fuselage is from a Focke-Wulf 190-D, the famous "long-nose" Focke-Wulf, which has been restored and is on exhibit at the Air Force Museum in Dayton, Ohio.

In time, Butler buildings like this one were provided, but the space left a lot to be desired, and there was a great deal of apparently unnecessary shifting about. Left outside are the Dornier Do 335 "Pfeil," a push-pull twin-engine aircraft that has since been restored by Dornier in Germany, and is currently on exhibit in the Deutsches Museum in Munich. At its right are a genuine Grumman TBF "Turkey," now in Building 23, and a Curtiss SB2C-5, now on loan to the Naval Air Museum in Pensacola, Florida.

Many of the aircraft were left outdoors in these tar-paper-covered boxes, which not only provided no protection from the weather but actually acted as humidity chambers.

Behind Building 7 there was greater disarray. The area was shared with the now defunct Armed Forces Museum, and was littered with cannons, missiles, bombs, trucks, whale bones, and what have you. From the left is a Beech D-18, the highly modified Grumman XP5M-1 "Petulant Porpoise" (a take-off on the well-known Lockheed P2V "Truculent Turtle"), and the hull and center section of a Sikorsky JRS-1. The Grumman was traded to Darryl Greenamyer for his world speed record-breaking Bearcat, *Conquest I.*

In one of the rearrange-ments, the *Sacred Cow* wound up next to the Douglas XB-43 *Versatile II,* the Dornier Do 335, and Northrop P-61 *Black Widow.* When time and money per-mitted, canvas tarps were laid over the canopies and engine areas, but often these were blown off and forgotten.

Space was not always used well and had to be shared with other Smithsonian agen-cies. Here a Bücker Bu 181 Bestmann lines up in front of a Heinkel He 162 Volks-jaeger. The strange rudder and fuselage at the left of the photo don't belong to a secret airplane—they are half of a plaster cast of a whale.

aircraft, it did not occur to them to insist that they have a crane of proper size and capacity for the job. Instead, they would use ancient forklifts dripping oil and hydraulic fluid, pipes, levers, and slings to literally manhandle the aircraft from one point to another. They had an antique crane built by the Clyde Company, anthropomorphically called "Clyde" in affectionate respect to this day, with which they could work wonders—at the risk of their lives. They would routinely lift twice the normal capacity of the crane by the use of levers and extra counterweights, and Clyde never let them down. If they had to build an A frame for an aircraft engine overhaul, they did not call up a steel warehouse and order what was needed. Instead, they would go to some junk yard to scout out rusted I-beams for reuse.

It was admirable in a Quixotic way, but it led to a set of values and standards that reinforced the dismal image of the facility and caused further estrangement with the rest of the Smithsonian establishment.

Soon a split developed, whereby the people at Silver Hill regarded themselves and were regarded as blue-collar renegades, necessary, but somehow not a part of the Smithsonian. Garber and an ill-paid staff were plagued by duties "downtown" and the even smaller, less well paid staff labored on almost autonomously at Silver Hill. It reached the ludicrous stage where the very individuals who had restored the aircraft that were being put on exhibit downtown were not invited to the ceremonies marking the occasion.

Of course the people at Silver Hill resented these slights. They developed a fierce independence and truculence that reinforced their differences with the "downtown" establishment. Sadly, at the same time they found themselves victims of internal strife. The place became a hothouse of feuds, anonymous phone calls, complaints on safety, and occasional trumped-up charges of some sort of criminal activity. Aircraft sat out in the open with the canopies slid back, rainwater pouring in and rust water pouring out; bushes and trees, vines and ivy grew up through once proud fighters and bombers, while the black covered boxes slowly self-destructed. Internally there was corrosion, in both man and machine.

Despite the unhealthy conditions, a small nucleus of workers at the facility maintained a high sense of duty, ignoring the slights, which were often grotesque in their unfairness. On one occasion it was learned that a contract had been let—finally—to erect a large building at Silver Hill in an area where dozens of aircraft were currently stored. Typically, word had not filtered down to the Silver Hill crew until fifteen days before the start-work date. It was an impossible task, but four men, Ed Chalkley, later head of the whole facility, Walter Roderick, who would become chief of Restoration and Preservation, John Parlett, a master of equipment moving, and Bill Green, an incredibly strong and efficient man who retired recently, started in. Working fifteen-hour days, seven days a week, they shoved and pushed the boxes and aircraft from one point to another with their primitive equipment.

Miraculously, they finished on time, and their boss, Walter Male, was so elated that he put all four of them in for a performance award. The reply that came back from the Smithsonian award-evaluation committee stunned them, for it recommended that the four workers be fired, as they had obviously done the work unsafely by completing such an impossible task in the time allotted. It was also proposed that the supervisor who submitted the recommendation be fired, for permitting it to happen. The reaction was absurd, cruel, and unfortunately typical for the time.

No one really knew or cared how hard and how well the Silver Hill crew was working. Had it been in existence, OSHA would have shut the place down. When the first plane to fly the Atlantic, the massive fabric and wood Curtiss NC-4, was being restored, it was necessary for the men doping the broad wings to lie down on little wheeled stretchers so that they could reach across each wing. There was a rigid deadline for the project, and the whole crew was hustling to get it done. Ventilation in the shop was so bad that a system had to be set up to wheel groggy or unconscious men outside on their stretchers to recuperate, while someone else took their place on the job.

What sustained these people throughout was the quality of the work they were doing and the importance of the task. It was a curious fact—one that persisted for a long time—that the men at Silver Hill had a far better sense of the importance of the collection, of the need for preservation and the requirement for self-sacrifice to do the job, than did much of the curatorial staff. Funds were always very limited, but it was amazing how often when funds could not be found to buy two-by-fours and plywood for Silver Hill, there were still funds available for curators to take a trip to Europe, in the pompous and probably accurate words of the time, "to have intercourse with their peers."

Fortunately, external events would lead to a general improvement in the physical, if not the psychological environment. Sentiment had grown to favor what now would be called the National Air and Space Museum, and in 1962 money was appropriated by Congress for its construction. The Vietnam War intervened, however, and the project was put on the back burner; only very limited funds began to trickle out to Silver Hill for the improvement of facilities. Generally speaking, things remained at the poverty level for an industrial establishment. There was no new equipment; what was available was Army/Navy surplus. There was no safety equipment, no safety procedures, and no prospect of any. A general malaise of hostile indifference affected many of the workers.

Yet, against all reason, in the midst of this depressing environment, there remained that hard core of capable, concerned craftsmen who knew what needed to be done, knew how to do it, but were never asked for their opinion. In time they would turn Silver Hill into a masterpiece, but there still were tough days ahead.

Eventually, two events focused the spotlight of public attention on Silver Hill and forced some relief. The first was a brilliant article in the influential *Flying* magazine's March 1969 issue. In it, James Gilbert castigated both the government and the Smithsonian for disgraceful neglect of the national collection. He said, to quote only in part,

. . . The Air and Space Museum leaves you with the impression that it is very nearly dead. But there is worse to come. What we have seen [at the downtown site] is only the peak of the iceberg, the bulk of it lies underwater, almost literally, for most of the Smithsonian's 207 planes repose in what can only be described as a junkyard in a suburb of Washington called Silver Hill, Maryland . . . it is a shame and a disgrace . . . lying about the facility are dozens of unique and priceless airplanes simply exposed to the weather to rot. . . . All this, we are told, was a vast improvement over a year ago, when practically everything the Museum had was sitting out in the open. . . . The Air Museum people seem to have been expecting work to start on the new building every day for 20 years or so, and in consequence put off any real work of importance until then. . . . Is Silver Hill, then, to be with us forever? It would seem so. . . .

Gilbert went on to compare the National Air and Space Museum unfavorably with the London Science Museum, the Musée de l'Air, and the Air Force Museum at Wright-Patterson Air Force Base. It was a telling article, savagely done, but with the correct intention.

The second major event was a scathing indictment of the facility in the *Congressional Record*, the result of a Congressional inquiry which analyzed the situation with crystal clarity and even put the finger of blame on members of the Museum management, who had actually spent money on instrument flying lessons that could far better have been spent for preservatives to spray the derelict hulks at Silver Hill.

Such was the intensity of the controversy that the flow of funds at last began to improve. S. Dillon Ripley, the current Secretary of the Smithsonian Institution led a long and sometimes lonely battle to win a place on the Mall for the Air and Space Museum. More importantly, however, the new National Air and Space Museum building seemed to be assured, and if it were to be built it would certainly need some restored planes to exhibit.

Upper Smithsonian management had long been dissatisfied with the supervision of the Air and Space Museum, and recognized the critical importance of choosing a new director who would be able to reverse the trend. They selected Mike Collins, the astronaut who had circled the moon in the spacecraft *Columbia* while Armstrong and Aldrin made the first lunar landing from Apollo 11. Mike was perfect for the job, having rapport with Congress, stature within the Smithsonian, and the good sense to be able to hire good people and then delegate to them the myriad tasks of getting the huge new museum open. It was Mike who insisted on careful review of the architect's plan and then enforced adherence to it, resulting in the new building coming in on time and under budget, a phenomenon still talked about with admiration in the Capital.

The smooth flow of work inaugurated with the new building was matched by an increased tempo at Silver Hill, as the immense restoration requirements came to be clearly perceived. By 1975, the lovely pink Tennessee marble structure on the Mall was substantially complete, and it was possible to begin filling the enormous galleries with the artifacts from Silver Hill and elsewhere.

Twenty-three galleries had to be filled with air- and spacecraft, ranging in size from tiny World War I fighters to a Douglas DC-3, and from the bowling ball–sized Sputnik replica to the 52-ton Orbital Workshop. The exhibits had to be gathered not only from Silver Hill but from repositories all over the United States. They had to be routed to the Museum, assembled once inside the 30-foot entrance door, then suspended in compact arrays, all in sufficient time to permit the elaborate exhibit that would explain the artifacts and set them off.

The rancor and the difficulties of the past seemed to inhibit the process—the management at Silver Hill was kindly and well intended, but still cursed with a legacy of backbiting, informing, and what amounted to almost industrial sabotage. Silver Hill's problems were the only thing over which Mike Collins would lose his even, almost detached manner; his jaw would work, and he would express total frustration at the apparently insurmountable personnel problems.

The principal difficulty was a curious communication phenomenon, in which instructions would be both given and accepted with the best will in the world. When they were passed on, however, they had somehow been skewed to 90 or 180 degrees of what had been intended, with occasional wildly comic foul-ups resulting.

One of the productivity problems was that discipline had been slackened drastically in an attempt to improve morale. Work normally began thirty to forty-five minutes late, there were long coffee breaks, longer lunch hours, and a general inclination to leave a bit early to make up for coming in late.

When the first schedules were drawn up to determine how to fill the galleries with restored aircraft, it became evident that a far tighter integration of management between downtown and Silver Hill was needed. Obviously it was not going to be possible to achieve the desired number of restorations and get them installed without a new management system and new managers at Silver Hill. The problems and the solutions both resided in the people there.

The first problem—and a formidable one, given the vagaries of the federal civil service—was how to move the existing managers out of the way without actually hurting their careers, or their paychecks. There was no question that the people involved had not been doing their best, but also that they had in many ways been the salvation of the place in times of adversity. They suffered from the fact, however, that management had always been brought in from the outside; there had never been any promotions from within, and resentment was rife. The solution was to create new jobs, out of the mainstream, and to move the managers into them on a lateral basis. It was done—not without some *angst*, but it was done.

Picking the new managers was not so difficult. Over the course of several months three men had identified themselves as being clear thinkers, highly motivated, and totally dedicated. The challenge was to get them to see themselves in the same light.

Ed Chalkley, one of those who had been recommended for dismissal because he had done such a good job, is a smiling, fast-talking, humorous man with a quick temper and loads of compassion. In 1974, he had every capability except confidence in himself as a manager. He could paint an airplane, move a C-54, rebuild

The change, when it came, was almost miraculous. Aircraft were taken from their decrepit snake-
and bee-filled boxes, and installed inside newly painted buildings with sealed floors. The exhibits inside change from time to time, but it was a quantum improvement for the facility.

One big advantage that the Paul E. Garber Preservation, Restoration and Storage Facility provides is the ability to exhibit aircraft that were formerly on exhibit downtown, and which have their own following. Two of those are shown
here: Al Williams's Grumman *Gulfhawk* and the Boeing P-26 Peashooter.
Both of these aircraft are now back downtown, and in their place stands a
huge aluminum box that serves as a temperature- and humidity-controlled
chamber for pressure suits.

an engine, or suspend a DC-3 from the ceiling with complete confidence. He possessed tremendous qualifications to manage Silver Hill, for he could do any job and he knew how well anyone else could do any job. He liked the people, and was totally, absolutely honest. He ultimately got the nod to become the new chief of Preservation and Restoration, and he was the key man in the process of installing the aircraft in the new Museum.

Walter "Rod" Roderick was a slightly different story. Walter was retiring, almost reclusive. When asked to become shop foreman, he flatly refused. Yet Walter had hands of genius. He personally restored the Douglas World Cruiser to better than new condition, and, like Ed, could do any job in the shop. Walter had been hurt in the past, and he didn't want any exposure beyond his daily tasks. But he was left no choice, being literally ordered to become the shop foreman. To his own amazement, he turned overnight into a really expert manager.

Walter works continuously and takes care of his people like a mother hen. He treats the U.S. government as if its budget were his personal responsibility, and worries about every contractual dime that is spent as if it came out of his own pocket. When he is not on the phone checking to see if he can't get a better price on some supplies, he is on the floor helping the craftsmen. If there's nothing else to do, he grabs a broom and sweeps—he is always busy and the shop shows it. He has a deep human compassion that always comes through. Although it is psychologically costly for himself, he gives and gives to everyone in the shop, even the occasional person who doesn't respond and who requires discipline. When Walter has exhausted his own resources, or perceives that the government is not getting a fair shake, he resolutely but firmly goes about setting the person straight. Most of the time, though, he spends in counseling, advising, and helping, and at this he is the best.

Then there was Al Bachmeier. "Watch out for Bachmeier," they told me, "he's a crazy Bolshevik!" I personally found Al to be very even-tempered—always mad. Then I found out the reason that he was always mad was that he knew exactly what had to be done, and how to do it, but was never permitted to do what was necessary.

Al was made chief of Warehousing, and placed in charge of the movement of artifacts. We never had another problem in either area, and Al continues to come up with idea after idea, all of them good. He is the mastermind behind the National Air and Space Museum's

Building 20 is home to a wide variety of aircraft, now jammed more closely together than shown here. The Caudron G.4 hangs above a French-built Fiesler Storch; on its right are a Saab J-29 Flying Barrel, Republic P-47 Thunderbolt, and Kugisho P1Y2 Francis.

current inventory project, and if the truth were known, behind a substantial part of the entire Smithsonian inventory effort. He is a wild, irascible genius, sometimes; at other times a soft-hearted, benevolent caretaker of the Museum's treasures and the Museum's people.

Al had largely won me over in the first months of our association, but he completely convinced me one bitterly cold December day working in the historic tin shed behind the old Smithsonian Building where the main objects in the Aeronautics collection had been displayed for so long. The building was already half torn down and the sharp D.C. winter wind was whistling through the gaps. The challenge was Chuck Yeager's Bell X-1, which was mounted at a steep angle of bank on a 12-inch steel pipe, which in turn was attached to special fittings on the landing gear.

There was no way to "get aholt" of the first aircraft to go supersonic in its current 45-degree bank angle, so the first task was to get the wings reasonably level. Al took a welding torch and cut a large angle out of the steel pipe—big enough to work with, but not so big that the *Glamorous Glennis,* as Yeager had named the X-1, would break the pipe. He then took the torch and gently stroked the pipe with flame. As the heat took hold, the X-1 slowly started to settle into a straight and level position. When he had finished, the X-1 was right for the crane to pick up, and the angle cut in the pipe had disappeared. Al's estimate of the angle had been done by eye, and accurate to within a centimeter. He convinced me totally, right on the spot.

Almost overnight Silver Hill took on a different complexion. Work rules were tightened, and they needed to be. The new regimen called for work starting at 8:00 A.M., no breaks, lunch from 12:00 to 12:30, and work ending at 4:30, again with no breaks.

There were immediate prophecies of revolt, mass desertion, and probable fraggings. In actual fact, after a few days grumbling, the whole crew liked the new discipline; after a few months, with productivity soaring, coffee breaks were reintroduced. Things began coming together in a way that surprised everyone.

Perhaps the best tonic for morale was new

equipment instead of worn-out Army surplus. Retrospectively, it's a wonder that anything had got done, given the wretched tools the men had to work with. When they were in the process of disassembling the Boeing B-29 *Enola Gay* at Andrews Air Force Base, they had to use a compressor to provide power to some of the pneumatic tools that were necessary to de-mate the wing. The compressor was so old, and so difficult to start, that the work crew usually spent two to three hours urging it to life, then had to rest for an hour to recuperate from the genuine physical exhaustion the process had caused.

As the tempo of work picked up, so, understandably, did the self-esteem of all the employees. The fact that the three critical promotions had all come from within was extremely important. For the first time in the history of the facility it seemed possible that there really was a promotion ladder.

Nine months had been allotted to finish the restorations for installation and to bring all the artifacts into the Museum and suspend them. More than two hundred major artifacts, ranging from the fragile-looking Wright Flyer and the beautiful Hughes racer to the bulky and difficult-to-handle North American X-15, were installed in just six months, well ahead of schedule.

The process of "stuffing" the Museum appealed to a large cross section of people. In addition to the people from Silver Hill, there was a dedicated contingent from the Corps of Engineers at Fort Belvoir, Virginia, and some extremely skilled workers from the United Rigging Company. The scheduling of the artifacts became more and more complex. On many occasions two aircraft would be in the process of suspension, a third in assembly on the floor, a fourth being off-loaded from a truck at the entrance, a fifth waiting in the street, and a sixth en route from a distant location.

Silver Hill went from strength to strength, and morale soared as the personnel gained a reputation for being able, literally, to do anything. The whole facility was churning with an immense amount of the right kind of inertia, vast reservoirs of human kinetic energy.

Then suddenly, the task was done—everything that the people from Silver Hill could do for the new Museum was finished. It was time for the exhibit builders and the audiovisual types to take over.

Mike Collins approved a plan to turn all this talent and energy to a new task: CLEAN UP SILVER HILL. He wanted to get rid of the desolate sight of derelict aircraft moldering in the open air, of black boxes collapsing on their valuable cargo, and to create a new museum for the true buffs, the aficionados, the lovers of airplanes in the raw.

Undaunted, the troops at Silver Hill turned to with a will, and even the rigging contractor got caught up in the enthusiasm. He made an offer that he would open up the black boxes, move the aircraft into storage, and clean up the debris in six weeks, all for $18,000. It was the bargain of a lifetime. The only proviso was that space be cleared inside the buildings to permit him to operate.

Within a few days, the contractor realized he was going to take a bath. The black boxes housing the aircraft, which looked so fragile with their gaping holes and flapping black tar paper, turned out to be tougher than the Maginot Line. A gang started with huge chain saws, sawing, cutting, cussing, and trying to pull the severed remains apart with huge cranes. The boxes simply wouldn't let go—sometimes it would seem that there was nothing that hadn't been cut by chain saws, and still the box would hold together, fastened by yet another hidden oak four-by-four.

Hordes of hornets had established homes in the boxes, and it was not unusual to see a bare-chested workman waving a 24-inch chain saw over his head like a flag as he fled a swarm. Snakes abounded, but the toughest task remained simply cutting apart the twenty-five-year-old packing crates, reducing them to tiny pieces that filled the area with unending debris.

In about twelve weeks, though, every aircraft but two was inside. The Douglas C-54 *Sacred Cow*, President Roosevelt's aircraft, was to be moved to Dayton, and so remained outside for a few more weeks. Jack Kennedy's campaign aircraft, the *Caroline*, a Convair 240, was also left outside because the John F. Kennedy Museum in Boston had expressed an interest in acquiring it.

The same expertise that had filled the new building downtown was now put to work assembling and hanging aircraft at Silver Hill. A simple austere layout was made for two Butler buildings, and a total of $800 spent on materials. In less than six months, by January of 1977, the Silver Hill Museum was ready to open.

Fittingly for Silver Hill, it was a bootleg operation from start to finish. Ordinarily, to open a new museum one has to go through an interminable chain of command within the Smithsonian and through congressional channels for approval. The Silver Hill Museum was suddenly there. Once opened, it was so obviously worthwhile, and had been done so inexpensively, that nothing was ever said, although a few disapproving, wondering, heads were shaken.

With the opening, a whole new life began for Silver Hill and its people. No longer were they considered renegades. Instead, they were known as the Museum's fire brigade, thrown in whenever some high-quality work had to be done in a hurry. Morale kept improving, leavened by television crews that came out to watch them work, by magazine articles that praised instead of condemning. Today, the whole plant looks more like the clean room in an electronics facility than an industrial shop, and even the tired old metal buildings have received a bright new coat of paint.

The secret of the entire process is the extraordinary caliber of people who work there. Their productivity is so high that, if set up as a private corporation, Silver Hill could make a handsome profit. When all the overhead costs, utilities, salaries, and materials, are computed at Silver Hill, the annual budget runs to about $750,000. It has the capability to carry out six full restorations a year, if other Museum support work were not required. At the going price of $150,000 to $200,000 for restorations of Silver Hill quality, it is easy to see that the government could have a money-making proposition on its hands. Later, we'll take a closer look at how the people do this. But first let's see how they fit into the larger scheme of the National Air and Space Museum.

2

The Museum Downtown

The concept of a museum as a musty place where nothing much happens certainly doesn't fit the dynamic activity going on every day in the National Air and Space Museum on the Mall in Washington, D.C. The whole complex pulsates from morning to night, alive with the 30,000 people who pound through its halls on an average day (85,000 on a big day!) and with the 200 staff members who create the exhibits, do the research, protect the collection, and maintain the cavernous galleries in Disneyland-clean state.

At the heart of NASM's success are the exhibits that place the artifacts in thematic galleries, bringing them alive with information and detail presented in an imaginative way that eludes many other museums. In just a little over its first five years of operation, the Museum attracted more than 50 million visitors, and it is often said to be the most popular museum in the world today. NASM has received rave reviews from the media since its inception, and has a national following that is unique for a Washington-based museum.

The artifacts are priceless, irreplaceable, and in almost every instance the genuine article. There are no replica aircraft in the Museum—they are the real thing, as are most of the spacecraft. For space artifacts, where the original was either destroyed upon reentry, has departed the solar system, or is still in space, a genuine back-up article is exhibited. The only exceptions are in the case of certain Soviet spacecraft, like the Sputnik, which, in keeping with Russian practice, are models.

But as attractive as the artifacts are, their worth would be diminished if they were not presented in a way that catches the attention of the visitor forcibly. Some studies have indicated that the average tourist visiting the vast Smithsonian complex on the Mall spends an average total of only two hours and forty minutes there. Of this, an individual museum, either NASM or the National Museum of American History, for example, gets about an hour and ten minutes. Inside the individual museum, each exhibit gets an average of twenty *seconds* of the visitor's attention. It is imperative, then, to grab his or her attention, hook it by some attractive scheme, and then seduce the person into learning something about what is being shown. The increase and diffusion of knowledge is after all the reason for the Smithsonian's existence. Education is inevitably a major part of the Museum's mission.

It is far easier said than done. Museums of the past, particularly science museums, often followed the stuffed owl in a glass cage approach. You simply took an artifact, dusted it, identified it with a small typed label, and left it to the visitor to look or not as he chose. Today, some more progressive museums have abandoned this for the direct opposite, an extremely interesting hands-on approach, which works very well if the visitor flow is numbered in tens and hundreds rather than in thousands.

At NASM, thousands of hours go into the creation of an exhibit—often in a *two*-year interactive process between management, curators, designers, and the people who actually

In about five and a half years since opening, more than 50 million visitors have passed through the doors of what some people call the most popular museum in the world. To celebrate the fifth anniversary of the Museum on July 1, 1981, several special events were held, including band performances like this one by the "Hot Mustard" group. The crowds love being in the Museum at night, walking under the original Wright Flyer or around the *Columbia*, the Apollo 11 spacecraft. Here the two craft sit, about 30 feet apart, separated by sixty-six years in time. One started aviation with a successful series of flights, the longest of which was about 120 feet; the other started the exploration of other planets with the first manned landing on the moon. Incredible.

Paul Garber does what he likes best, making kites and explaining the process to young people. Paul heads up the Smithsonian's annual Kite Festival, which grows in size and diversity every year.

fabricate the exhibits. The overall purpose is to dispense knowledge about every aspect of air and space, but even the huge 635-foot-long, 83-foot-high, and 225-foot-wide building is limited in what it can show. Consequently there is real discussion, often surprisingly heated, about what will be selected for exhibit and how it will be done.

The first step in the process is a decision on what each gallery should cover. The whole panorama of aviation and space history is reviewed, and compared against what is already on exhibit. Melded into this process are the individual interests of the curators, who ultimately will have the responsibility for selecting the artifacts, writing the exhibit scripts, and so on. When the Museum was originally set up the process of selection was not too difficult, for major exhibits dealing with such subjects as Apollo, World War I, or Air Transportation were almost foregone conclusions. Now the task is made more difficult, for one must choose not only what might go in but also what must come out.

The latter is a real problem. Most of the individual galleries have built up constituencies over the years, and any notice of removal brings an immediate protest. Decisions are usually based on such tangible factors as visitor flow, the results of questionnaires, and so on, as well as certain intangibles such as a sense of imbalance in the ratio of aviation to space galleries, or the need to take account of current events like the journey of the Voyager spacecraft.

Silver Hill provides some relief for the situation, for artifacts that are removed one day from the Museum usually go on exhibit the following day at Silver Hill, and a diehard F-86 freak, for example, can still see the object of his affection, even if he has to drive another 7 miles to do so.

The overriding decision as to what goes into a gallery usually revolves around what is not being adequately covered in the Museum. A

Guided tours are available during much of the day at the Museum. Here Bobby Dyke, one of our most popular docents, is telling a group about the Gemini 4 (lower left) and the North American X-15 (above). On June 3, 1965, Edward H. White II left the Gemini 4 spacecraft for the first American "walk" in space. The X-15 was one of three of the type; they flew higher and faster than any winged aircraft, reaching out beyond the atmosphere. Top speed attained was 4,534 miles per hour, and top altitude was 354,200 feet, or more than 67 miles.

Still another big night was the January 20, 1981, Inaugural Ball. Vice President George Bush heads for the speaker's stand; Mrs. Bush is at his left.

typical example would be the Jet Aviation Gallery, which opened to celebrate the Museum's fifth anniversary. We recognized that this most modern period of flight had not yet been well covered in the Museum, and that in the forty years since the flight of the first jet aircraft—a tiny Heinkel He 178 on August 27, 1939—jet aviation had in fact considerably changed the world. Despite the evident natural technological bent of the Museum, there is considerable concern about depicting the social and cultural effects of flight, and surely jet aviation had an impact on every aspect of modern life.

Once the basic theme was decided upon, a curator was assigned the task of developing a concept script. This is a brief preliminary treatment, perhaps six pages in length, which outlines what and how he thinks the gallery should teach the public about the subject. The concept script is reviewed by everyone concerned with the process, then the curator starts working closely with the talented team of designers whose task it is to present the aircraft in a setting that will induce people to learn.

It's a curious thing that the curators, who presumably know everything about the subject, and the designers, who presumably know everything about the design, eventually come to agreement, but only after dozens of arguments. The curator, given free rein, would stuff the galleries with dozens of artifacts, without regard to visitor flow or communication. The designer would probably tend to limit the gallery to one artifact, perfectly set. But a synergistic effect takes place, and oddly enough, whenever there is an absolute donnybrook, a stand-off where neither designer nor curator will compromise, it is usually the designer who is right and who wins the "argument."

Once the concept script has been generally approved, a "unit script" is usually prepared jointly by a single curator and one designer. The curator has reviewed what artifacts are appropriate and available. In the case of the Jet Aviation Gallery, opened in 1981, we would of course have liked to have had the very first jet plane of all, the Heinkel He 178 in which Erich Warsitz made the first jet flight in 1939. Unfortunately, it had been destroyed in

an air raid on Berlin. We would have liked to have had the first British jet, the Gloster E28/39, but it is now permanently on display at the Science Museum in South Kensington. We already had the first American jet, the Bell XP-59, on exhibit in the Flight Testing Gallery. This lack of "firsts" meant that we had to take another tack.

The choice was easy, for we had two glorious fighter planes of enormous importance available. One was the world's first operational jet fighter, the lean and mean-looking Messerschmitt Me 262, first flown in Germany in 1942. The other was the prototype of the first U.S. operational jet fighter, the Lockheed XP-80 *Lulu Belle.*

These then became the centerpieces of the gallery, their size, shape, and colors presenting the designer with immediate challenges. Meanwhile the curator went shopping to see what other relevant artifacts he could bring into the gallery to convey his messages.

The designer began work on how the gallery would flow, giving consideration to safety, viewing, accessibility, maintenance, and production costs. Sketches and preliminary models were made, alternatives presented. The audiovisual units, essential for a public brought up on television, were planned early on; for the first time in any museum anywhere, videodisc units were used. Within each gallery there is usually an attempt to have sufficient interactive units to draw visitors from one point to the next, and the Jet Age Gallery ultimately provided cockpit simulators, films, and computer-driven "Design-a-Jet" machines.

With approval of the unit scripts, the curator now launched into the most time-consuming part of the creative process, the writing of the actual labels with the educational content of the exhibit. Every fact has to be cross checked, research has to be done to tremendous depths, most of which isn't used, and finally, the curator's natural bent for scholarly, technical language has to be transformed into simple, interesting text for the average visitor.

There are two forces at work here; on the one hand, the curator has a love for his or her subject that at times borders on madness. He (or she) wants to tell all he knows, in depth, *ad infinitum,* and unfortunately often *ad nau-*

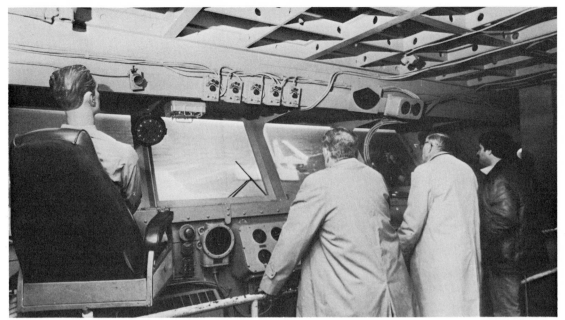

The Museum features some dramatic audiovisual effects. Here visitors stand on the navigation bridge of the U.S.S. *Smithsonian*, CV-76, a commissioned vessel in the U.S. Navy, and watch launch operations from a carrier. All of the hardware items shown are authentic, from the carrier *Hancock*. The films showing launch operation were taken on the U.S.S. *Eisenhower*. This is the Sea-Air Operations Gallery, which combines such audiovisual features with the hangar deck of an aircraft carrier, where four small-size aircraft are exhibited.

Even the most jaded visitor shows a sense of awe at actually touching a piece of the moon. This was returned to the earth in December 1972 by the crew of Apollo 17. It is a hard, fine-grained basalt, produced by volcanic activity approximately 4 billion years ago, and still not showing the wear of millions of visitors' fingers.

The Skylab Orbital Workshop in the Space Hall, an exact duplicate of the original manned space station launched into earth orbit by the United States on May 14, 1973. The huge structure, 52 feet high, had to be moved into the building in three sections, and then reassembled.

seam. Yet nothing turns the layman off more swiftly. As a result, the labels have to be structured in a sort of three-layer cake. The first layer is a grabber, a hook in bold print, which tells the visitor the most essential facts that he or she can comprehend in that self-allotted twenty-second visit.

The second layer of the label goes into more detail; if the visitor is reading it at all, he must be interested, so the curator gets to expand. The type may be slightly smaller, and words slightly more complex to accommodate any technical jargon that is not otherwise easily expressed.

The third layer gets down to the meat of it. The curator has the visitor hooked, he can expand on what he wants to say, and he can even become more technical.

An opposing force to this orgy of curating is the design requirement to limit both text and photographs, and to present the artifact and its associated graphics in a visually attractive manner that enhances communication. The curator typically wants to use 150 photos to tell a story; the designer knows that at most 50 can be handled within the space available to that portion of the exhibit. There then begins a real synthesis of talent, the trade-off of facts versus content, the test of wills of designer and curator.

Inevitably, a compromise must be the result, but fortunately the Museum provides a way out. The research that goes into an exhibit does not have to be concentrated there; for every new gallery several publications result, into which can be poured all that the curators have learned. For the visitor who wants to go beyond the level of knowledge available from the exhibits and its labels, these publications provide new answers. In addition, the Museum library on the third floor stands ready to provide further information.

Experience has shown that one of the nicest things the Museum does for many people is done inadvertently during this period, and that is making mistakes. In creating a gallery in which there may be forty individual units, perhaps eight hundred labels, and thousands of facts, mistakes are inevitable. The Museum has an extensive internal and external review process, by which all of the text is closely scruti-nized by experts in the field, but errors still occur. Some are simply typos, some are matters of context, and others are mistakes, pure and simple. Nothing gives the interested visitor greater pleasure than to call upstairs with a correction. Oddly enough, the curator is usually (not always, they are human too) glad to be informed of the error so that he or she can correct it.

While the process of writing the scripts, gathering the photos, restoring the artifacts, etc., is going on, the designer is wrestling with the design problems. It is not too difficult to create an environment for a Rodin sculpture, for the Hope diamond, even for a ship model. It is something else to take four full-sized jet aircraft, seven huge jet engines, a number of models, and a huge assortment of photos, films, and graphics, and place them in a gallery 110 feet wide and 55 feet deep that still manages to look inviting. It is even tougher if you have done almost thirty galleries in the past, and this one must be new and different.

The hardware of the Jet Aviation Gallery was especially difficult to handle. There is a sleekness, a lethal quality about fighter planes that could be a turn-off, and jet engines themselves are not intrinsically interesting. The designer has to create an attractive ambiance around what might seem to some as instruments of terror.

The solution lies in disposition, color, form, lighting, and unity of concept. The designer sees the gallery in neutral terms. He is not caught up in the mystique of fighters or the thrust of the engines. He (or she) can use colors to soothe, shapes to lead, and forms to entice so that the visitor is moved through the exhibit, aware of the artifacts and almost unmindful of the artifacts that make them attractive.

While the designer is working at this, he has to keep production costs in constant consideration. Anyone can spend $100,000 on a single unit and make it attractive; the trick is to spend $5,000 and make it so. In doing this, a designer often uses colors or materials to transform shapes, for a subtly colored rectangular shape is much less expensive to produce than a starkly colored round one. These methods become almost instinctive. But sometimes the integrity of a gallery, or its flow, calls for the creation of a costly production shape, and then the designer has to defend his choice.*

Eventually, all the label scripts, photos, artifacts, designs, and blueprints are ready; all of the aircraft have been laboriously moved in, assembled, and perhaps suspended. The exhibits production crew at Building 13, Silver Hill, has been constructing pre-fab units as the drawings were released, and now everything begins to come together. The only thing moving faster than the construction pace is the calendar, for an opening date has to be set months in advance. When the final week rolls around, there seems to be at least three weeks of work remaining, but, inevitably, the work gets done, though sometimes the last hammer falls just a minute or two before the first guest walks in on the night of the opening party.

The next big question is, How will the public like it? And, less important, How will it be received by the media? The Jet Aviation Gallery has been a big success so far; only the curator and the designer know what improvements remain to be done.

This whole process goes on continually at the Museum, for there are numerous exhibits each year, yet it represents only about 20 percent of the total Museum effort. At the same time, research is being done on lunar and Martian landforms, on the history of astronomy, and on myriad other air and space subjects. Just as in universities, these result in articles, books, and such typical academic flourishes as seminars and symposiums. It is not a publish-or-perish atmosphere, but there is a compulsion toward writing and research.

Less visible yet perhaps even more important are the collections management activities. Museums, by definition, exist for their collections, but acquisition of specimens is only a small part of the total problem. Every item collected requires space, maintenance, and record keeping, all costly items. As a result, one of NASM's most difficult tasks is how

tactfully to refuse most proposed donations. It becomes necessary to determine exactly what the collection should consist of in terms of historical importance and technological interest, and then bravely to decline to accept things outside that determination. Donors, always with the best will in the world, will call up wishing to provide us with Uncle Don's flight helmet, used when he was a navigator in the Air Force in 1949. Well, Uncle Don's helmet might fill an important void in the flight-clothing collection, but more probably it will duplicate one already there and must be turned down with regret.

Acceptance carries with it hazards also. A donor will provide an artifact, perhaps a magneto for the Fokker D VII; it may fit perfectly into the collection, but is not necessary for exhibit. The very next time the donor comes into town, he expects to see his gift displayed prominently next to the Wright Flyer, and if not, we—and his congressman—hear about it.

One of the most difficult tasks in collections management, aside from preservation and restoration of the aircraft, which will be dealt with in the next chapter, is the care and preservation of documents. Paper products are self-destructing, made of organic compounds that have been treated with acids and alkalies as a part of their creation. It is heartbreaking to see an original letter from Wilbur Wright slowly, inevitably being destroyed by its own chemical constituents. The life of such an artifact can be stretched by proper treatment, storage, and handling, but in the long run it will decay. As a result, important material has to be microfiched for permanent record, a costly and time-consuming process, and one that the researcher often resents, for it is far more rewarding to handle original documents than it is to peer through a reader, or work with hard copy reproductions.

Still, there is no way out. Repeated handling (and the odd pervert, who destroys or steals original material) merely accelerates the inherent organic process. Microfiche methods have been vastly improved, and when tied to computer retrieval, actually speeds research efforts. The best thing about it, of course, is that microfiche copies of entire files can be prepared and sent to outside researchers far

---

* The design process was not always so controlled nor so basically tranquil. Paul Garber suffered his first heart attack when an irate Museum director threw a two-by-four board through an exhibit case which Paul had just completed and which somehow didn't catch the director's fancy.

more cheaply than actually trying to research their requests in house. This places the burden on the researcher to find equipment by which to read the microfiche, but also provides him or her with the opportunity to see far more material than could otherwise have been requested. The cost to the government, even if no charge is made for the microfiche, is less, for it permits the archivist to handle many more requests. Normally, however, the cost of the microfiche is charged to the requester.

The Museum has perhaps the best and most extensive aviation photograph collection in the world, one that is growing constantly as private collectors learn that their collections will be maintained and made accessible if donated or willed to the Museum. There are 1 million-plus photos, ranging from priceless Curtiss and Wright glass-plate negatives to spectacular photos of Saturn's rings. There are storage and retrieval problems with photos and negatives, too, and these are currently being resolved by a massive program to place all the photographs on videodiscs. This five-year project will be of tremendous importance to researchers and to other museums and universities, for the entire collection can be reduced for storage on ten or fifteen videodiscs. At relatively low expense, these can be reproduced and sent to other research centers, effectively placing NASM's collection at the disposal of the world.

A researcher will be able to sit at a computer terminal and flick through the entire collection, or at least through his own area of interest, in a comparatively brief time, retrieving the photos he needs in hard copy and not damaging the originals by handling. Much of the joy in research is the serendipitous finding of something that you didn't know existed, and the videodisc will enhance this prospect.

In a similar way, the Museum plans to set up a central source for indices of all the major aeronautical collections in the world, an "Index of Indices," if you will. Researchers will be able to come to NASM to plot their itineraries for research tasks, saving them the familiar fate of journeying to an expected source only to find that what was expected is not there. The long-range plans—which depend upon some advances in the art of microform copy, and, as always, upon the budget—envisage a true research center, where microfiche copies of the actual content of all the world's major collections will be on hand. The attraction of such a prospect is that this aggregation of information will be available not only at NASM but also, at very reasonable cost, at other museums around the world. Microfiche itself is relatively inexpensive. The cost lies in the actual compilation, indexing, and filming of the material. Once this is done, perhaps by a system of grants, the microfiche copies can be duplicated at negligible expense, and data processing can be used to transmit both soft and hard copy.

Collections management also involves such mundane tasks as inventorying the collection. A genuine hands-on inventory had not been taken at the Smithsonian until 1978, when NASM began a modern, computer-oriented identification of every item in its collection. A year later, Congress instructed the Smithsonian to have all the other museums follow suit, and many of the techniques developed by Al Bachmeier have been applied elsewhere.

By January 1983, every item in the Museum's collection will have been identified, photographed, treated, and placed in appropriate storage. The inventory process has brought many benefits not originally considered. Thousands of items not known to have been in the collection have surfaced; in the same way, a smaller number of items that were either duplicates or had deteriorated to the point where restoration was impossible have been removed. The careful administrative process ensures that nothing of value is lost to the collection, while also channeling duplicate items into the hands of other museums.

The inventory has demonstrated some potential savings, too. During the process of setting up the museum for opening in 1976, an effort was made to obtain flying clothing from all the major combatants in World War II. Lengthy negotiations, at considerable expense, provided uniforms from Germany, England, and elsewhere. Then, in the course of the inventory, a huge unidentified box was opened, and found to contain all the uniforms needed, and more. No one knew they existed, except for one of the "old guard" who had forgotten

The various galleries are done thematically; here you see the World War I Gallery. The Fokker D VII at the left was captured at a front-line aerodrome near Verdun. The Albatros D Va at right is one of the Museum's very best restoration efforts.

Lockheed XP-80. Painted in English regulation green: When the aircraft was being built, Lockheed was temporarily out of the standard American olive drab and "borrowed" the paint from a production line building aircraft for England.

The Hughes racer is considered by many to be the most beautiful piston-engine aircraft ever made; it hangs in the Gallery of Flight Technology. The sleek low-wing monoplane set a land speed record of 352.322 mph in 1935, and a transcontinental speed record in 1937. Howard Hughes had a large part in the design of the aircraft, and flew it for almost all of its forty-four hours of flying time.

about them. Similarly, a special portion of the automatic direction-finding radio in a Messerschmitt Me 262 was fabricated, at considerable expense; during the inventory no less than *one dozen* identical radios were found in mint condition.

Another surprising benefit of the inventory was the great saving in space requirements. When an artifact was shipped in by a loving donor, it usually came in a giant package. Quite often a box the size of a foot-locker would contain nothing more than a well-wrapped and completely padded altimeter, perhaps in a 6-inch-square container. After the item had been cleaned, identified, and photographed, it is placed in a special protective box tailored to its exact size, with a resultant saving of several cubic feet of floor space.

Retrieval time of artifacts has been reduced as well. Previously, it might take three days to three years to locate an item, for the process depended mainly on the ability of the man who handled it last to locate it again. Now any item can be picked up from an exact storage location in about twenty minutes.

The use of the automated printout and photograph has been a big help in research. A curator can scan a series of entries and photographs to determine the suitability of an item for exhibit, loan, or study. Before, he would have had to go to Silver Hill, unearth the item from whatever mysterious location it was in, uncrate it, and then make a determination. As the original documentation was spotty at best, this often entailed going through half a dozen items before something suitable was found.

But perhaps the biggest beneficiaries of the inventory process have been other museums, via NASM's extensive loan program. The inventory has been able to determine just how many of each item are in the collection. Should there be more than are needed for exhibit or study, these can be made available for loan to bona fide non-profit museums around the world.

Everything about a museum is implicitly educational. But the Education Services Division at NASM creates programs tailored to specific teaching needs. When NASM was built, the architect tried to make all the areas equally ac-

cessible for the handicapped, and exhibits were designed in a similar way. This is essential, but it is somewhat passive, so the Education Services Division also has tried to devise many active programs to make the Museum serve the disabled better.

The visually impaired visitor is offered a number of devices that can enhance his or her experience, ranging from taped cassettes of the labels to thermoform models, essentially Braille representations of the artifacts, which give a tangible sense of what is on show. Analogous programs exist for the hearing-impaired.

Yet, for all the exhibits, and even the artifacts, many visitors leave the Museum most impressed by the feature films they have seen on the giant five-story screen. A process called IMAX permits the flooding of a huge screen with brilliant, crystal-clear images of flight and gorgeous scenery. The first film, *To Fly*, has achieved a cult status—almost 6 million visitors have seen it. It is basically a simple story of the chronology of air and space travel, told in swift-moving travelogue vein, with just enough thrills and hokey humor to make it memorable. Some visitors brag of having seen it hundreds of times; some few say "never again" when their stomachs rebel against the inverted flight scenes.

The second film, *Living Planet*, has been almost equally successful, even though it departed completely from *To Fly* in style, and presented a message on the beauty and the fragility of our environment.

A third film is currently in the works. It has a tough task, for it must be as good as *To Fly* without repeating it. We shall see.

Each one of these activities at NASM creates demands upon the staff of the Garber Facility. First and foremost, of course, is the preparation of restored artifacts for exhibit. The Museum develops a five-year plan for exhibits, and artifacts must be prepared to go in place when the exhibit is ready for them. As a single job of aircraft restoration might take from twelve to twenty-four months, the restoration schedule has to precede the exhibit schedule by that amount of time.

When the gallery is ready to receive the restored artifact, it must be disassembled, placed

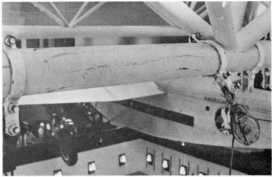

The DC-3 went through several test lifts to determine that the weight and balance were correct, that the various devices were positioned correctly, and that all of the cables were fastened securely. It looked just fine . . .

With a crack like a rifle shot, one of the clamps holding a rigging pulley opened and shot along the pipe girder, smacking into the triangular bracing . . .

The movement of the clamp was sufficient to let the left wing of the DC-3 drop—along with our hearts and our hopes. E. J. Thomas had been standing right where the wing touched down, but he was watching and when the wing moved, so did he. At this point we didn't know how badly damaged the aircraft was—if we had to remove it for repairs, we would not have had time to bring it back to the Museum before opening day.

A sad crew. Author is at far left, next to the Museum director, former astronaut Michael Collins, who endured the trauma with his usual cheerful stoicism. E. J. Thomas, for once without a hat, is next to him; at far right is Hernan Otano, one of the prime movers in opening the Museum, and wizard behind the audiovisual effects.

The following week, fully repaired, the DC-3 goes up again. The lift was tricky, as the right wing had to go up and over the balcony, while the left had to fit within the vertical pipe beams at the windows. The man with forefinger extended is Frank Murray, who directed the rigging operations, and without any exaggeration is a full-fledged genius at the business.

on a flatbed truck, and transported through the dark Washington streets at two o'clock in the morning to avoid daylight traffic jams. Once inside the Museum, it has to be moved to its gallery, often involving a crane lift to the second floor, and then placed in position and reassembled. Inevitably, some dings are inflicted en route, and these must be touched up. Then the question of positioning the aircraft arises. If it is simply mounted on the floor, there isn't much of a problem; but if it has to be suspended to fit in with the design, a number of considerations arise.

In the first place, aircraft weren't designed to be hung in museums, and most don't have suitable pick-up points. No one likes to alter an artifact, so a pick-up device has to be created that will fit some natural strongpoint on the aircraft—the engine mounts, the wing spar, the landing gear trunnion, or whatever. Then the right place in the ceiling has to be found, and usually there isn't any, as the gallery roofs are crisscrossed with sprinkler systems, heating ducts, and lighting tracts.

Typical Silver Hill skills are called upon, however, and "strongbacks"—large steel I-beams—are laid out in such a pattern that the aircraft can be supported. Then the exacting, sometimes frightening task of lifting the aircraft into position, securing it, and letting it hang begins.

The Silver Hill crew has the method down pretty perfectly now, but it still involves a great deal of strain to place the only remaining example of an airplane 10 feet in the air, suspended by cables that are swedged in place, and know that the public will be walking underneath. The solution is uncompromising insistence on quality material, redundant cabling, and continuous cross checks to ensure that everything is done correctly.

The track record has been pretty good so far, with several hundred objects ranging in weight from 5 ounces to 17,500 pounds successfully hung, and only two untoward instances. The first one occurred during the suspending of the Douglas DC-3, and we learned a lot from it.

The process of suspension had been pretty well defined by the time we got to the Gooney Bird, the heaviest item hanging from the Museum's circular pipe girders. A special set of lifting cables, used previously on the Museum's "Qué Será Será," the Navy version of the DC-3 that had flown at the South Pole, was used as the primary method of suspension, while a secondary set of cables was rigged directly to the landing gear structure.

The cables had been checked, the fittings had been magnafluxed, and the pipe clamps that secure the lift cables to the girders had been X-rayed. A procedure had been devised for the lift, so a series of short lifts was begun, raising the gleaming DC-3 a few feet off the floor while the cables and fittings were checked. Everything looked okay.

On the day of the lift I foolishly put out a notice that the staff was invited to watch, and the second-floor balcony was packed with people. Everything seemed fine, and the Gooney Bird had risen majestically to a height of 15 feet off the ground when what sounded like a rifle shot cracked, the left wing dipped, there was a crunch and a shudder. The DC-3 hung in a 45-degree angle from the girders, one wing pointing futilely up, the other bent grotesquely on the floor. (Don't ever believe the old story that in moments like this your past flashes across your mind—it is your future that stares you in the face.)

I jumped down from my perch on the balcony to see if anyone was hurt (miraculously, no one was) and then we assessed the damage. The DC-3's wingtip was bent up, but the wing itself was not hurt. It was the moral equivalent of a fender-bender.

Upon analysis, it turned out that the rigger had placed some side stress on one of the circular pipe clamps being used to raise the aircraft in place. This had opened it just a little, but sufficiently to permit it to shoot along the circular pipe girder like a bowling ball down an alley; the slack it thus provided the cable allowed the wing to drop and I became the first man ever to damage a wingtip on a Gooney Bird inside a building.

The U.S. Air Force quickly responded to a call for help, furnishing us with a replacement wingtip from the C-47 stores at Robins Air Force Base, Georgia, the very next day. Two days later it was installed and polished out, and a week after that, with a careful rehearsal and an inspection to ensure that there were no side loads, the DC-3 went up like the lady she is.

The other incident was minor. A small model, not an artifact, was hung in an exhibit. The swedge, a small lead fitting that mashes into cable to form the bond, didn't hold, and the model plummeted to the floor, causing quite a bit of damage to it but not to anything else. It was absolutely inexplicable, for we had hung hundreds of items weighing far more with exactly the same methods. Investigation revealed that the swedging tool had been loaned out and abused in the process; it couldn't effect the clamping forces necessary to form the lead bond. Another lesson was learned: Sequester all tools used in the suspension process, and keep them calibrated at all times.

The general success of the suspension operation, during which plane after plane went up like weights on a clock, was due primarily to the cooperation generated by the professional rigging crews and the in-house Smithsonian personnel. The professional crews were led by a charming black Irishman named Phil Kelly,

who promised you everything and somehow delivered, and the Pavarotti of crane operations, Frank Murray. Perhaps Toscanini might be a better allusion, for Frank directed the mammoth crane through intricate maneuvers with the slightest motion of his fingers, snaking a 70-foot boom attached to a 10,000-pound airplane through invaluable artifacts and a tangled tracery of existing cables. On the NASM side, Ed Chalkley and always be-hatted E. J. Thomas, Ed's close friend and mentor, ran a tightly disciplined but fun-filled ship.

Oddly enough, of all the problems they tackled, the most difficult proved to be disassembled aircraft which had to be lifted to the second floor. A fully assembled aircraft has a center of gravity, usually exactly defined, and often pick-up points that permit easy movement. A disassembled aircraft is entirely different. It seems to become alive, and can cause serious, dangerous problems by its nervous intractability.

Perhaps the worst case ever was the fuselage

One big delight of working at the Museum is the opportunity to meet legendary figures of the past, here one of the greatest test pilots and businessmen of all times. Brigadier General Harold R. Harris set many records before becoming an airline pioneer, and today still has a marvelous if sometimes ribald sense of humor. From left, Donald S. Lopez, chairman of the Aeronautics Department; General Harris; his granddaughter Stephanie Stevens; and the author.

of the Spitfire Mark VII, which seemed to heave with a malevolent spirit, anxious to turn upon anyone attempting to move it.

The big Merlin engine naturally made the wingless Spitfire extremely nose-heavy, and this was thought to be compensated for by a series of weights and tiedowns, which presumably would keep the nose from bobbing down or the tail from bobbing up. Somehow the Spit seemed to have an insane vertical center of gravity as well. (It did. Of course, all things do, but in most cases this simply doesn't matter for rigging purposes.) The Spitfire, normally the most tractable of airplanes by reputation, had become a "Jaws" shark of rigging.

The pretty airplane made its first attempt to bite the crew loading it on the flatbed truck for the move downtown, lunging at them as it was maneuvered into place by the forklifts and crane. It seemed ready to leap out and crush anyone nearby, its tail swiveling and fuselage rolling. No matter how many tiedown straps were used, it seemed to maintain a capacity to hurt. The unloading process at the Museum was similar; every attempt to move the aircraft resulted in wild gyrations that threatened itself and anyone within arm's reach. Finally subdued by sheer force, it was ready for the lift upstairs, over the vulnerable glass balcony wall, for transportation into the World War II Gallery.

The camouflaged fuselage was rigged carefully at what seemed to be its center of gravity, and tag lines, ropes to control the movement, were passed out to the strongest workers to apply force in whatever direction was needed to keep the maverick Spit under control.

The next few minutes reminded me of Victor Hugo's story of the cannon loose below decks on the rolling sailing ship. The Spit fuselage buckled like a gaffed salmon and seemed ready to leap out of its moorings. Every time it moved one way, one of the tagline holders would ride herd on it, inducing another oscillation in the opposite direction. Within a few minutes it had exhausted everyone, including the crane operator who felt the gyrations transmitted through his lifting boom.

The fuselage was placed on the floor and shored up in a vertical position while a whole new lifting jig was fabricated. It was intended to pull the c.g. (center of gravity) back toward the tail, and so provide an easier means of controlling with tag lines.

With the new rig the Spitfire went up like a subdued pony, nibbling at freedom, but firmly held in check. There was a collective sigh of relief when it was finally deposited in a cradle and fastened with multiple tiedowns for the short trip down the hallway to its new resting place.

From that point on, it was a piece of cake—the airplane went together easily, with no more trouble. It stands in the World War II Gallery now, proud, and confident of a long tenure, for no one will want to go through the hassle of taking it out.

The people from Silver Hill learned from every incident like this, and went on to do extensive exhibit work, something outside their usual line. Whenever there is a task too difficult to specify for a commercial contractor, the Silver Hill gang is called in to handle it. It may be placing two dozen propellers in varying sizes on a 50-foot-high wall, or building a staging area from which to view a mural, or simply getting a gallery finished on time. But the gang, like the Marines, is always ready.

Still, the main focus of their work is at the Garber Facility, where the essential restoration process goes on. And this is what we'll be looking at next.

3

Restoration at Silver Hill

On a trip to the Garber Facility, you are immediately struck with the tempo of operations, the cleanliness of the surroundings, and the variety of things going on. In the first building, 24, a small team of men may be in the process of assembling Bevo Howard's Bücker Jungmeister, the white and red biplane in which he entertained thousands with his aerobatic skills, and in which, sadly, he crashed fatally in 1971. Outside, down the narrow, grass-bordered road leading to the main workshop, Building 10, you might find a completed World War I de Havilland D.H. 4 being systematically photographed by Dale Hrabak, recording the accomplishment of yet another restoration. To the left of Building 10, George Genotti, *our* "Italian Stallion," and Dale Bucy might be rinsing down an ancient English engine, while through 10's open doors you could spot Mike Lyons's derrière disappearing inside the fuselage of a Focke-Wulf Fw 190.

Inside the shop there is the same sort of ordered pandemonium. A crackling stream of sparks flashes from the welding shop where iron-man Bill Stevens is creating yet another metal jig to support the next plane entering the system. Down the way, Reid Ferguson is methodically fitting together one of the biggest jigsaw puzzles of all time, the intricately structured Northrop N-1M Flying Wing.

Crossing over, past Harvey Napier hunched intently over a lathe, Garry Cline is using his surgeon's fingers to reassemble *Minerve*, a delicate tracery of jeweled sculpture that depicts a fanciful balloon/ship/household in flight. To his right, Wil Powell runs the bubbling tanks of the corrison-control shop like a sorcerer, with Bayne Rector, a Magnum look-alike, as his rather tall apprentice.

In the office, Carol Lockhart calmly keeps everything and everyone on schedule.

All this is only a portion of what is happening at any one time. Downtown there is a crew lifting a spacecraft into position; another is in Building 22, disassembling the only remaining Japanese Nakajima B6N Jill in the world. The Jill was almost destroyed during thirty years of exposure to the elements at its Willow Grove graveyard, but it is now guaranteed protection and ultimately restoration.

Work goes on, too, in the warehouses, where a mixed crew of Garber workers and curators generates the seemingly endless inventory.

Like a shepherd circling his flock, Walter "Rod" Roderick moves fluidly from spot to spot, bringing a needed tool, a manual, a bit of advice, or the latest instructions from "downtown." Rod is the leaven that causes the spirits of the shop to rise as well as the binder that keeps it together. It is not uncommon to see him telling a craftsman exactly how to approach some delicate combination of wood and fabric work, while at the same time dusting a display case. He's in perpetual useful motion.

This constant stream of activity goes on without end, for the task at Silver Hill, roughly figured, would take the present crew another hundred years to complete, even if one as-

An important photo, though no one knew it at the time. Two of the three fine managers of Silver Hill are at work on their first project, Wiley Post's *Winnie Mae,* now on exhibit in the Gallery of Flight Testing. The baby-faced young man at the far right is Ed Chalkley, who is now chief of Production Operations for the entire facility. Next to him is Walter Roderick, chief of Restoration. These two men, along with Al Bachmeier, have contributed more to Silver Hill's success than anyone else, and they've done it by dint of long hours of hard work, innate good sense, and the best possible motivation.

The three key men today—Ed Chalkley, Al Bachmeier, and Walter Roderick.

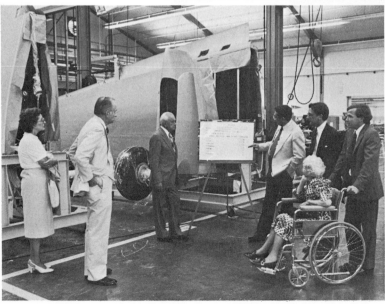

One of the genuine pleasures of Silver Hill is the distinguished visitors it attracts. Here T. Claude Ryan tours the facility, and as is usually the case with such towering pioneers, he knew some inside information on virtually every aircraft there. The chart is the "bogey board" used to keep the restoration crews on schedule in regard both to calendar time and man-hours expended. The aircraft in the rear is a Nakajima Irving night fighter. From left, Mrs. Shillito; Mr. Barry Shillito, chairman of the board of Teledyne, Inc.; Mr. Ryan, the author; Mrs. Ryan; Mitchell Stanley; and Neil Hammersmith.

sumed that no new tasks were added. There are at least a hundred aircraft that require preservation or restoration, and at least twice that many engines, and even the productivity of the Silver Hill crew can handle only so many at a time.

The task is made less daunting for Roderick and Chalkley by several factors, however, for Silver Hill management disposes of some unique assets. The first is an extraordinarily well motivated crew—this outfit lives and breathes aircraft. Most of the men either own an airplane or are building one, or incredibly detailed models of one. Second is the remarkable overlapping bags of skills. Many of the senior men—Joe Fichera, Charlie Parmley, Ferguson, Cline, and others—are skilled in not one but several of the necessary disciplines for a first-class restoration. Each of these men is a master craftsman in woodworking, metalworking, fabric working, doping, painting, jig building, tool building, engine teardown, airframe assembly, and so on. As a result, there is a flexibility in scheduling that an ordinary engine and airframe repair shop couldn't possibly have.

Even with these artists, Silver Hill puts additional demands on talent, for it is basic to NASM's philosophy that aircraft should be restored exactly as they were built, using the same materials and the same methods that went into their original construction. A team working on an Albatros D Va from 1917 will do the rib stitching just as the German worker would have done at the Albatros Werke in Johannisthal, and the cotter pins on the Mercedes engine will be turned in just the manner demanded by the inspector at the German plant. In effect, this preserves technology as well as artifacts, and may be equally important.

The same team that put the Albatros together might next be called upon to do a Japanese aircraft, and with little more than a change in position and a different tool box, will do the same level of replicative work.

So precise are these craftsmen that when, reluctantly, a part must be replaced instead of repaired, it is always stamped "Duplicate part by NASM," or "Repaired by NASM," with the date, so that perhaps two hundred years from

now scholars will be able to tell what really was original and what was replaced.

The patience and skill required for restorations like these are demanding. Garry Cline spent two years thoroughly immersed in the Albatros, and finally became so nervous that he turned to his next project, some less demanding exhibit work downtown, with real relief.

A major concern to NASM's top management is the eventual replacement of these talented artists. (Note the word "artist," rather than "artisan." The people at Silver Hill are artists in every sense of the word, from the implicit dedication, training, and care to the demonstration of unique talent.) The average age at Silver Hill is about fifty and many of the men have worked there for more than twenty years. Fortunately, the place is immensely attractive to would-be restorers of all ages, and there is a continuous stream of applicants who want to go to work. Some say they will work for nothing, and there has been more than one case of a highly paid executive seriously pleading for a chance to leave his lucrative profession and make a mid-life career conversion to start work as an apprentice.

As a result of a little planning, a sufficient number of talented young men have been hired to create what is in effect a guild system. From hundreds of applicants, Roderick and Chalkley have been uncommonly lucky in selecting a half dozen young men and women who meet their stringent screening. The first thing they demand is a willingness to work, to cram ten hours' work into every eight-hour day, and do it willingly and with good cheer. The second thing is adaptability, for work one morning might mean standing in freezing weather levering a 7,000-pound fuselage off an 18-wheeler, and the afternoon might mean scraping rust from the fins of a sixty-year-old rotary engine.

The new men are put through a series of training experiences, working side by side with the experts. The older men pass on their skills and methods, and let the younger men pick up the heavy end of the labor. Oddly enough, the climate of Silver Hill is such that the older men are more than willing to listen to the younger troop's ideas and, if they are good, adopt them. It doesn't happen often, for the senior workers have seen most things come around more than once, but it is implicit at Silver Hill that anything worth adopting will be adopted, regardless of its source. The "not invented here" philosophy is not permitted.

As the tasks of the shop permit, the younger workers are rotated from job to job, and in the course of time pick up all of the skills, with special emphasis on the ones they are most interested in.

All this talent is purchased at bargain rates, for the U.S. civil servant classification system is not designed to be able to reward talents as exceptional as these. A carpenter in another museum, whose biggest challenge is knocking together two-by-fours for a room divider, gets paid the same rate as a Silver Hill man with the same length of service, even though the latter

can take apart the gossamer wings of a 1911 Blériot and replace them with the same ash-cap strips, antique brass nails, and new glue. It's exploitation of a sort, but nobody leaves Silver Hill—that's where they want to be.

The twenty-eight-person work force at Silver Hill undertakes myriad tasks, but they break down into six main missions. First and foremost is *restoration*, which is the fun and the soul of the place, and which has come to have a certain meaning, as this chapter explains. Second is *preservation*, which approaches restoration in importance, but doesn't have quite the same degree of challenge or interest. Preservation and the additional four missions—the Museum itself, warehousing, exhibit support, and the physical production of exhibits—will be covered in the next chapter.

Restoration

The Garber Facility *is* restoration in the minds of many people who work there, and certainly the facility's primary reputation is based upon restoration.

The job of restoration involves taking a museum artifact—an airplane, an engine, an instrument, a spacecraft—and with absolute care and fidelity restoring it to the condition it enjoyed during its active career. This is easier said than done, for many aircraft have had more than one career. Charles Blair's Mustang, *Excalibur III*, started out as a stock P-51C; it was modified for racing, and Paul Mantz won the Bendix Trophy Race twice in it before Blair acquired it and further modified it for trans-Arctic flights. It would look great in any configuration, but its most important work was really the later navigational exploits. It was decided to reproduce it accordingly.

The process of restoration involves an enormous amount of preplanning. The selection of the aircraft to be restored is a matter of endless discussion. The requirement to restore an aircraft usually results from the need to exhibit it in the Museum downtown. Because exhibit galleries can be conceived, written about, and produced in less time than it takes to restore an aircraft, a great deal of forecasting must be

done—forecasting that begins with the five-year master plan for exhibits.

Once an exhibit gallery has been decided upon—The Golden Age of Flight, for example—members of management and the curatorial staff must determine which aircraft should go into the gallery to best represent what they wish to show. Often restored aircraft are ready to be exhibited, but sometimes there is an essential one that *must* be in the gallery and must therefore be restored.

When an aircraft is selected for restoration, a whole series of parallel processes begins. The plane itself is carted from storage to Building 10, where it is carefully cleaned and disassembled. During this process a senior craftsman, Joe Fichera perhaps, will supervise, making voluminous notes. He will determine if there are any parts missing, if there are any bogus or incorrect parts attached (surprisingly, not too rare an occurrence), if there have been any non-standard repairs, and if there is any damage that must be repaired by other than conventional techniques, such as welding a magnesium component.

Each stage of the disassembly is photographed, from major subsection, as in the demating of wing and fuselage, down to individual minor components, like the washers, springs, pistons, plungers, valves, pipes, and so on that make up the hydraulic mechanism of a retractable landing gear. This is essential even for these master mechanics, for often no documentation at all exists on the artifact, and something that seems straightforward on disassembly becomes a nightmare of miscellaneous parts when it's time to put it back together again. A good example is the carburetion system of a Japanese engine—not too different in appearance on simple inspection, but a devil to reassemble without photos.

While this is going on, the curators will be determining in what guise the aircraft should appear on exhibit. The rule, normally, is that it will appear in its most appropriate markings and colors for the purpose of the exhibit. In general, NASM follows a practice of *not* refurbishing aircraft in the markings of another, more famous aircraft of the same type. We would not, for example, restore our P-38 in the markings of Major Richard Bong, the leading U.S. ace of World War II, with forty victories. If we had Bong's actual airplane, we would, of course, be delighted to do so. The fear is that taking such a liberty, even if it were well explained in the labels, would inevitably lead visitors to some false conclusions. Instead, we attempt to chose a "plain vanilla" airplane, one with representative markings of the time that can be well documented.

If the exact markings of the plane can be determined, no matter who flew it, these will often be reapplied, as is the case of the Messerschmitt Me 262 now in the Museum.

As soon as the disassembly process is done, an inventory is made of all missing parts, and of all major repair work required. Bob Mikesh, prolific author and the Museum's Curator of Aircraft, has a wide network of contacts to seek out missing parts; he also prepares a curatorial package that will place on record the desired work and final markings.

At this point, a solution to a management problem peculiar to Silver Hill surfaces. In the past, one of the few hazards managment had was that a person would fall in love with a project, and do more and better work than necessary. When we were restoring Amelia Earhart's Lockheed Vega, a young man named

Norman Goldstein was putting the finishing touches to it. He waxed it, then rewaxed it, then waxed it again, although it was already burnished to a firelike glow. He was needed on other projects, but I came in one morning to find him headed back to the airplane, wax and rags in hand. We had a little heated discussion, in which he noted that my desire for perfection could be compared unfavorably with the men who produced Edsel automobiles. It ended with me telling him, "If you put one more coat of wax on that Vega, you're fired!" He stopped, but it was clear that the Vega, which looked perfect to everyone else, including the old heads in the shop, still wasn't ready in his eyes.

The fact is that the staff have a firm concept of their duty to give the Museum their very best work, and if something is not 110 percent perfect, they're not satisfied. In the past we've used a historical analogy to make the point that what is done should only be done as well as production aircraft of the time. Imagine, we told them, that you are a German worker at Messerschmitt in late December 1944. You're building 262s on a line in a forest, without even a roof over your head; you've lost your son on the Russian front, you know the war is lost, you hate the Nazis, you haven't had a decent meal in years, and you're working seventy-two hours a week in freezing weather. It is unlikely that you'll make a part better than necessary to be safe (for you're still a patriotic German) and to pass the inspector. It's a cinch you won't spend your lunchtime polishing out the back of an inspection panel that no one will ever see.

Well, the men listen to the story—but they still want to polish the back of the inspection panel, for this isn't for the Third Reich, it's for the National Air and Space Museum, and for posterity. Their name is figuratively on the project, and they want perfection.

The danger of this approach is that too many hours will be spent on that extra 10 percent of perfection that could be better applied to another project. To offset this fascination with perfection, but still not inhibit it, the team assigned to a project is required to estimate the total number of man-hours required to complete it, and then break this estimate down into time required for each of the major components, wing, fuselage, etc.

This estimate is reviewed by the shop management, and usually revised upward, based on past experience. It becomes a self-imposed bogey, one that helps determine the completion date of the aircraft.

If, for example, a total of 6,600 hours is estimated for the Messerschmitt Me 262, with 2,000 hours for the fuselage, 2,200 for the wings, and so on, it begins to serve as a guide. Suppose the team has put in 1,600 hours on the fuselage and it is only 50 percent complete, they know they are going to have to come up with some improved methods to reach their own target. As it is implicit that they won't skip on quality, new and more efficient techniques are the result.

As might be expected, the idea of a bogey was not well received at first, but in time the crews came to like it, and take great pride when they can improve the forecast. Practice has shown that in most cases the actual hours come out within 15 percent of the estimate, a pretty fair record. In some cases, where perhaps some totally unexpected corrosion problem exists, the estimate gets revised upward to meet the new knowledge.

For most restorations a two-man team is assigned, with specialists called upon as needed. Within the individual case, the two men decide who does what and in what general sequence. They develop a task list for each component, then set about in a methodical way that provides for the most cost-effective handling.

One essential task that facilitates the restoration is done at the time of disassembly: this is the fabrication of special stands on which to mount the major components of the aircraft. Many of the airplanes came to Silver Hill mounted on huge oak skids, and these have deteriorated over time. One of Al Bachmeier's first ideas was to custom-fit steel skids to each component for easier handling and storage. He'd been derided for suggesting it, being told the cost of the steel was too much. When he pointed out the hundreds of man-hours it would save in handling, he was laughed at. As a result, a great deal of further damage was done to airframes when the wooden skids broke, or when the forklifts attempting to move them jabbed the structure.

Now the very first task on disassembly is to fabricate the stands. I am not personally a craftsman, having five thumbs on my right hand and six on the left, but over the years I have purchased a great deal of equipment for the government. I know that I could go to a local manufacturer and specify that I would like to buy a frame that would accommodate the fuselage of a Focke-Wulf Fw 190 A-8, one that could be rolled about the shop by two men, and that further would have the capability of rotating the fuselage through 360 degrees so that it would provide a convenient work station.

Any one of a number of manufacturers would jump at the chance to build it, and the quotes would come back for delivery in three months, at an estimated cost of perhaps $15,000. Then, a few weeks after the order was let, a query would come as to whether we wanted the stand built of steel or balsa wood. If I want steel, of course, it's $7,000 extra and another four weeks for delivery. An exaggeration, perhaps, but not by much.

At the Garber Facility, the two-man crew would approach the Focke-Wulf Fw 190 fuselage with several lengths of 6-inch I-beam steel, a welding torch, a plumb bob, T Square, and a fine eye for detail. Four days later, there is a beautifully executed steel skid, on casters, painted yellow, with pick-up points, weights, and so on marked, with a simple structure that rotates and can be pushed around the shop, fuselage on board, by two men. In short, triumphant Yankee ingenuity of the very best sort. The cost: about $600 worth of materials and eight man-days of labor, or another $800.

Since there may be as many as five restorations going on at any one time in the shop, all of which require special machining and corrosion-control effort, it becomes necessary for Rod to act as a focal point to ensure that a sensible schedule is maintained. There is a lead time in obtaining many of the scarce parts and even scarcer materials, and it takes a master chef's sense of the recipe to keep everything moving smoothly through the shop.

Corrosion Control

The first crunch point is Wil Powell's corrosion-control shop, through which will pass almost every metal part of a restoration. And part means every tiny subcomponent, the washers, rings, valves, pistons, springs, retainers, turnbuckles, wires, etc., which in their thousands are part of even relatively ancient aircraft. An affable, quiet, smiling man, Wil is an interesting study, even for Silver Hill. He is an accomplished pilot and mechanic, but he wanted desperately to work at Silver Hill in restoration. When he applied there was only one job available, in the corrosion-control department. We had previously employed a GS-9 to do the job and his efforts had been lamentable, for his biggest concentration of effort was on becoming a GS-11, while the work piled up.

Wil didn't know any more about corrosion control than any pilot would, but he came on board as a GS-7, willing to learn. He plunged himself into his work (a little in-joke among the dip-tank workers of corrosion control) and into a fearsome study program. He rearranged the shop for a better production flow, and in six months had the place clicking as it never had before. In a year he was confident, doing things in-house that had previously had to be sent out to contractors; in two years he was a recognized expert, whose advice was sought by museums around the country.

Wil's task is extremely difficult. Not only does he have to work with corrosive liquids, in steaming vats that look like a Cubist set for the witches' scene in *Macbeth;* he also has to accommodate to an endless flow of similar-looking parts, often without any information as to their material content.

While almost anyone can differentiate a Zero from a Mustang in appearance, it becomes increasingly difficult to tell what belongs to which as their parts are disassembled. By the time you are down to the interior mechanism of flap-retraction gear, one washer begins to look very much like another, even though they are completely non-interchangeable.

As the parts come in, Wil has to maintain absolute control over their identity while they pass through a process that will involve cleaning, rinsing, etching, rinsing, plating, rinsing again, and polishing. In addition, the myriad parts are often made of unusual materials; they are not always simply steel or aluminum. Wil

has to detect what they are made of before he starts, for the wrong material in the wrong solution can result in reactions ranging from dissolution to explosion.

There are larger problems, too. Some materials are so corroded that further cleaning will destroy them unless they are precisely handled; you cannot simply throw them into the vat for an overnight soak. Other components are miniature batteries, raging with electrolytic corrosion. The German and Japanese specimens present special challenges in this regard, for by 1945 they did not anticipate airplanes lasting thirty days, much less thirty years, and would cheerfully bolt aluminum to steel without even paint as a protective sealer. In these instances Wil is forced to deviate from original practice, for it would be insane to clean them up, then bolt them back together to start the whole process over again. Instead, he will coat the two materials with an appropriate buffer, an epoxy perhaps, and make a note in the log that is kept on all restoration activities.

Wil has the temperament to stand long hours in front of stewing cauldrons, and the

The corrosion-control shop is not especially impressive-looking, consisting of fifteen or twenty vats, some bead-blasting equipment, and so on, but it is the single most important area of the facility. Here Wil Powell dunks an assembly into an aluminum acid deoxidizing tank. Wil took on the job of corrosion control with only a general working knowledge of what was required. He went into an intensive study program, and within two years was an expert.

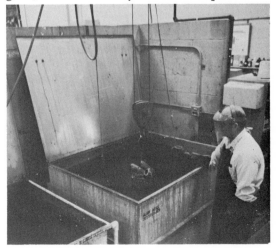

Bayne Rector came as an apprentice, and quickly took on an important role as an apprentice in the corrosion-control shop.

patience to etch and rinse, etch and rinse, sometimes for days, to remove the patina that an aircraft acquires in thirty years of outdoor exposure. He does have a temper, rarely excited but awesome when he is really ruffled, usually by someone undoing his carefully completed work.

He also has an excellent apprentice in Bayne Rector, who somewhat reluctantly agreed to begin to understudy Wil when he was hired. Bayne wanted to get into the regular shop work, painting, doping fabric, and so on, but we needed someone to back Wil up, and to learn for the future, and the younger man agreed. It's been a tough course, but he is now far more experienced in the intricacies of corrosion control than most men twice his age, and he will probably be brought into the shop to expand his experience in the next few years.

Machining

The other choke point in the shop process is machining. This is Harvey Napier's domain, and he rules it with an iron hand and an odd cackle. Harvey is one of the world's greatest machinists. He learned his skills over the years in a wide variety of important positions, including working on the original equipment at the atomic test site in Alamogordo, New Mexico.

Talking to Harvey is an experience—he makes Casey Stengel seem like a master of clarity. He provides long circumlocutious combinations of words that convey feeling, but not much meaning, to the listener, delivered with a fixity of eye and intensity of purpose that is riveting. Harvey has regarded the upgrading of equipment in the shop with some misgivings; he enjoys the new machinery, but somehow misses the challenge of the old. He had one lathe, a veteran at least of World War I and more probably the Spanish-American War, donated to the museum when the Naval Gun Factory shut down. It was as idiosyncratic as Harvey sometimes is, and only he could keep it accurate by aiming well-directed kicks at certain points as it turned.

Harvey is a rare combination of gloom, doom, and optimism. He has foreseen death and destruction in every change made at Silver Hill, once arguing himself successfully out of a promotion everyone else was determined to give him. On the other hand he goes out hope-

Harvey Napier at work on his lathe. Harvey is an incomparable craftsman, capable of doing Cellini-like work in any metal. He is also skilled in many other areas. Silver Hill is one of few such facilities to have its own art gallery, which can be seen across the shop on the wall.

fully to hunt deer each year, with rarely a kill to his credit.

When you want Harvey to do something, you have to approach him with the correct mixture of a little humbleness, a little kidding, but most of all with a real challenge. If you take him the breech mechanism of a German machine gun that is damaged, you have to determine early that you are going to tell him that it probably can't be repaired, that we don't have any documentation to go on, that it would be better to contract it out to some commercial firm at an exorbitant price, and that he is probably far too busy to do it anyway.

He'll grab it out of your hand, mumble something about "Why don't they get busy on earthquakes, it never did look good out there, if one man tires but nobody listens," and walk away with it. At this point you *do not* tell him how you think it should be done or when you need it.

A few days later he'll signal you to come over and with a quiet gleam of pride hand you back exactly what you wanted, having remembered that a Swiss machine gun in our collection had the same breech, and having copied it with absolute fidelity down to maintenance scratch marks. He'll gruffly accept any praise you dare offer, and go back to work.

Underneath all this brusque, almost unfathomable exterior is a wonderful, hardworking family man who has faced some severe personal health problems with his children with dogged determination. He is unique and, many of us fear, irreplaceable. We have other machinists, masters by most ordinary standards; but they don't have Harvey's Cellini-like ability to create almost from thin air exactly what is needed.

Roderick has the same scheduling problem with Harvey that he does with corrosion control, for there is literally a flood of things to be done and very few outside shops with the capability to do them. As a result it is necessary for him to manage Harvey's time with real precision, and make sure that any ordinary machining tasks are done by others or contracted out. One minor difficulty is that Harvey is not too happy when someone else uses his tools, so work is often done at night to keep him cool.

Two Master Metalworkers

The emphasis I've placed on the quality of work done at Silver Hill would be diminished if the extraordinary quantity of work were not also noted. The jewel-like quality of the restorations would be worthwhile almost irrespective of the time required, but Silver Hill marches to the master clock of history; its people are aware that their treasures, the artifacts, are literally being devoured by time, and there is an atmosphere of charged urgency to get the job done. As a result, the place hums like a World War II munitions factory, with people moving at a fast clip from one spot to another. One reason for this is Ed Chalkley, who has only one speed, full throttle. But there is also a general sense of seriousness that pervades the place. Two master mechanics and metalworkers, Bill Stevenson and Bob Padgett, seem to personify this spirit. Wherever they work, there seems to be a blur of activity. Both start early, work late, skip lunch, and take few breaks. Both have to be dragged from their

Dale Bucy, left, is a master metalworker, who can take a few hand tools and duplicate an intricate modern aircraft structure. Bill Stevenson on the right is perhaps the hardest working man of the hardworking crew; he too is an expert metalworker, but his forte is the construction of jigs and tools. With a few I-beams and a welding torch, Bill can create anything from lace to a bridge.

One of the "old guard," John Parlett combines an in-depth knowledge of safety procedures with an uncanny warehouseman's eye. He can estimate to the millimeter whether an airplane will fit into a certain spot, and if you have to move aircraft from one part of the country to another, he is the man to consult.

work periodically, just to rest, and both occasionally have flare-ups with outsiders—contractors perhaps, or civil servants from some other Smithsonian office—who don't keep up with their pace. Chalkley, a hard driver and a tough taskmaster, constantly has to keep on them to slow down so they don't make themselves ill. This probably seems like malarky in a world used to Oliphant cartoons showing bloated civil servants with their feet on the desk, and to Senator Proxmire's Golden Fleece awards, but it is the literal truth and can be verified any day by inspection.

Stevenson was stolen from another museum not by the promise of more pay but by the promise of harder, more challenging work. He is a little inconvenienced by some physical problems that might have invalided another man, but he steams at flank speed through the

Soft-spoken Bob Padgett is an instructor pilot, with multi-engine and instrument ratings. He sacrificed his full-time flying career to come to Silver Hill to work on historic aircraft. With Stevenson, he forms a one-two punch that literally rips into work. Here he is disassembling the equipment in the cockpit of the Nakajima Irving.

shop, leaving vortices of energy in his trail. Oddly, he always seems perplexed when he is complimented on his work, and is somewhat apologetic that he's only done the work of six men instead of eight.

Padgett, tall, lanky, quiet, but with a devastating sense of humor, is an instructor pilot for multi-engine aircraft, and has instrument and commercial ratings, but he came to work at Silver Hill just to get his hands on the artifacts.

The two men form an incredibly innovative team. They have undertaken a dozen tasks that would have stumped conventional engineers, then executed the metalwork necessary to bring each about. A typical example was lifting the 8,000-pound McDonnell FH-1 Phantom jet fighter up 10 feet into the air into a minuscule corner of the Jet Aviation Gallery. There was about 1 inch of play in all directions, but Stevenson and Padgett engineered a lifting sequence that placed the Navy jet up on slender metal slings, perfectly safe and solid.

Markings and Camouflage

I've digressed somewhat from the restoration sequence, but it was necessary to cover the ancillary events that go on.

Once the aircraft is cleaned, disassembled, and placed on stands, the work begins in earnest. One task that must be done with extreme delicacy is eliciting the original markings from beneath the layers of bogus paint, so that they can be reproduced on the finished aircraft.

Many of the foreign aircraft in the collection came to the United States at or near the end of the war. These were routinely painted over for maintenance or display purposes, with little or no regard for the original paint colors and markings. A typical aircraft might have three to five layers of American paint over its original German or Japanese markings, and all of the basic warning decals, instructions, and stencils with which all warplanes are so liberally covered will be completely overpainted.

To reach these important markings requires a knowledge of where they might be and a sanding technique reminiscent of that for removing dirt from around a fossil in an archeological dig. Hand sanding, gently done, gets rid of the covering paint and reveals the faint outlines of the original markings and paint. Samples of that original paint are then taken and analyzed spectroscopically to determine exactly what the colors were.

The markings and camouflage paint lines are recorded by another means. A translucent material called pounce paper, very similar to that used in dressmaker patterns, is applied over the newly uncovered markings, which might be a swastika, a squadron marking, a Japanese stencil, or whatever. The pounce paper is carefully keyed to prominent features of the aircraft—rivet lines, panels, grounding wire holes, and so on. The markings are then copied exactly, with voluminous notes on color, width, height, and spacing, and with particular attention to any anomalies, for there is no desire to improve on the markings—just to reproduce them exactly.

Camouflage patterns are reproduced in exactly the same way, an essential task since there is so much controversy and so many opinions on colors and squadron markings. Hobbyists and buffs tend to take factory specifications as gospel, and react violently if a finished reproduction doesn't measure up exactly to what was specified in the official directive. What they forget is that in the field, especially in the latter days of the war, literally anything could happen. Supplies were short, manpower was short, and the urgency of the situation transcended the need to have precisely measured outlines on national insignia. If standard-issue paints were unavailable, substitutes were used, and camouflage patterns were often supplied freehand rather than in strict conformance to instructions. There was a great deal more individuality than might be expected, and the only thing that you can say for sure is that "It might have been this way."

Taking the information directly from the aircraft avoids most of these problems, but not always, and sometimes not in cases that seem relatively routine. Charles Blair's *Excalibur III* is a case in point. Everyone knew it was a maroon, but just what shade? Colors fade on aircraft, and they also fade in memories and in photos. It is difficult to determine exactly what is the correct shade unless you do a chemical analysis.

In the case of Blair's airplane it was possible to do this, and furthermore, the original manufacturer of the paint was still in business. Paint was obtained which had an almost certain chance of duplicating that of the original. Except that when Charles Blair walked in, he said, "Hell, that's the wrong color!"

Intensive Cleaning

Once all of the detective work has been done, the pounce paper marked and stored, the intensive cleaning can begin. The paint is stripped by chemical and mechanical means, and the real corrosion-control problems are brought into focus. These can range from superficial, a mere requirement to treat and finish, to catastrophic, as in the case of Blair's Mustang.

Blair had been exceptionally thoughtful to the Museum. Before donating his beautiful racer, he had a commercial firm do a corrosion-control job on it. Unfortunately, commercial firms work for profit, and this one applied its efforts only to easily accessible areas. Combined with the fact that the P-51 had been modified to have a "wet wing" (the wing itself was used as a fuel tank), there was far greater corrosion than had been imagined. The landing gear trunnion was of magnesium, and badly corroded. A trunnion from a wrecked P-51 was found, but when brought in, it too proved to be damaged. Fortunately the damaged area was not the same as the corroded area on Blair's airplane, and it was possible, with some skillful cutting and welding of the magnesium (no easy task, as anyone who has seen magnesium burn knows), to replace the gear.

The Messerschmitt Me 262 was another case where corrosion exceeded the most pessimistic expectations. The 262's wing spar was steel, to which thick aluminum plates were attached. Padgett and Stevenson had to remanufacture the wing, literally, treating it all the while, to achieve the restoration.

Treatment of corrosion control sometimes becomes a problem due to sheer size. If the object—a wing section or fuselage—is too large to dip into a chemical bath, it is necessary to treat it in the open, alternately squirting it with liquid chemicals, then washing it with water to get rid of the residue. Mike Lyons, a skilled modeler and ardent historian, solved the Me 262 fuselage problem by draping it in a gigantic plastic tent, donning a respirator, then stepping inside the fuselage to burl it with powdered walnut shells delivered from a pneumatic gun. Mike spent over a hundred hours bringing the inside of the 262 to burnished perfection. He was the last man to see his work except for Rod, when he inspected it; and he will probably be the last man to see it for another century. But he knows it's right.

Missing Parts

The replacement of missing parts is a twofold challenge. If they exist in the collection, or anywhere in the world, it is preferable to run them down and bring them in for reinstallation, for the cost of location and transportation is inevitably less than the cost of remanufacture and, besides, they are in fact original parts. In some cases, no parts exist. In others, they turn up with serendipitous timing, as in the case of the Albatros D Va, for which a passing visitor contributed an otherwise unavailable magneto.

Replacing sheet-metal parts can mean either simple body and fender work or a tremendous challenge. Sometimes the missing part has severe compound curves and carries a portion of the structural load. It would be relatively easy to brace the structure and dummy up a fiberglass molding to replace the original part. No one would know, and an entry could be made in the restoration logbooks defending the action. Naturally, this is anathema to the Silver Hill crew.

A case in point was a piece of the left nacelle covering the Messerschmitt Me 262's Junkers Jumo 004 engine. It was a complex piece, with multiple compound curves, and it was designed to carry structural loads. Dale Bucy, who is a master metalworker, took a photo of the right-hand side and blew it up to full size. This was still not a plan, as it was a flat portrayal of a multi-curved surface, but it enabled him to begin. He reversed the negative, then cut out a larger than full-size copy in metal. By skillful measurement, bending, beating, and adroit use of eyeball guesses, he created a mirror-image duplicate.

Sometimes the creation of the tools to duplicate the parts takes far more time than the making of the part itself, once the tools are ready. When Rich Horigan was rebuilding the Albatros D Va fuselage, he faced what seemed an impossible task. The seventy-year-old plywood had delaminated and disintegrated, and there were but bits and pieces of the original fuselage intact. The Albatros had been built with a sophisticated system of formers wrapped with three-ply wood, some of it molded to fit the compound curves of the streamlined shape. Rich had first to create the male and female molds, using plaster, and carefully cutting and fitting to obtain the same shapes. Once the molds were complete, special plywood of the exact thickness of the original was obtained from Finland, and this was placed in the molds. The molded shape was then fitted and glued to the fuselage, a process much less time-consuming than making the molds themselves.

In a similar way, George Genotti, the smiling Italian, had to fabricate male and female dies to recreate the stringers used in building the nose of the Me 262. The original stringers had been stock material, turned out by the mile by German factories. George had to create the dies from metal, then painstakingly hammer out the stringers, foot by foot, so that he captured the exact size and appearance of the originals. George also fabricated new gun mounts for the 262, using another aircraft's parts as a pattern.

George is a very bright man, capable of deep insights both into his work and into society; he raises bees, makes wine, and can do anything with his hands. His volatile temper renders him something of a target for Chalkley's practical jokes. It's a rare day when George's lunchbox is not welded to the ceiling, or his tool box weighted down with lead, or a composite photo made up showing George in completely phony—and funny—compromising positions. George bears it all in good humor, eating his hot pepper lunches, and more often than not getting his revenge the same day with an astute application of salt to somebody's coffee.

The degree of disassembly of the aircraft is surprising even to the knowledgeable. George Genotti, an intelligent, sensitive man who might in another time have been a writer, can reproduce any metal part; he also can reassemble any equipment components, no matter how intricate or unfamiliar.

Once all the disassembly, corrosion control, and detective work has been done, a project generally seems to dissolve into the general background of activity of the shop. Progress is made day by day, but it is elusive and more easily noticed on the management charts than on the airplane itself. Dings are removed, equipment replaced, instruments found and installed, woodworking redone, fabric reapplied, and so on. It is exactly the same sort of work that would have gone on in the repair depots of the Luftwaffe, the Regia Aeronautica, or the Royal Air Force during the active service life of the aircraft. But there comes a time when all of the component parts are ready to be finished—and then the project seems to come alive again.

There are half a dozen excellent painters in the shop. Since "Handsome Charlie" Parmley is one of the best, he is usually called upon to do the finishing work. Charlie is the salt of the earth, a retired U.S. Air Force master sergeant, former crew chief, farm owner, collector of antique aircraft, sometime pilot, and inveterate storyteller. He can be depended upon for an amazing quantity of work of the highest quality, along with the ability to totally embarrass you and any important VIP you might be bringing around. I have this recurrent nightmare in which for some reason I'm showing the Queen of England and the Pope around Silver Hill, and as I round the corner, there's Charlie. I don't know what he's going to say, but I know it will be dreadful—and I know the Queen and the Pope will both laugh.

Charlie has a never-ending stream of stories, and if you had only a casual conversation with him, you would think he was a loafer, but his productivity equals or exceeds anyone else's in the place. He is particularly at ease with the

The smile is not there because a picture is being taken—Charlie Parmley is always smiling, and always has a joke to tell, usually bad. Charlie has become the leading expert on restoration of aircraft of the 1903–14 era.

aircraft of the very earliest period of flight, and in a single year restored the Curtiss Pusher on exhibit downtown. He is now engaged in a Museum first: we have all of a 1910 Benoist biplane except for the fuselage, and Charlie is recreating that from some drawings and photos.

A man who shares Charlie's deceptive work pattern is Reid Ferguson, a big, jolly, lumbering bear of a man who can do any job in the shop, but is regarded as the foremost plastic worker in the country. He has fabricated the intricate protective plastic shields around the various spacecraft in the Museum.

When you watch Reid work, the first impression is of very slow, deliberate effort. He doesn't move swiftly, and one gets the feeling that he wouldn't finish quickly. The essential key is that Reid never makes a false move; he never has to make anything over, never has to look for a tool, never has to take a second measurement. He is almost machine-like in his precision, and his deliberateness translates into speed.

Museums all over the world demand his talent, and we have had to become less generous in loaning him out than we were. A Japanese

group once borrowed some spacecraft from the Museum for exhibit in Japan, and had shipped them to a commercial firm on the West Coast to have the same sort of lexan covering placed over them that Reid had created for the Museum's exhibits. Six weeks and several thousand dollars later there was an emergency call from Japan—would we please send Reid to the West Coast to bail the company out, for they had not been able to duplicate the necessary lexan covering.

He is currently working on the Northrop N-1M, the only remaining Flying Wing of its period, and one that was intended only to be used for test purposes for two or three years before being scrapped. It is a complex structure, designed both for lightness and strength, but not for mass production, and it is literally becoming unglued. Reid patiently takes apart the numberless parts, scrapes the dried-out glue off, reglues them, clamps them back, and then reassembles the structure. Where the parts are missing in an area of several compound curves, Reid has devised, with John Cusack, a simple string measuring device that permits him to reproduce the surface exactly. Reid broke his legs in an automobile accident a few years ago, but as soon as he could get some steel rods inserted he was back on the job, hobbling from one task to another at his own deliberate (but swift!) speed.

Once Charlie has finished the paint work, and Reid has reinstalled any plastic or Plexiglas, the reassembly process begins, and it is here that some of the final frustrations surface. Parts that came apart with reluctance seem to go back together with hate. It becomes a matter of sweat, cursing, and tears to induce a thirty-year-old landing gear to retract again. Hydraulic seals burst, worn gears stick inexplicably and when unstuck do not hold at all, doors that seem to match and should close simply hang up. But eventually everything comes together, factory fresh, working well.

The question inevitably arises whether Garber Facility aircraft are restored to flying condition. Here, like any good bureaucrat, I'll waffle a bit. In the case of certain aircraft whose history is known, and whose condition is good prior to restoration, it could be said that they are brought back to flying condition. Ex-

amples might be the Blériot XI, whose low-time Gnôme Rhône rotary engine would run if properly prepared with lubricants, and whose airframe is in as good a shape as the day it left the factory; or the de Havilland D.H. 4, which needs only a new ignition harness and proper fluids to be ready to go.

In other cases the Museum has to recognize that there is an opportunity-cost in restoration, just as there is in investment. The hours put into the restoration of one artifact are not available to the restoration of another, and so decisions have to be made as to how close to flying condition an aircraft will be taken.

When the Vought Corsair F4U was restored, it was found that one of the big R-2800 engine's pistons had a crack in it. Rather than replace this piston, with the attendant expense and with full knowledge that the engine would never be run up again, the repair was not made, although a notation was inserted in the aircraft's curatorial file. The reasoning was that we have mint R-2800s available in case they were ever needed, and the additional time and expense required for repair would add nothing to the value of the aircraft as an exhibit or study item.

Similarly, if a minor crack were found in the wing spar of an aircraft being restored—one that would ground it from flight but not interfere with its being suspended or otherwise exhibited—it would probably not be repaired. It is simply a question of available man-hours.

Each aircraft is fully restored in the sense that all wiring and hydraulics are hooked up, all controls properly connected, and gears, flaps, and other parts can be made to operate. It would be wasteful to spend time restoring such things as radar, radios, and instruments to full operating condition, inasmuch as they would never be used and some of them operate on frequencies no longer in existence. All the parts and components of such equipment are preserved and reinstalled, however; if it were necessary for some legal or scholarly reason to make them work, they could be brought to operational status.

When fully assembled and touched up, the aircraft is rolled out for a complete photographic record session, and is then either placed on exhibit at Silver Hill or brought downtown. Once completed, it is a source of pride for the men who did the work; but after a few days it is somewhat forgotten as they immerse themselves in the next task.

In this description of the restoration process, I've tried to weave in some of the people who do the work as a narrative device. The truth is that everybody at Silver Hill deserves some discussion. Take Joe Fichera, for instance.

Joe is a graying (well, silver-haired) Italian phenomenon of sixty-plus years, recovered now from flying his antique Arrow Sport into the Maryland countryside on a return trip from the annual Ottumwa, Iowa, fly-in. Joe's knowledge of aviation at each phase of its progress is extraordinary. He knows the woods, dopes, and metals that were used in the 1920s, what techniques were developed in the 1930s, where the military differed from civil practice, where parts needed to repair the planes of the 1940s are, what new methods were introduced in the 1950s, and so on. He can look at a badly rusted component and tell you that it is of English manufacture, modified in the United States, and that "so-and-so" in Kansas has a matching piece.

The godfather of the shop, Joe Fichera. Joe is a veteran pilot and antique aircraft owner, and has definite ideas about how things should be done. If anyone runs into difficulty with a restoration, or with obtaining a replacement part, they usually come to Joe for help.

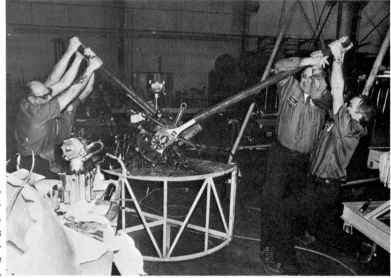

In a classic "get a bigger hammer" routine, Harvey Napier, Dale Bucy, Joe Fichera, and Mike Lyons tackle a nut on a Focke-Wulf's BMW engine assembly.

And Joe is sometimes the least little bit irritable, especially if you happen to contest what he is saying, for he is used to being right and to doing things his way. It is the prima donnaism of the maestro, and easily tolerated. He serves now as a sort of father figure to the entire group, usually engaged in doing his own restoration but available for consultation to anyone having a problem. With Joe, as with most people at Silver Hill, the main concern is to see that he doesn't overdo: he hates the thought that he no longer can grab the end of a 350-pound wing and manhandle it around.

Garry Cline is another example of unlimited talent. Shy, soft-spoken, and unassuming to an almost painful degree, Garry's work can only be described as brilliant. From a few photographs, he can recreate the cockpit of an F-18 fighter, instrument faces and all. His incisive mind works things through before ever he puts a hand to metal, and once he begins work, the chips fly like marble being sculpted. He is a first-class researcher, writer, and speaker as well. One of the big problems at Silver Hill today is how to keep his services in the restoration shop when his talents are equally in

The most challenging and perhaps "most perfect" restoration to date has been the Albatros D Va. Rich Horigan (left) did the primary work on the fuselage, while Garry Cline (right) did the wings. They collaborated on most of the rest of the aircraft, forming an ideal team. Both are soft-spoken gentlemen, anxious to please, demanding of themselves, and highly skilled.

Rich Horigan at work on the de Havilland D.H. 4 wing; this restoration was relatively easy. Note the meticulous repair of the woodworking.

Hang glider pilot, home (not home-built) restorer, musician, sometime vegetarian, Karl Heinzel is shown applying a brace to the de Havilland D.H. 4 landing gear. Heinzel's patient, steady work pattern and cheerful good humor complement his high degree of skill in working with wood and fabric aircraft.

demand downtown to help put out the Museum's *Air and Space* magazine.

Rich Horigan and Karl Heinzel have been a team on several airplanes, including the Bellanca C.F. and the de Havilland D.H. 4. Rich is soft-spoken and quiet, while Karl bubbles with nervous energy and likes to chat a bit. Together they turned out some of the most beautiful restorations in the history of the facility, moving from one to the next with an ease that utterly belies the difficulty of what they do.

The others involved at the Garber Facility are covered in the various captions of photos accompanying the text; all deserve special mention.

Now let's take a look at the rest of the jobs and the rest of the people at Silver Hill. The work they do is not quite as glamorous as restoration, but it is fundamentally just as important.

4
Nitty and Gritty

Restoration may be glamorous, and it might just distort the picture of what Silver Hill really does. There is undeniably something fascinating about seeing a moldering pile of fabric, plywood, and twisted metal resume its original shape and color as a World War I fighter. There is a mystique also about the detective work involved in determining how an aircraft should be finished, and there is no doubt of the tangible reward when a newly resurrected aircraft shines in all its burnished glory.

Yet other missions at the Garber Facility are equally important and equally demanding, even if they lack the glamour. The second most important job is like restoration without its glory; but perhaps, because of the extent to which it is done, it is in fact even more important.

Preservation

Preservation encompasses much of what is involved in restoration. The artifact is cleaned, checked for missing parts, and has a storage stand created for it. Corrosion is arrested, and preservatives ranging from the standard Softseal to brand-new exotic products that cost as much as $100 a gallon are used. The essential difference between restoration and preservation is that the dings aren't removed, and no finish work is done. These are the time-intensive aspects of restoration, and as a result, considerably more items can be preserved in a given number of hours than can be restored.

This is the reason that restoration sometimes has to give way to preservation. The Museum by its nature must think in terms of centuries, and many of the aircraft in the collection would not survive if they were not preserved now. Many will perhaps not reach the full restoration cycle in the next thirty years, given

the limited level of manning and funding that the Museum has, so it is essential to be sure that they are preserved *now* for restoration *then*, even though then is not yet defined.

Certainly much of the hard, knuckle-breaking work of restoration is found in preservation. It is no easy matter to remove a Japanese torpedo bomber from the rotten wooden skids it was placed on thirty years ago, and then to find just the right pick-up points so that a steel skid can be built. The bolts holding the engine to the fuselage are just as solidly rusted for a preservation job as for a restoration, and the same sort of sweat and strain must be exerted to do the job properly.

Fortunately, the degree to which corrosion can attack is vastly reduced when an aircraft is inside a dry building, with a coating of Softseal applied. The former abuses at Silver Hill are brought into sharp relief when it is seen just

Steven Wittman's famous *Buster* hangs in a place of honor in Building 24. This little aircraft had a sensational racing career. It began life as *Chief Oshkosh*, and competed for over twenty-four years in class races and in free-for-all races. The designer pilot, Steven Wittman, was always a contender in the National Air Races, flying aircraft of his own design, and he still flies and races today.

In 1939, Fritz Wendel, flying a special Messerschmitt Bf 109R, set a world's absolute speed record of 469 mph. The war precluded any further record attempts, and at the end it was clear that the jet engine was the wave of the future. As a result, for thirty years, and apparently for ever, the world's absolute piston-engine speed record remained in German hands. Darryl Greenamyer determined to capture that record, and modified this Grumman F8F-2 Bearcat to do so. He succeeded, setting a new record of just over 483 mph.

One of the most exotic aircraft in the collection is this Horten flying-wing design. This is the Gotha Go 229 V3, a pre-production prototype. It was intended to have a top speed of over 620 mph and a service ceiling of around 50,000 feet, formidable performance for 1945.

Jean Roché designed the Aeronca C-2, the first true American lightplane. Powered by a tiny two-cylinder Aeronca engine of 26 horsepower, the C-2 had a top speed of about 80 mph. Instrumentation was austere, and there were no brakes—the pilot could, if he wished, and if he wore gloves, reach out and grab the tire to slow the plane down. A French Morane-built Fiesler Storch is below the Aeronca.

Back by popular demand, the famed Lockheed P-38J Lightning rests under Frank Hawks' Franklin glider. The P-38 was assembled because of the many requests by visitors to see one; it was cleaned up and given a coat of preservative, but was otherwise not restored. It looks pretty good considering it rested outside in the rain for more than twenty years.

Every year the Museum is deluged with congressional inquiries as to why the Republic P-47 Thunderbolt is not on display downtown. The inquiries are triggered by constituents who are "Jug" fans, and who feel that their favorite aircraft has been slighted. The truth of the matter is that the P-47 is just bigger than the Mustang, and if it were installed instead in the World War II Gallery, not one but two aircraft would have to come out. As it is always the curator's desire to have more, not fewer, airplanes, the P-51 will probably stay in place.

how easily simple precautionary measures can be taken. A perfect inadvertent example exists in Building 22. A beautiful gull-winged Grace—an Aichi B7A Shooting Star to the Japanese, perhaps the best and certainly the fastest torpedo bomber of the war—was stored disassembled out of doors. It was arranged in such a way that one wing section was accidentally bathed in leaking engine oil, while the other was not. Where the oil protected the spar, there was no corrosion; the other one is almost destroyed. It illustrates in simplest terms how much might have been done by spraying the aircraft with drain oil begged from local filling stations, if nothing else had been available.

Preservation encompasses much besides aircraft. The facility has an "engine farm" where several score engines are packaged in their shipping cans. They had been stored like this for years, but on their first inspection were found to be filled with water. All of the cans were emptied, the engines pulled, cleaned, and preserved, and then reinstalled in the cans. New seals and plugs were added, and each one is now inspected periodically to make sure the preservatives are in good order.

Besides major components, there are thousands of instruments, maps, machine guns (locked away under a special surveillance system), navigation instruments, and tools. An advanced invention installed under Al Bachmeier's enlightened guidance are two huge aluminum, air-conditioned, temperature- and humidity-controlled storage chambers, where art works and fragile items like pressure suits or oxygen masks are stored. Even Gilmore, Roscoe Turner's stuffed pet lion, is happy there. Two more boxes will be installed soon, and the vast NASM documentary collection will at last be housed in the sort of storage it has been needing for thirty years.

Al is a tough taskmaster, and he has an especially difficult job because of the lack of glamour of the assignment. His crew is as talented as those in Building 10, but they don't get the same sort of press and television notice that occurs when a new restoration rolls out. As a result it takes a special effort to keep them motivated—one usually found by assigning them the most demanding tasks the Museum has to offer. If an aircraft has to be moved at short notice from Silver Hill to the second floor of the Museum, it is Al's people, working with

The Silver Hill crew also was responsible for moving the aircraft from the facility down to the Museum, and many a D.C. citizen was startled early in the morning to find himself trying to pass a land-bound aircraft. Here the DC-3 is pulled past the nation's Capitol at 2:00 A.M.

One of the two examples of the type remaining, the Sikorsky JRS-1 is an imposing specimen. The other survivor is an S-43 that belonged to Howard Hughes and was crashed by him into Lake Mead when he was practicing to become the pilot of the Hughes Flying Boat. It has been restored recently, and is on the West Coast. A Bell UH-1B nestles under its right wing.

An extremely interesting test aircraft, the quarter-scale Martin PBM Mariner. Powered by a single Martin-built Chevrolet engine that drove the two propellers by means of belts, the little aircraft was used to supplement wind-tunnel tests. Oddly enough, similar experiments went on in secret in England and Germany at about the same time, and for about the same reasons: doubt that wind-tunnel and hydrodynamic tests would provide adequate data.

steady and capable John Parlett, who will mastermind the job. They also have a continuing assignment to straighten up the remaining storage buildings so that these can be opened to the public too.

The secret of this last task is to make as much space available as possible without seeming to crowd the aircraft so closely together that they cannot be photographed and enjoyed. Bill Reese, Ed Marshall, and Carrol Dorsey have become expert at this, visually translating the limited horizontal and vertical distances within the Butler buildings into the best accommodation for the sometimes huge artifacts. One of the major difficulties, of course, is that the buildings are already chockfull, and it is difficult to move a large twin-engine amphibian like the Sikorsky S-43 around to make room for a Swedish Saab J-29 "Flying Barrel"

when the way is impeded by an XF8U-1 Corsair and the Lockheed XC-35. (To an airplane buff, this mixture of exotic iron sounds like a heavenly fantasy. To the Garber facility crew, it's all in a day's work.) The men use a great deal of preplanning and a certain intuitive sense about what will work and what won't. The results are uncanny, for they are able to transform a jammed hangar into an attractive museum setting, and put more airplanes in at the same time. Part of the secret lies in using the vertical area, by suspending light aircraft and missiles from the beams, and by taking into consideration the differences in the vertical height of the artifacts themselves.

As a result, five buildings have been made available to the public; open seven days a week, they attract the true believers.

Warehousing

Perhaps even less glamorous than preservation is the warehousing. Silver Hill has only ten small Quonset hut–type buildings and must make the most of them. Steel racking has been installed, which permits the use of every inch of vertical height, with a central pathway left open for a fire lane and to operate a forklift. The Museum's engine collection, almost certainly the most comprehensive in the world, is displayed in pristine array in these small buildings, one mounted above the other in racks, glistening with preservatives. You can go from the biggest piston engine ever built, the thirty-six-cylinder, nominal 5,000-horsepower Lycoming "Super Corn-Cob," to a tiny three-cylinder rotary, to untried jets. If you are an engine freak, it is an unforgettable experience.

Everything else, from flying suits to sextants, has to be both properly stored and easily retrievable. This is where Al Bachmeier's inventory system comes into play. Each item is inspected, photographed, and preserved, and an entry made in NASM's computer system. The location of the item is noted, and when it is stored, it is placed in a secure area in a numbered bin. When required, it is easily available. And Al, the former Bolshevik madman, is now a national authority on the subject, having been covered in the *Wall Street Journal, Time* magazine, and TV talk shows.

He still comes in for plenty of heat, for one of the toughest jobs is to face the fact that certain artifacts are no longer worth storing. This can come about because of duplication, or just deterioration, but Al's team has to raise the issue with curators, who then go through an agonizing decision process as to whether to keep or to throw out.

Putting a Thud on Skids

Perhaps the very toughest challenge to the warehousing crew is the movement of a large aircraft from its destination airport, usually Andrews Air Force Base just outside of Washington, D.C., to the Garber Facility. There are certain practical limits on this, dictated by the

bridges, underpasses, and highway clearances, and in the future it is almost mandatory that the Museum acquire a large industrial facility at an airport to handle really enormous aircraft like the 747 or its space counterpart, the Space Shuttle. In the meantime, no matter how big they are, Al Bachmeier and his crew know how to move them.

Some of the most deteriorated-looking elements of an aircraft needing restoration are such items as tires or, as shown here, self-sealing fuel tanks. It takes all of Wil Powell's expertise to bring these shapeless, cracked masses back to an almost normal state.

The Mad Bolshevik himself: Al Bachmeier, a man of many talents, and a fundamental contributor to the success of the Museum. Junior Marshall is at the left, and Joe Fichera is driving the forklift, supported by Larry Motz. You'll find Al dressed like this or in Hickey Freeman suits, depending upon his needs for the day.

Moving the fuselage of the Fairchild Republic F-105 Thunderchief from its Andrews Air Force Base home to Silver Hill was a major accomplishment. The Silver Hill crew made use of the chief structural components of the aircraft—the forward landing gear and wing attachment points—to fit heavy-duty steel supports that attached directly to the truck bed. The ability to accomplish moves like this saves the government thousands of dollars every year.

Bill Reese, shown here with his first major project—the restoration of the engines of the German Messerschmitt Me 262 jet fighter—has proven equally capable in any phase of the Garber Facility's operations. In addition, he is an excellent writer, who can summarize a project in a succinct but comprehensive way.

The most difficult task to date has been the enormous Fairchild Republic F-105, officially named Thunderchief but more affectionately called Thud. This huge 64-foot long, 27,500-pound gross weight fighter was made available for transfer from Andrews Air Force Base to Silver Hill. The 113th Tactical Fighter Wing of the Washington, D.C., National Guard provided its usual friendly assistance, but there were some grave doubts raised as to whether or not the Thud could actually be transported to the Garber Facility. This was not so much because of the size or weight, but because there was no apparent way to break it down for transport, and it was too big to be towed intact.

John Parlett, master of a thousand previous moves, and Junior Marshall, our truck driver, got the necessary permits ready. Ed Chalkley took a team consisting of Bill Stevenson, Bob Padgett, and Bill Reese to inspect the F-105 and do some preliminary planning.

After a little consultation, they decided they could move the airplane onto the Museum's lowboy trailer without the use of a rented crane. There were a number of reasons for this, including the cost of renting the crane, but the principal challenge was to move it safely, easily, and with a minimum of stress. The Air Guard personnel, while helpful and hopeful, openly doubted the Museum's ability to do the job.

There was sufficient clearance between the F-105's belly and the trailer to permit the latter to be backed underneath it; an extra 8 inches in height was obtained by over-inflating the landing gear's oleo struts, extending them to their limit of travel.

Three days later, the actual work began. Junior Marshall helped Padgett and Reese fabricate the base, which was made up of 8-inch I-beam sections, and would support the fuselage. Five-inch box beam members were used as uprights, with 3-inch channel iron being readied in place for the support legs. Suitable 8-inch triangular gussets were welded into place. Next day, with the help of the Air Guard, the F-105 was broken down into its main components, with the stabilizer, engine, vertical fin, and drop tanks removed. The aft section of the engine was pulled and placed onto a standard F-105 maintenance dolly. These sections were then transported to Silver Hill.

The following day, the crew pressurized the aircraft's pneudraulic (combination hydraulic and pneumatic) accumulator, and the plane was towed over to an inactive runway where crucial welding was to take place.

An I-beam had been readied to support the nose of the F-105; the nose was jacked up, the nose-gear shock strut removed, and the lowboy trailer backed into place. Uprights were bolted to the base of the stand, support legs were cut to size and bolted into place, and the nose gear was then fastened to the lowboy's steel base plate. The Thud was now firmly tethered by its nose to the trailer.

The Silver Hill crew moved to the midpoint of the airplane, working smoothly together— and getting unfeigned admiration from the Andrews Air Force Base personnel who wandered out to watch. The uprights at the rear were bolted to standard jack pads, making three firm attachment points holding the F-105 to the trailer. The main oleo struts were then deflated, taking the weight off the wheels, and leaving the airplane supported solely by the trailer. Now it was a piece of cake to drive the airplane back to the flight line and remove the wings for transit, collapsing each gear and storing it.

The rest of the trip was no more than a truck ride, for the F-105 was firmly captive. The warehousing crew had done in a few days and at a few dollars' expense what a commercial unit would have charged several thousand dollars for. And they had done it elegantly, in the style that becomes them.

Other Missions

The entire contingent at the Garber Facility constitutes a "fire brigade" capability for the Museum. When, due to some overoptimistic scheduling and unfortunate exhibit revisions, the Jet Aviation Gallery seemed to be heading for a postponed opening (a real misfortune, for it was intended to be the big event in the 1981 five-year anniversary celebration), the crew from Silver Hill was called in. With hammers flying, saws singing, and welding torch smoking, six men swarmed over the exhibit. Within two weeks it was ready to open on schedule.

One of the unusual results of this sort of added mission is the synergistic effect it has on other workers at the Museum. There is an evident quickening of tempo, due in part to the fact that the Silver Hill people set a rhythm that cannot be ignored, and also to the fact that they are apt to run right over you like the Steeler offensive line if you happen to be just standing around.

The way the Silver Hill team operates is easier to understand if one is aware of exactly how far the place has come in terms of equipment and working conditions. Just before the new Museum downtown opened, Silver Hill had reached new heights and new depths. In terms of activities and funds, things were at a peak; in terms of appearance and services, it could hardly have been worse.

Working conditions were absolutely subhuman. There was no dressing room; some lockers were randomly disposed on top of the rundown office space, and men dressed and undressed in the open, confident that the women on the staff would gladly look elsewhere. The bathroom was a decrepit, two-fixture hole in the wall that stank, and had the additional feature of backed-up sewage for much of the winter when the lines to the outside sump froze.

Safety conditions were abominable. There were no sprinklers—an absolute must, as the tragic San Diego Air Museum fire proved. Garber was a safety inspector's nightmare of ancient wiring, inadequate fusing, improper lighting, hazardous ventilation, open paint spraying in the shop, no safety shoes, no safety goggles, and worst of all, no safety discipline.

All of this changed as Silver Hill blossomed. The necessary equipment was purchased, and John Parlett applied his extensive knowledge of safety practices to bring the place into shape. Today it is regarded as the model for the Smithsonian.

And there is a nice well-tiled locker room, complete with shower facilities (oh heady luxury, hot water), an immaculately kept restroom (with, a real novelty, one for men and one for women), plus all the amenities standard for U.S. industry but so long denied to Silver Hill. It makes a difference.

The Garber Facility is a classic warehouse as well as a warehouse of classics. The place is kept in immaculate condition by workers who care. From far left, Sikorsky XR-4, Northrop Gamma, Huff-Daland, Curtiss Jenny, and Curtiss Robin. Above are two missiles, the Pou de Ciel, a Bowlus Baby Albatross glider, and the Sisu glider.

Part Two

THE
COLLECTION

The genuinely intense pleasure that a true airplane buff gets from visiting the Garber Facility is, I think, enhanced by two factors not often found in most aviation museums. One is the immediacy: at Silver Hill you must walk around and through the aircraft, and all of the admonitions of the docents and the tour leaders cannot keep you from the inevitable surreptitious caress of a love object's wing or tire when you really must surrender. The other is diversity. Most museums make a virtue of some sort of logical arrangement, whether by chronology, type, or manufacturer. At Silver Hill, because of the requirement to cram as many airplanes into as small as space as possible, and because there are so many changes, the airplanes are placed in a helter-skelter intimacy that heightens their effect. You'll find a Custer Channel Wing over a Lightning, a Bell Helicopter in the wing-pit of a Reliant, a Messerschmitt Me 163 under a Helioplane. It doesn't make any historic sense, but it is somehow still aesthetically pleasing. Writing about the individual airplanes is a little different, however. There should be some logical presentation, and for that reason I have rearranged the aircraft in print into what seem to me to be logical groupings. First, the Classics.

5
The Classics

Here we are on dangerous ground, for almost all of the airplanes at Silver Hill are considered classics by someone, and by definition are almost such by being included in a museum. But the next few pages will highlight individual stories of airplanes which have a special mystique that elevates them to the classic role. The mystique could stem from specific flights, or from being an example of a beloved type, or from being flown by a glamorous pilot; but no matter, it endows the airplane with what in a human being is termed charisma.

Selecting just five "classic" aircraft was not easy; the case could be made for any of several score within the collection. But each of these five—the Curtiss Jenny, Curtiss Robin, Northrop Gamma, Laird RT-14 Turner Racer, and Spad XIII—represents broad categories of aviation.

The Jenny was America's only indigenous contribution to World War I, and provided the basis for the first generation of "barnstormers," a term often misused but inevitably synonymous with gypsy Jennies.

The Robin was a genuine landmark lightplane, one that had profound influence on American design, and would have had an even more important career if the Depression had not slowed its rapid sales.

John Northrop's Gamma was an extension of the configuration and type of construction he had initiated with the slightly smaller Alpha, and it was to have profound aeronautical, political, and military effects. Although the Gammas themselves were built in limited numbers, they were flown by very influential pilots, and were in the very forefront of aviation's headlines as well as aviation technology. From the Gamma, and its Alpha predecessor, were developed the basic wing used on the Douglas DC-1, -2, and -3 transports, and these aircraft literally revolutionized air transportation throughout the world. Airlines either purchased the aircraft from Douglas or a Douglas licensee, or pirated the design by virtually duplicating the aircraft, as the Russians and Japanese did, or by having their manufacturers create near-Chinese copy versions. Still, the most important developments of the Gamma were the military ones, which led to the Northrop A-17 attack plane and the Douglas SBD dive bomber.

Roscoe Turner remains one of the most fascinating characters in aviation. A complex man, he deserves better treatment than to be remembered only by the myths which he joyfully helped create.

Turner's silver racer—RT-14 being one of its several designations—was intended to sweep him to victory in effortless circuits around the Thompson Trophy course. He wanted an airplane that would win without forcing him to wrest victory from other equally determined pilots by risking his life on every turn. In typical Turner fashion, it didn't work out that way, due in large part to his own freebooting methods of financing (at other people's expense), his carefree approach to design (against other people's advice), and his impetuous nature. But despite the limitations of the aircraft as it finally developed, Turner won races with it, once again taking the margin of victory out of his psychic hide.

The final classic, the Spad XIII, blends all desirable museum characteristics into one remarkable artifact. It is unique, being the only World War I Spad XIII still in its original fabric; it had an important history, being the mount of Captain Arthur Raymond Brooks, an ace and a hero; it is representative of an important type, both in design and in service; and finally, it looks great.

The Spad XIII is hallowed in the memory of every World War I aviation buff, but it was far from flawless as a fighting machine, and has suffered some necessary debunking in recent years. Nevertheless, one has only to peer into its tiny utilitarian cockpit, more of a foxhole than a place from which to fly an airplane, to sniff its oil-soaked fabric, and one can hear the wires sing. It is tattered, but alive.

The Curtiss JN-4

The importance that manufacturers have attached to aircraft names through the years cannot be overestimated. Even in today's sophisticated world of multi-billion-dollar armament sales, an appropriate name is always sought—one that will somehow convey the mission, or the preeminence of the design, or an aviation heritage. Thus General Dynamics was pleased to have its F-16 called "Fighting Falcon," a relatively small but fiercely combative bird. McDonnell Douglas departed from its ghostly line of Banshees, Demons, and Phantoms to name its F-15 the "Eagle," symbolic both of America and of the F-15's air-superiority role. Grumman demonstrated a bit of good-natured humor in accepting "Tomcat" as the name for its swing-wing F-14. After years of tough-cat images ranging from Wildcat through Hellcat, Tigercat, the unlamented Jaguar, Panther, and Cougar, it engagingly selected "Tomcat," with its swinging image of an amatory street fighter, an image that young naval aviators like to project on occasion.

Many names don't catch on, usually because the pilots think another one is more appropriate. Thus the Thunderbolt became the Jug, the Thunderflash became the Hog, and the Thunderchief became the Thud. No one ever called the B-52 a Stratofortress, despite years of public relations, but BUFF, for Big Ugly Fat Feller (or something) caught on instantly. And last, whoever named the C-47 Skytrain had obviously never seen a Gooney Bird.

Affectionate names like Gooney Bird are not bestowed lightly, and rarely are they the ones offered by the manufacturer—the Piper Cub being an exception. In the case of the Curtiss JN-4 series, Jenny was a natural both because of the phonics, and because the airplane looked and acted as you suspect a girl named Jenny would look and act in the second decade of the twentieth century. The name fits, as does its nostalgic importance. America has for more than eighty years been infatuated with automobiles, and there has always been a search to find an airplane that corresponded in folklore to the Ford Model T. The Jenny comes closest to this. It was a simple airplane, forgiving of many sins, occasionally intractable, just as the Model T was, but able, with a lot of help from its "driver," lots of roadside repairs, and above all, lots of luck, to get most places its pilot wanted to go.

The JN-4 was the most important aircraft that America was able to contribute to World War I. The de Havilland D.H. 4, a combat plane which, as we will see, was built in substantial numbers and actually fought at the front, was more important as a demonstration of American potential than as a warplane, but it was, of course, an English design. The Jenny, in its own unspectacular way, did more for the American and English air effort by training thousands of cadets to fly.

When its wartime task was done, the Jenny, in awesome abundance, dominated civil aviation in America for six or seven years after the war. It was available, it was inexpensive, and it was forgiving—a combination that did much to make pilots out of amateurs—and it pro-

An evocative picture of the famous Curtiss JN-4 in Air Service markings. The Jenny had a lot of wires and struts—built-in headwind—but once airborne it was an effective trainer, and made the most solid contribution to the World War I aviation history.

A classic photo, showing how, like Charlie Brown's kites, Jennies were attracted to trees. The pilot could have landed almost anywhere within a 10-mile radius, but luck or nature drove him into the tree. He probably survived the crash, but may have had difficulties negotiating the remaining 30 feet to the ground.

A scene straight out of the first Oscar-winning film, *Wings*. That could well be Gary Cooper up there, casting a shadow over the remainder of the camp! Note U.S. star insignia applied well inboard on wings; cocardes were used overseas.

vided for the first time a sense of aviation to the vast country that had originated the science.

But perhaps as important as either its military or civil roles was its sociological contribution to folklore. The Jenny appeared in articles, books, movies, and paintings. More than this, it was indelibly in the American memory: an entire generation saw and remembered the Jenny as its introduction to flight. Thousands of people convinced themselves that their first flight was in a Jenny, when they perhaps never even got near one. Jenny had become the generic term for the open cockpit biplane.

And Jenny was a felicitous name for an aircraft of felicitous timing. Curtiss brought the JN series into being by an amazingly convoluted route for the time, when many aircraft were simply lofted one week and flown the next, and its final configuration reflected the many sources of design input.

The complicated design history of the Jenny speaks more for the primitive state of American aeronautics ten years after the Wright brothers' first flight than it does for anything else. Glenn Curtiss, the arch rival of the Wrights, who had become the leading designer and manufacturer of aircraft in America, was still more comfortable with the A-frame pushers he had been building and flying for seven years than with the more modern designs appearing in Europe, with which he was fully familiar. Yet at the few military flying fields in the United States, pushers had become notorious for their high fatality rates. It was possible, even in a minor accident, for the rear suspended engine to break loose and crush the unfortunate pilot. Of the fourteen military airmen licensed to fly, eight had been killed. In 1914 the Signal Corps banned the pusher for training work.

Curtiss had built the Curtiss Military Tractor in 1912, and others, including the Burgess Company and Glenn L. Martin, had built excellent examples of the type, with the Martin TT especially well liked at the Army's principal training field in San Diego.*

The importance of the new design to Curtiss

---

* The tractor biplane was always claimed as the personal invention of our eccentric hero J. V. Martin (see page 100), who in fact had a Queen Martin (a sort of Blériot in a Farman suit) built for him in 1912.

was so great that he was unwilling to take a chance, and sought to cover the bet of his own design, the Curtiss Model G, with one from an experienced English designer, B. D. Thomas. Thomas, who had worked for Avro and was currently employed by Sopwith, had just completed the Type 137 biplane to British Admiralty specifications, and the Model J he designed for Curtiss naturally resembled its predecessor.

The Model N soon followed the Model J, differing only in detail, and the best features of the two were improved upon and combined in the Model JN, which was developed successively into the JN-1, JN-2, JN-3, and JN-4. These were not the only permutations en route, however, for Curtiss had established a subsidiary firm in Toronto, where a Canadian model was developed. It was designated the JN-4Can, and soon was called just the "Canuck."

The heart and soul of all of these designs was the Curtiss OX water-cooled engine, which in its OX-5 variant was to power many postwar aircraft. The Curtiss V-8 engine was considered very reliable for its day, and so it was, comparatively speaking, although every pilot trained behind it experienced engine failures as a matter of course. Its biggest deficiency was a single ignition system, and one of the major modifications to the engine in its postwar use was the retrofitting of a dual ignition system. Vibration also played havoc with its cooling system, wrenching hoses loose, inducing leaks in radiators, and providing an unwanted hot shower for the pilot at regular intervals.

Curtiss's firm, despite the fact that he was the king of American aviation manufacturers, was always capital-limited. Inevitably, when it tried to expand OX engine production to meet rapidly escalating U.S. and British requirements, it ran into difficulties.

By 1916, the war in Europe was finally beginning to make an impression on the American public and upon Congress, and there was a slow but dawning realization that an air force would ultimately have to be created, for which a training base was an essential prerequisite. Thus while only one each of the JN and JN-1 types had been built, there was a demand for 10 JN-2s, 104 JN-3s, 701 JN-4s, and 781

Not a twin Jenny, à la North American F-82, but two cadets who had been looking in the wrong direction. Crashes like this were usually survivable, because the Jenny had a great deal of structure that acted as shock absorber.

JN-4As. Five JN-4Bs were built, and one JN-4C—but then came the deluge.

In Canada, 1,260 JN-4 Canucks were constructed, while in the United States, Curtiss and five licensees built 5,303 examples of the Jenny in all of its models, primarily JN-4Ds, but including the U.S. Navy's float-equipped N-8 and N-9 series. More than 8,100 of the basic type were delivered in four years, the vast majority in 1917 and 1918.

The JN-4D series was the initial synthesis of all that had gone before in the JN line. It had finally settled on the standard Esnault-Peltrie stick and rudder control system favored by the British and French, which served over the next two years as the basis for a further series of variants. (Curtiss had always favored its own control types, with a wheel to control the rudder and pitch, and a yoke to control the ailerons; later, it used a Deperdussin system employing a control wheel instead of a stick.)

Despite basically angular lines and a forest of wires and struts, the Jenny managed to be a rather handsome airplane, and has become even more so as the years pass and the excellent workmanship can be appreciated. The fuselage was a basic wooden, wire-braced structure, fabric-covered, with large wooden engine bearers to carry the 90-horsepower

OX-5 engine. The wings were of uneven span, the upper being 43 feet 7 inches long and the lower just a little shy of 34 feet; they offered the Jenny a wonderfully contradictory combination of low wing loading and low power-to-weight ratio. The 1,920 pounds of a JN-4D were spread over 352 square feet of wing area and 90 horsepower, giving a wing loading of 5 pounds per square foot and a power loading—or a lack of power loading—of about 21 pounds per horsepower. If the power loading would get you into trouble, the low wing loading might get you out.

There was an enormous control surface area, again both useful and detrimental. At the low speeds at which the Jenny operated, you needed barn door–size controls to be effective, but smaller and lighter surfaces would have made handling easier.

The Jenny could be stunted, if sufficient altitude was gained to acquire entry speeds and to provide a margin of safety, but it was really best suited to the straight and level mode, where it flew very steadily. It was forgiving, for it took a lot of effort and back pressure to make it stall with wings level (not so in a turn), it gave lots of warning that a stall was imminent, and it recovered quickly. (Note that these are all comparative statements about an

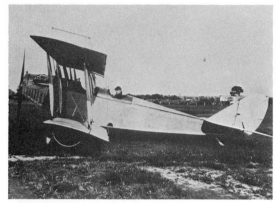

After the war, surplus Jennies became the route by which countless would-be pilots became airborne. This is an Air Service instructional JN-4 in use at the School of Military Aeronautics at Princeton University, but it is like thousands of others released in 1919 and after to a public hungry for a $500 airplane.

airplane that had only a 30-mile differential between stall and top speeds.) Perhaps best of all, it had sufficient structure around the pilot to absorb the shock of any but the most disastrous crashes. If you could avoid going straight in, or headlong into an obstacle, you could often walk away from what was little more than a pile of debris.

Yet the Jenny's record was a good one for the time, in terms of serviceability, hours flown, and fatalities sustained. At the peak of the flying effort, there were an average of 2,000 training planes, mostly Jennies, on hand, of which more than 1,100 would be serviceable at any one time. Hours flown rose from just a few hundred per month to more than 362,000 per year in preliminary flying schools; overseas, further training effort added another 170,000 hours in 1918. All of this training was not without its cost: pilots were killed at the rate of 1 per every 1,140 flying hours, and for observers, the figure was 1 per every 2,377 flying hours.

The many crashes reflected the convulsive effort to catch up made by the United States. Forty-one flying schools were opened, twenty-five in the United States and sixteen overseas; twenty-eight for mechanics were founded, and an equivalent number for observers, gunnery, and so on. In that brief, brilliant interval between April 1917 and November

1918, 22,689 eager cadets entered ground school programs, most of whom had never seen an airplane before the broad wings of the Jenny cast their shadow over the tent cities. Of these, 17,540 graduated, a remarkable 77 percent success rate, which reflects the care given in the recruitment process, as well as the enthusiasm with which young Americans greeted the prospect of flight. The monumental buildup was designed to sustain the Air Service to a total of 358 squadrons in 1919, though the Air Service itself thought that 202 was more feasible.

Despite this massive pipeline of effort, a total of only 1,415 American pilots were at the front by the time the war ended, out of more than 4,000 in France. There was a monumental head of pressure in the pipeline, however, and these few were but the elite advance guard of thousands to come if the war had continued.

The Jenny was developed into a number of important subtypes by the installation of a different engine or different equipment. It turned out that the new and highly respected Hispano-Suiza 150-horsepower engine could be adapted readily to the basic Jenny structure, and the much more useful JN-4H (H for Hisso) aircraft resulted. Special gunnery, bomber, observation, and fighter trainer versions appeared, and in these the speed range went from 41 to 93 miles per hour, compared to the 45- to 75-mph band of the JN-4D. The OX-5–powered Jenny would lumber to 2,000 feet in ten painful minutes, and had a 6,500 foot ceiling. You can imagine what the figures were like on a hot day at a high elevation, although the real relationship of air temperature and density to performance would not be fully known for years to come. The much more businesslike Hispano versions could lumber all the way up to 18,000 feet, if the conditions were right, and could climb to 6,500 feet in ten minutes. Best of all, from the pilot's point of view, the Hisso Jenny was much more responsive.

The margin of power made the equipment of the H Model Jenny an easier task to suit the particular mission, for a few hundred more pounds could be carried. While the JN-4D had a maximum gross weight of 1,920 pounds, the JN-4H could carry up to 2,284 pounds in the JN-4HB bomber trainer version, and 2,269 in the JN-4HG fighter trainer. The 350 extra pounds wouldn't mean much on a B-52, but for the Jenny it meant that the same bombsights and bomb-release mechanism used on de Havilland D.H. 4s could be installed, or that a forward-firing Marlin and rear cockpit Lewis guns could be included. A radio was standard. These "Super Jennies" were absolutely necessary for the campaigns planned in 1919, when large quantities of multi-crew aircraft, including the de Havillands and the larger Handley Page and Caproni bombers, would need a full complement of observers, "bombers" (as bombardiers were then called), navigators, and gunners.

As the Jenny swung into near mass production by at least six other manufacturers in addition to Curtiss, the price for the aircraft stabilized at around $4,750 each, although this sometimes varied from contract to contract depending upon the quantity ordered and the equipment specified. The engines were purchased separately, many from the Willys Overland Automobile Company, and were "government furnished equipment."

All in all, the Jenny gave sterling service throughout the war, training thousands of cadets. It had one last fling of front-line immortality when the United States Post Office inaugurated official air-mail service between Washington and New York. The service began on May 15, 1918, when Major Reuben H. Fleet, later founder of Consolidated Aircraft, flew from new York to Washington, and Lieutenant George L. Boyle flew, if not to oblivion, then very close to it (he was trying to reach Philadelphia), Waldorf, Maryland. Boyle had landed, wrecking his aircraft and totally confused, only 25 miles from his takeoff point, and the mail was transhipped to a train. Boyle did better on his next attempt, this time flying 125 miles in the wrong direction to Cape Charles, Virginia. Inasmuch as he had been lost twice, and demolished two airplanes in forced landings, he was detailed to other duties. In general, however, the Jennies served well carrying the mail, just as they had served well in all their other functions.

When the war came to an end, the government had thousands of all subtypes on hand and no further use for most of them. It was decided to retain an ample number of the Hispano-powered aircraft for future training needs, but the remainder were declared surplus, along with large quantities of OX-5 engines. Standard J-1 trainers, grounded during the war because of their unreliable Hall-Scott engines, were also put up for sale, but with surprising restraint the government did not offer many of its high-powered models for civilian use, anticipating that they might be too much for the average citizen to handle.

The postwar period found a lot of newly trained flyers who no longer had airplanes to

The Jenny was used a great deal for experimental work after the war. Note, in this one at McCook Field, the triple rudders and what appear to be antennae sticking out in front of the wing.

fly, and a whole country filled with youngsters longing to become aviators, there was a constant flow of new designs for aircraft offered to the marketplace, all naturally more advanced than the Jenny, but none that could compete with the give-away prices of the latter. Within a few years prices fell as low as $500 for a virtually new JN-4, with engine, along with sufficient flying instruction thrown in for the would-be pilot to get his new airplane off the field. It has to be remembered that there was no FAA or any predecessor agency in those days. Pilots and planes both were unlicensed, and you could fly anything you had the guts to tackle.

Many of these early fledglings got no farther than the airport boundary before cracking up, but others went on to teach themselves to fly and to become barnstormers. It's chilling today to recall that a pilot would solo after three or less hours instruction one day, and begin taking up passengers for hire the next. For every Lindbergh who emerged from his Spartan self-taught school of hard knocks there were probably two hundred others who had a brief romance with flying, savored its joys and trembled at its frights, and then went on, if they survived, to more sensible, more rewarding occupations.

The late Brigadier General Benjamin S. Kelsey, the fabled test pilot and engineer, who was NASM's second Lindbergh Professor of Aerospace History, had an enduring love affair with the Jenny, and often spoke and wrote of it. Ben describes how the Jenny had very positive limitations and flight characteristics that were adapted to the primitive conditions of the time. With no brakes, the aircraft depended upon big square grass fields to provide sufficient scope for takeoff and landing, for these were of course always made directly into the wind. You needed room to taxi, also; cross-wind taxiing frequently became a series of circles, using the wind for part of the turn, and then gunning the engine for power for the remainder so that you could meander generally in the desired direction.

General Kelsey recalled that the tail skid worked well on the grass fields, even though it flopped freely from side to side from 15 degrees of center. It was highly advisable to walk the length of any field from which a takeoff or landing was planned, to spot the ditches, stones, fences, soft areas, and so on that would turn a Jenny right over on her back.

A good Jenny, Ben said, climbed at 300 feet per minute maximum, although takeoff was quick except for hot days or high elevations. Once airborne, the 90-horsepower OX-5 would just barely flog the accumulated drag along; at the end of a 2,000-foot-long field, you might have only 30 feet of altitude after takeoff, and for the next mile you still could not expect to clear tall trees. As a result, takeoff

Any landing you can walk away from is a good one. This Jenny landed "wheels up" at McCook Field; across the field you can see, dimly, the two Martin bombers— one J.V., one Glenn.

planning had to take into consideration distant ridges, housing buildups, and so on. The flashy chandelle after takeoff was simply not part of Jenny's character.

The large and unbalanced control surfaces made stick pressures very heavy, and Ben felt that response to control input was sluggish. This was partially offset by the fact that the same characteristics made straight and level flight rather easy; in some contemporary aircraft, any diversion of attention from the flight path could result in an immediate spiral dive, or screaming stall.

Ben liked to do aerobatics in the Jenny, never minding the fact that you had to gain enough altitude to be able to enter the maneuver with speed gained from a dive. An expert could make graceful loops and barrel rolls, but more advanced aerobatics were impossible.

The Jenny, as noted, had a predictable stall, easily recognized and somewhat difficult to maintain. Once entered, the spin was controlled by use of the rudder alone, with a quick recovery secured by simply releasing the rudder and putting the stick forward. The turns of the spin were slow and wide, and altitude loss was minimal. One unusual feature was that you could go from a spin in one direction to a spin in the other by simply reversing the rudder and maintaining back pressure on the stick.

The temperamental OX-5s made forced landings an ever-present probability, and much hangar flying was devoted to the best way to live through one over unfavorable terrain. Some people advocated picking a tall tree and "pancaking" into it, while others thought it best to land between the trees and let the wings be ripped off to absorb the shock. It was definitely *not* a moot point.

Just starting the aircraft was not without hazard, for a malfunctioning switch could cause the OX-5 to kick over. The famed aviation artist Douglas Rolfe suffered this experience. A grounded magneto let the engine start as he propped it, slamming into him with such force that he lost his leg and the use of one arm. Less tragically, it was the fate of more than one pilot to be propping his Jenny through, only to see it start up without him, and either taxi to destruction or fly away like a giant free-flight model.

The Jenny brought an awareness of flight to all parts of the country, at a time when the stuttering sound of an OX-5 would bring people running outside to watch a genuine airplane go over, a phenomenon we may see again if fuel prices keep going up. The lucky few who were able to get rides in the barnstormers' airplanes formed an impression of the reality of aviation that did much to promote its future growth. The Jenny was ubiquitous, and while it may have been uncomfortable to ride in, it was comfortable to live with.

The Museum's Jenny, serial number 4983, is

The Jenny today at Silver Hill. It is still in its original condition and remarkably fit, a tribute to the American materials used in its construction. New tires have been fitted, part of a Museum-wide practice to enlist the help of major tire manufacturers to make these odd-sized antiques.

perhaps one of the best examples extant of the high quality of materials used in American World War I aircraft. Built in 1918, and delivered to the 46th Aero Squadron of the U.S. Army Air Service, it served as a trainer. It was donated to the Smithsonian in 1918 and has been on exhibit ever since, either at the old display in the Arts and Industries Building or at Silver Hill. It is more than seventy years old and still looks very fit; only a bit of checkering on the varnish gives a clue as to its age.

As a final bit of nostalgia here are some "humorous notes" on how to fly a Jenny. This is probably just one version of a more ribald set, and the author is unknown, but it does give some insights.

"How To Fly a Jenny"

1. Inspection: It is best not to inspect this ship. If you do, you will never get into it.

2. Climbing into the cockpit: Do not attempt to enter the cockpit in the usual way. If you put your weight on the lower wing panel, it will fall off, and besides, your foot will go through the wing, probably breaking your leg. The best way to enter the cockpit is to climb over the tail surfaces and crawl up the turtle back. Be sure to brush the gopher and squirrel nests out of the cockpit. Take care not to cut your hands on the remnants of the windshield.

3. Instruments: after having carefully lowered yourself into the cockpit and groped in vain for the safety belt, take a good look at the instruments, both of them. The one on the right is the tachometer. It doesn't work. The other one is an altimeter, and it functioned perfectly until 1918, when the hands came off. Look at them, for when the engine starts you won't be able to see them because of vibration.

4. Starting the motor: The switch is on the right. It doesn't work because it's not connected. However, it gives a sense of confidence to your mechanic who is pulling the prop through if he can hear the switch click when you say, "Switch Off." If for some reason the motor doesn't start, don't get out to pick up the cut and bleeding mechanic.

5. Warming up: Don't warm up the engine. It will only run a few minutes anyway, and the longer it runs on the ground the less flying time you have. After the throttle is opened, do not expose any portion of your body outside the cockpit. It is no fun having your face slapped by a flying rocker arm, or being peppered with small bits of piston rings, valves, etc. that are continually coming out of the exhaust stacks.

6. The takeoff: The takeoff is in direct defiance of all the laws of nature. If you have a passenger, don't try it.

7. The flight: After you have dodged trees, windmills, and chimneys until you are over the lake, you will note a large hole in the left side of the fuselage. This hole is to allow the stick to be moved far enough to make a left turn. Don't try one to the right.

8. The landing: The landing is made in accordance with the laws of gravity. If the landing gear doesn't collapse on the first bounce, don't worry, it will on the second. After you have extricated yourself from the wreckage and helped the spectators put out the fire, light a cigarette, and with a nonchalant shrug walk disdainfully away.

The Curtiss Robin

The Jenny launched the firm of Curtiss directly into a key position as a supplier of military aircraft. After a brief flirtation with a civilian type called the Oriole, Curtiss concentrated on building fighters and attack planes for both the Army and the Navy. However, the lure of the "Lindbergh boom" was too much to bear, and the proud Garden City, Long Island, firm finally decided to reenter the civil market.

Among the thousands of types of aircraft that have been churned out over the years, there have been many thrilling, many chilling, and even a few amusing examples, but very few that could characteristically be called happy. The new Curtiss entry, the Robin, a rather angular high-wing design, was one of these, for fortune seemed to smile upon it in all of its many versions.

The Robin had a relatively long production run, more than seven hundred being built at the Curtiss-Wright plant in St. Louis, and it was adaptable to a series of engine and equipment changes. It was used in many roles throughout the country, including flying oil pipelines, training, floatplane work, and so on. Best of all, it was used in a long list of record flights and gained a sort of immortality with Douglas "Wrong Way" Corrigan, of whom more later.

The Robin was Curtiss's first civil aircraft to receive an airworthiness certificate. It was launched early in 1928, when new aircraft were appearing like daffodils in the spring, and despite its angularity, was much more modern in appearance than many of its contemporaries. The high-wing monoplane cabin configuration was strongly reminiscent of the Ryan *Spirit of St. Louis,* a real advantage in 1928, and Curtiss had done its usual systematic engineering to create an efficient design. Wind-tunnel analysis showed that it had a relatively low drag coefficient for the period, when most of its competitors were somewhat larger biplanes, and it achieved a good performance even though the initial version retained the Jenny's obsolete Curtiss OX-5 water-cooled engine. With this throwback to World War I,

the Robin cruised at 85 mph with three souls on board. The use of the OX-5 engine permitted a bargain price of about $4,000, and helped Curtiss use up stocks of the engine.

Curtiss, one of the few manufacturers of the time also making engines, had further engine-marketing plans for the Robin. It soon installed the Curtiss Challenger air-cooled radial engine, which in its various versions ranged from 160 to 185 horsepower. Performance naturally was much improved, with top speed going to a creditable 115 mph, while the price went up almost $3,500.

Public acceptance of the aircraft was immediate, and by 1929 Robins were rolling down the production line at the St. Louis plant at the rate of seventeen per week. Then the Wall Street crash had its inevitable effect, and Curtiss, like so many others, had to suspend production until orders reduced inventory. Prices ultimately dropped to a clearance-sale low of $2,500. Within a few years, used Robins could be purchased for $300, with virtually no flying time on them.

More than seven hundred aircraft of a single type made a big impression in the 1930s, however, and the Robins were to be seen at airports all over the country. The cost of flying and flight instruction was inordinately high then, even compared to today, and the numbers of Robins began to dwindle. But they were still attractive to adventurous youngsters who wanted to emulate Lindbergh, Doolittle, and others. One such was thirty-one-year-old Douglas Corrigan.

Corrigan was a brash young man, single-minded and possessed of mechanical ability, flying skill, and an unusual amount of chutzpah even for an Irishman. He had worked on the *Spirit of St. Louis* when it was being built, and had shaken hands with Lindbergh prior to his flight. The transformation of Lindbergh from lean, likable mail pilot to a world figure in a matter of 33 hours and 30 minutes had impressed Corrigan mightily.

The young Irishman purchased a relatively low-time Robin in 1933 for $325, and over the next five years modified it with increased fuel tank capacity and a used Wright Whirlwind engine (the same type used by Lindbergh on the Ryan) to give it a transcontinental, even transoceanic range capability.

He improved himself, too, taking instrument flying lessons at a time when they were rare, and honing his navigational skills. He played footsie with the inspectors from the Department of Commerce, conning them into believing that he was interested only in flying from New York to Los Angeles and back, and securing limited licenses to do so.

Corrigan made a really impressive and often overlooked non-stop flight from Los Angeles to New York in July 1938, and then submerged himself while Howard Hughes made his spectacular around-the-world flight in his Lockheed 14. On July 17, Corrigan took off again with a full load of fuel, flew across the Atlantic, and with either luck or foresight landed in Baldonnel, Ireland, where his preposterous "I flew the wrong way" story elicited exactly the roar of amused approval that the public and press required at a time when most of the

stories coming from Europe were doleful tales of the next war.

The 180-degree-out-of-phase pilot was lionized, and the Department of Air Commerce was embarrassed. It managed more gracefully than most government agencies might have, however, and merely made sure that he did not attempt to fly back. Corrigan skillfully parlayed the flight into a modest fortune, even starring himself in a film about his adventure, then settled down as an orange rancher, comfortably out of the public's eye. His Robin still exists, reportedly in excellent shape, perhaps the most famous of its breed.

On display at Silver Hill is what is probably the second most famous Robin, and in truth, it performed even more remarkably than did Corrigan's.

Called *Ole Miss,* and flown by the Key brothers, Fred and Algene, its contribution to history was an epic 653 hour, 34 minute non-stop flight over Meridian, Mississippi, from a noon takeoff on June 4, 1935, for twenty-seven days until landing on July 1.

The flight was typical for the day in its in-

The Curtiss Robin *Ole Miss,* flown by the Key brothers on their record-breaking 653-hour flight in 1935. The tubular structure around the engine is a stand that permitted airborne maintenance, including oil changes, plug changes, and lubrication of the Wright Whirlwind's flailing rocker arms—a windy task that almost caused a tragedy.

tent, which was to promote business at the local Meridian Airport, and to stimulate aviation in general. The Key brothers jointly managed the airport and were competent, businesslike pilots. They had seen the spate of endurance records set since the Army Air Service had startled the world with the 150-hour flight of the *Question Mark* in January 1929, and realized that a new endurance mark was at least a possibility for them to achieve.

Much of the charm of the golden age of flight lies in this realization of the possibility for attaining fame by the ordinary man. With the Granville brothers it was speed, and they created their brilliant, dangerous Gee-Bee racers; with Bill Piper, it was mass marketing, and he took the Taylor Cub and turned it into the most popular plane yet known; with Tex Rankin, it was aerobatics, or acrobatics as they called it when Tex was flying. With the Key brothers it was endurance, the physical ability to stay airborne within the confines of the tiny cabin monoplane and to do it for longer than anyone else had done.

The Key brothers did their planning well. They were loaned the Curtiss Robin J-1 Deluxe, with its 165-horsepower Wright Whirlwind engine, and they made a number of essential modifications to it for the flight.

The most obvious change was the construction of a rugged-looking catwalk on each side of the cockpit, out to the engine. The Whirlwind was not designed for endurance flying of the nature contemplated by the Mississippians, and they knew that they would have to lubricate the flailing rocker arms by means of alemite fittings. They would also have to change oil, change sparkplugs, or whatever as the Robin circled round and round the Meridian airport. A quick-drain oil change system was installed.

The gas-tank capacity was increased, and an extra 150-gallon tank, tailored to serve also as a seat, was fitted. A sliding hatch was placed in the top of the fuselage to permit the aerial transfer from a buddy plane not only of gasoline and oil but also food hot from home, supplies, and so on.

The Robin was not designed for extensive flight without frequent maintenance inspections, and certain fittings, including some on the stabilizer, were made oversize and overstrength, just for safety. This was a bit of provident foresight that ultimately saved the aircraft.

There were no probe and drogue or boom refuelers in those days, and gasoline had to flow down a manually held hose from another Robin flown by a friend, James Keeton. It was tricky business flying in formation in the turbulent summer Mississippi air, but they soon became so practiced that they could off-load 60 gallons of fuel in six minutes.

Endurance flights have their own set of problems, not encountered in other types of record attempts or in the routine two-hour hops of everyday flying. Strains develop in prolonged flying that are normally taken care of by routine maintenance, and perhaps worst of all, a record flight is committed to go on, regardless of weather, which can be suddenly violent in the South.

There were two unsuccessful attempts prior to the record flight. On June 21, 1934, the Key brothers were 123 hours into the flight when two cylinders blew off the engine due to detonation caused by bad fuel. On July 21, a second flight was aborted after 169 airborne hours when the weather became so bad that refueling was impossible.

It's times like these that dogged determination and real hunger for a record become essential. The time, expense, and preparation had been accented by the fatigue and ennui encountered in two long but non-record flights. No one would have been surprised if the Key brothers had gently kissed the entire program off.

Instead, they went back to basics, and spent a year raising money and improving their aircraft. They realized that the austere, primitive instrumentation of the Robin must be changed if they were going to survive in the inevitable Mississippi thunderstorms. Fortunately, help came from a distinguished source. Major Claire Lee Chennault (later to become General Chennault, leader of the American Volunteer Group, the Flying Tigers), Lieutenant W. C. "Billy" McDonald, and Lieutenant Luke Williams were members of the Army Air Corps aerobatic team known as the "Men on the Flying Trapeze." The group, in a probably totally unauthorized operation, lent the Key brothers flight instruments, and persuaded the Sperry Instrument Company to lend them an artificial horizon and a directional gyro, truly heady stuff in 1935.

The same careful preparations were made, but when the Robin took off on June 4, no one knew just how bruising the flight would become—a formidable combination of fatigue, boredom, and danger. In the course of the next 27 days there would be 107 transfers of fuel and 432 contacts in all. Formation flying, ordinarily not too difficult on a limited basis, became increasingly demanding as the days wore on and fatigue and nervousness set in.

The weather was often nearly impossible for flying in formation. A Robin was not the most stable platform in even moderately rough air, and in a thunderstorm it became a cork bobbing about, rocking the brothers back and forth for hours on end, and continually threatening to end the flight by preventing refueling.

There were other adventures. The battery caught fire, and Al Key had to switch off the engine to extinguish the flame; the Robin almost force-landed before the engine started again. The stabilizer braces, which had been reinforced, began to weaken dangerously, threatening a catastrophic structural failure in flight. As if this were not enough, Al developed an abscessed tooth that was painful in the extreme.

On the basis of radio instructions from the ground relayed by their father from a local dentist, and using a surgical needle that had been dipped in iodine, Al lanced the abscess himself, providing enough relief to carry on. As he remarked in a 1965 letter, "other than that, things went along real smooth."

Despite all of the irritations and general grief, including Fred's nearly falling from the catwalk during routine maintenance, the principal hazard of the flight was boredom and fatigue. You have to be dedicated to keep fly-

Looking even more dangerous in practice than in theory, one of the Key brothers works on the accessory section of the flailing Whirlwind engine. Fuel was introduced through a hatch in the rear of the cabin, and 107 transfers were made during the record flight.

In 1955, the venerable Robin was refurbished for some nostalgic recreation of the record flights, and then flown to Washington, D.C., for presentation to the Smithsonian. The service structure, which had been removed after the original flight, was reinstalled, and looks hazardous enough even at ground level. Here Fred Key is greeted by his brother, Colonel Al Key, after Fred's flight to Washington, D.C.

In his familiar role as acceptor for the Smithsonian, a smiling Paul Garber shakes Al Key's hand as the title to the aircraft is formally transferred.

A little heavier but no less proud, Fred Key visited the Robin when it was on exhibit in the old Arts and Industries Building. A former B-17 pilot, Key went on to a successful military career after the war, eventually becoming Air Attaché in Colombia.

ing on, hour after hour, hot, sweaty, tired, and grumpy, with the prospect of a record still hundreds of hours away. Still, the lure was there, and once they had passed the world's official endurance of 553 hours, they went after another unofficial record, recently set in another Robin, of 647 hours and 20 minutes. The record attempt by Forest O'Brien and Dale Jackson in the *St. Louis Robin* had been disallowed for a faulty barograph, but the knowledge of its existence was enough to keep the Key brothers going.

On July 1, 1935, it was obvious that it was time to return. After 27 days, after 653 hours, after lots of grueling in-flight refueling, flying through storms, and over-intensely personal companionship, the two brothers landed to the accolades of their friends and the nation.

Both men went on to successful careers, in flying and out. They were both B-17 pilots during World War II, and Al was elected mayor of Meridian in 1965.

Ole Miss was put into routine use after the flight, with the special equipment removed. In 1955, it was refurbished to reenact the epic flight on its twentieth anniversary (not a full 653-hour performance, however) and was then flown to Washington, D.C., for presentation to the Smithsonian. It is now on display at Silver Hill, and will very probably be brought back into the building downtown during the future Golden Age of Flight exhibit.

The Northrop Gamma—*Polar Star*

During the 1930s every Woolworth and Kresge dime store sold a small, 4-inch-wing-span cast-metal model of the Northrop Gamma. It was expensive, for the time, at a full dime, but it captured a delicate beauty that made it supreme among its competitors on the dark varnish–stained counters. No one I knew was rich enough to have two of these little jewels, but everybody managed to have at least one to hold and taxi and move through the air with appropriate mouthed engine noises.

None of us were aware that the real Northrop Gamma existed; it was enough that the model was realistic, promising, and obviously years ahead of its time. The point of all this reminiscence is that what was true of the model was true of the airplane itself. It was supremely beautiful, inspirational, and although only a few of this exact type were produced, it holds an immortal place in aviation history.

The Northrop Gamma was remarkable as a piece of modern sculpture, as innovative engineering, as an important military design, and as the useful tool of scientists, explorers, businessmen, and racing pilots alike. Some of the biggest names in aviation were associated with the type, including Jacqueline Cochran, Howard Hughes, Jack Frey, Bernt Balchen, Tommie Tomlinson, Frank Hawks, and that combination Jack LeLanne/Hugh Hefner of the day, Bernarr MacFadden. More than fifty military versions were built, most of which went to China, where they were regarded as wonderful war machines and used almost not at all.

The Gamma's greatest contribution—one that is often overlooked—was to American naval airpower, for from the Gamma derived first the Northrop A-17 attack plane for the Army Air Corps, and then, with modification, the Douglas SBD Dauntless dive bomber for the Navy. The Dauntless turned the tide of the war for the United States at the Battle of Midway, and every bomb that left the plunging dive bombers had been carried on wings that bore the familiar Jack Northrop signature.

The Gamma also had brilliant antecedents. Designer Northrop had begun his career as a hewer of wood and drawer of water for Donald Douglas. Never formally trained, he had an intuitive eye for design and for economy that was to place him in the forefront of aviation for thirty years. His first task was designing the fuel system for the Douglas World Cruisers, large heavy biplanes that were the first to fly around the globe. From there he went on to one of the most innovative careers in aviation.

His first major triumph was in the immortal Lockheed Vega, in which he combined new manufacturing techniques with a squeaky-clean design that enabled a host of pilots to set records, and to bring airline companies almost to the point of making money. Art Goebel, Lou Reichers, Lee Schoenhair, Wiley Post, Amelia Earhart, Roscoe Turner, Jimmy Doolittle, and Frank Hawks all flew Vegas. To give a crass dollars-and-cents idea of the lasting value of the airplane, it has joined the ranks of vintage Duesenbergs on the collector's market. One, probably the only remaining Vega outside a museum, was recently offered for sale for $340,000, more than twenty times its original factory price.

The Vega was startling, with its cylindrical, cigar-shaped smooth fuselage and its clean, Fokker-like plywood cantilever wing, and Northrop worked every possible design permutation from it in both metal and wood, as well as in combination. From the basic Vega design sprang the low-wing Lockheed Sirius, which Colonel Lindbergh and his wife flew north to the Orient and elsewhere; from the Sirius came its retractable gear offspring, the Altair. A quick switch of cockpit placement created the low-wing cabin Orion, and a few struts created the parasol-wing Air Express. Consolidated, under Reuben Fleet, unashamedly copied both the Vega and the Air Express, and did well with both.

Characteristically, Northrop was already looking ahead as the Vegas proceeded down the production lines. He saw metal construction as the key to the future, and formed his

The Northrop Alpha, shown here in Western Air Lines markings, provided the basis for a whole series of later designs. (Courtesy of TWA)

own firm to create the Northrop Alpha, which was to metal construction what the Vega was to wood.

The Alpha was a sleek low-wing monoplane, not only built entirely of aluminum but designed so that no expensive tooling was required for its manufacture. Its wing was Northrop's "multi-cellular" design, so strong that a steamroller would just ride up over it, and so successful that TWA specified its use in the design of the Douglas DC-1. If you compare the wing of the Alpha, the Gamma, the Douglas DC-3, and the Douglas Dauntless, you can see the unmistakable Northrop design features.

Like the Gamma, the Alpha was not built in large quantities, but it made the Northrop name a household word with its silver good looks and its frequent appearance in the newspapers. The sole remaining Alpha is suspended in the Air Transportation Gallery of NASM.

The firm Northrop had created became absorbed in the Boeing-Stearman corporate line-up, and Northrop left once again to form his own firm, this time in happy harmony with Douglas, which apparently regarded the Northrop Corporation as a research and development unit. It valued Northrop's ideas over the years, and served as a financial resource, as well as a production outlet.

Frank Hawks, whom I suspect was not really a very good pilot given the number of crashes he was involved in, and despite the rash of city-to-city records he set, was recovering from yet another accident in 1932, when he let

Northrop know of his needs for a really fast record-setting racer. Hawks did not participate often in closed-course races, but could be depended upon to lower the time from New York to Miami, or Washington, D.C., to St. Louis. He worked closely with Northrop during the development of the first of the Gamma series, the famous Sky Chief which carried the same Texaco logo that can still be seen on gasoline pumps.

Northrop expanded upon the basic Alpha concept, scaling it up and streamlining it even more to create the Gamma. The multi-cellular wing was combined with a slender, longer fuselage. The spatted wheels developed for the Alpha were retained, for in the speed range in which the Alpha and Gamma operated, the advantage conferred by the lower drag of a retractable gear did not offset the increase in weight and mechanical complexity. A variety of engines could be fitted. But the most distinguishing features of the Gamma were the huge sweeping fillets that enabled Northrop to perch the fuselage on top of the wing for maximum internal space, yet maintain a smooth airflow across the empennage.

Each of the Gammas that followed the number one airplane was different. Northrop was enamored of the Junkers-style floating ailerons for a while, as this gave him still more room for his generous flaps, and when the number two Gamma was rolled out, it was so equipped. Don Berlin, famed designer of the Curtiss P-40 and other airplanes, was project engineer for Northrop on the Gamma, and he recalls one

The first Northrop Gamma went to Frank Hawks and became the Texaco *Sky Chief.* The second was sold to Lincoln Ellsworth for Antarctic exploration, and was named the *Polar Star.* The Gamma was extremely adaptable and was flown on floats, skis, and wheels.

The *Polar Star* didn't log much time in its career, just a little over 200 hours. But it did endure some great extremes in weather, surviving Antarctic storms that might have overcome a lesser craft.

version which had the floating ailerons on the *leading* edge of the wings. This was used for one hair-raising trip around the pattern, and then it was back to a more conventional drawing board. No photo of the experiment is known to exist.

It's difficult now to recall the heady ferment of the 1930s, when these Gammas were called into being. The Lindbergh boom was in full spate, and the leading explorers of the day— Admiral Byrd, Sir Hubert Wilkins, and so on—were grabbing one headline after another as they sped off to chart whatever remained uncharted in the world. The Gamma was an obvious choice for exploration, due to its ruggedness, high speed, and long range, and it was chosen by Lincoln Ellsworth for his proposed 1934 Trans-Antarctic Flight. He named the second Gamma the *Polar Star.*

Ellsworth selected Bernt Balchen to be his pilot. Balchen was one of the most important and least written about pilots of his era. An intelligent man and a brilliant pilot, he suffered from a flaw unknown to almost any other aviator of the day except Lindbergh—he was modest. He has received far less acclaim than he deserves, and his modesty was in fact the reason that he endured some ignominious treatment which a lesser person would have rebelled against.

Balchen was credited with "more hours over ice and snow" than any other pilot, having acted as relief pilot on the Amundsen-Ellsworth Relief Expedition of 1925, the Amundsen-Ellsworth-Nobile Arctic Expedition of 1926, the Hudson Bay Expedition of 1927, and Byrd's Antarctic Expedition of 1928–30. During World War II he was everywhere north, staff adviser to the Finnish Air Force in 1939, flight lieutenant in the Royal Norwegian Air Force, commander of Bluie West 8 in the U.S. Army Air Forces, chief of Allied ATC to Norway, Sweden, Denmark, Finland, and the USSR, and—least known and most important—commander of clandestine air operations against the Germans in Norway from 1941 to 1945.

Between the lines of his biography, one finds that he also flew to the relief of the *Bremen,* in 1928, piloted Byrd on his near-miss trans-Atlantic flight in the *America* in 1927, and made the first flight with him over the South Pole in 1929. On the side, he acted as occasion demanded as operations manager of Norwegian Airlines.

From all of this you may wonder, as many do, why Colonel Balchen did not become Brigadier General Balchen in the U.S. Army Air Forces, or in the successor U.S. Air Force. The story has never been told, and perhaps never will be, but somewhere in his relationship with Rear Admiral Richard Byrd something went terribly wrong politically, and there was a bitter unspoken animosity that was ruinous to Balchen's career and harmful to Byrd's reputation. The controversy smolders to this day.

The Gamma at Silver Hill reeks of Balchen's adventures. Its logbook is filled with his flight notations, for he logged most of the aircraft's total of 201 hours of flying time. He signed its overhaul off "Deception Island, November 17, 1934," with his BB initials; yet, ironically, he was not able to participate in Ellsworth's eventual success.

In 1934, the Gamma was damaged while being off-loaded from the freighter *Wyatt Earp* in a paralyzing moment of suspense when, having been left on the ice overnight, it was almost lost as the ice began to break up. It came within moments of plummeting to the bottom of the sea when the ice floe broke up and drifted away. As it was, the airplane was beaten up so badly that it had to be returned to the United States for repair.

Today, the *Polar Star* waits at Silver Hill for its next trip—this one en route to the Museum downtown. Note the wrinkles on the skin, the result of a hard landing on its epic trans-Antarctic flight in 1935.

Balchen and Ellsworth, who had shared many an adventure together, had initially gotten along very well, but there soon developed a very modern-sounding argument about the proposed flight. Balchen wanted three men in the cockpit, while Ellsworth insisted there should be only two. It wasn't the flight duties that Balchen was concerned about, but rather the exhausting tasks of an Antarctic expedition, which included clearing away acres of snow, tamping down runways, and securing the aircraft against the fierce, sudden winds. Ellsworth was deeply aware of the physical requirements of the adventure, but felt that the weight of the third man and his supplies would detract from the amount of fuel that could be carried and was therefore a hazard. The actual flight would give some validity to his point of view.

The pair made a tentative flight in early 1935, but their strong differences remained, and Ellsworth felt constrained to choose a different pilot, Herbert Hollick-Kenyon, an Englishman flying for Canadian Airways and of course well versed in cold weather operations. Another Canadian, J. H. Lymburner, was chosen as back-up pilot and engineer, while Sir Hubert Wilkins, perennial polar adventurer, was in charge of the vital supplies and logistics.

Hollick-Kenyon and Ellsworth had a harrowing time, making three attempts to reach the South Pole. Their first flight was terminated when a fuel line broke. The second flight found them over a range of previously uncharted mountains, hampered by a howling headwind, and unable to see ahead or below. After two such missions, against the most hostile environment on the globe, both men were well aware of the hazards involved in a third. There were literally hundreds of thousands of square miles into which they could disappear if any possible malfunction occurred. Yet they pressed on, and on the third attempt suffered even more vicissitudes than on the first two.

The third attempt consisted of five individual flights, each requiring a hazardous takeoff and landing from unprepared, unsurveyed surfaces, any one of which could have concealed the fissure or the slab of ice that would do them in. The most grueling was one 13-hour, 55-minute bruiser that ended with a hard landing on the whited-out ice on November 23, 1934. The weight of the big Pratt & Whitney engine, multiplied by the long moment arm of its position in the nose of the long fuselage, caused serious wrinkles in the skin, and effectively introduced a down-thrust angle into the engine mount. A blizzard completely covered the aircraft with snow, the driving wind packing the interior so solid that it had to be dug out with cups and spoons after the arduous removal of the rear of the fuselage. The emergency radio failed, the primus stove didn't work, and the searing cold made every action a matter of survival.

One can imagine the anxiety of the pair after the nightmare flight and the subsequent bone-tiring fatigue from removing the snow as they went through their mental checklist and prepared to start the engine. There were no jump cables within a thousand miles—and there must have been a tremendous feeling of relief when the big propeller began to turn, the blue smoke streamed into the clear Antarctic air, and the pop-pop-popping settled into a steady roar.

The *Polar Star* when fitted with the "floating aileron" adapted from Junkers technique and full-span split flaps.

Eventually, the *Polar Star* got airborne again, only to run out of fuel 25 miles short of the South Pole. The last lap was made on foot to the welcome provisions and stores left behind at Admiral Byrd's famous camp. Ellsworth's ideas on the value of the third man versus his weight in fuel were vindicated; if the distance to travel had been 50 miles, they might well not have made it.

The recovery of the aircraft from its isolated position was almost as hazardous as the flight, but it was eventually shipped back to Floyd Bennett Field. There it was reassembled and repaired for a one-time flight to Washington, D.C., where it was turned over to the Smithsonian.

When the *Polar Star* was restored in 1963, great care was taken to retain the honorable wrinkles in its skin caused by the hard landing. In 1978, I had the pleasure of taking Donovan R. Berlin through the Silver Hill facility, and his eyes lit up when he saw the veteran Northrop sitting placidly on its wide skis. Don ran his hands over the wrinkled skin and said: "Damn it, I knew it would do that. Here's how we should have designed it." He began sketching out an improved design for the Gamma's forward section, some forty-four years after it had left the factory. It was typical of the nostalgic magic of Silver Hill, where the airplanes seem still to be ready for the flight line.

Roscoe Turner's Dream Machine

The lovely silver midwing monoplane sits as cockily at Silver Hill as it did in its racing prime at Cleveland. The Turner Racer was a champion in spite of its designers, its pilot, and at times, in spite of itself. Twice the winner of the most prestigious closed-course race in the world at the time, the Thompson Trophy, the sleek-looking airplane, like the hooker with a heart of gold, disguises a past that is filled with mistakes, greed, short-sightedness, lack of faith, and near tragedy. Fortunately, it was a past also filled with genius, guts, trust, and the cosmic *savoir-faire* of a tough, if practically unlettered, racing pilot who had promoted himself into a legend before his time, but whose legend endures today.

Variously designated the LTR, Laird Turner Racer, the RT-14, the Laird-Turner Special, the Turner Racer, the *Ring Free Meteor*, the *Pesco Special,* and *Miss Champion*, the famous racing plane now occupies a place of honor at the Garber Facility after a tour of duty in the downtown Museum. Close by its side, in air-conditioned, humidity-controlled comfort, is another part of Roscoe's act, Gilmore the Lion. Gilmore is stuffed, but in as fine a fettle as a stuffed lion can be, and of great interest because he represents a tender facet in Roscoe's volatile personality.

Roscoe acquired Gilmore as a tiny baby cub, and succeeded in convincing the Gilmore Oil Company that a great deal of publicity would result if the lion flew with Roscoe on record-breaking flights. It worked beyond their fondest dreams, and shots of Roscoe holding the cub, the cub wearing helmet or parachute, Roscoe and the cub registering at hotels, etc., provided grist for the eager media mills.

The young lion's amazingly rapid growth coincided with its decline in newsworthiness, and by the end of six months, Gilmore was too large (and probably too dangerous) to fly with Roscoe any longer. A lesser man might have consigned Gilmore to any zoo, and forgotten about it. Not Roscoe, who faithfully for the next nineteen years paid for Gilmore's upkeep, and paid him periodic visits that had nothing to do with publicity but spoke instead of Turner's gratitude. When Gilmore finally succumbed to old age, Turner had him stuffed by a taxidermist and brought him home. Gilmore was displayed next to the Turner Racer, and it was soon found that he lost all of his whiskers about once a week, not to moths, but to visitors who wanted a souvenir of a bygone era.

Turner was the prototypical heroic air-racing pilot. He was so influential that he inspired comic strips, movie plots, and hundreds of

What a man and what an airplane! Roscoe Turner dressed as the public thought an air-racing pilot should dress: crimson helmet, royal blue blouse, faun trousers, highly polished boots, diamond wings, natty mustache, and always, a gleaming smile. Roscoe could smile even when it hurt, and through the years he had a full measure of both hurts and triumphs. The clean design of the airplane is apparent; only the fixed landing gear is out of character.

imitators, most of whom never got close to anything more powerful than a J-3 Cub. He had adopted a gleaming smile that showed more ivory than even Terry Thomas possessed, a waxed spike mustache, and a completely fake military uniform suitable for the air arm of the Mystic Knights of the Sea. It consisted of a royal blue blouse, diamond-studded wings, faun-colored jodhpur flying pants, and glossily waxed high boots; his not-so-ring-free hair was surmounted with a glorious fifty-mission crush hat. And one must remember that Roscoe was resplendent at a time when most other pilots dressed like jerks in uncomfortable high collars, neckties, and baggy, oil-stained pants.

Turner brought style to racing, a style that was perfect for the cornball circus atmosphere in which air races were conducted; it worked well for him. Underneath the flamboyant trappings he was a dedicated pilot, determined to wrest a sufficient fortune from air racing to set himself up in a responsible, more long-lived business. He did just that, for after an action-packed free-spending, but generally poverty-filled racing career, during which he entered more Thompson Trophy races (seven) and won

A formal portrait. Racing pilots of the time sought endorsements by manufacturers, and accepted large decals advertising the products as a price for their free use, a practice that continues to this day. This is the final configuration of the aircraft, with neatly panted wheels, canopy closed, and a large Champion sparkplug decal on the cockpit side.

more (three) than any other pilot, he founded the Roscoe Turner Aeronautical Corporation in Indianapolis (for some reason the only town where he felt he would not be cheated) and established a successful business.

Turner was one of the few men to step from racing into a reasonably profitable career. Benny Howard did it, as did Steve Wittman, but for every Turner, Howard, or Wittman there were dozens of young men, equally enthused yet not equally skillful, who at best went on to other less glamorous businesses, or at worst were balled up in the flaming wreck that was for many in the crowd the real attraction of racing.

Turner's association with *Miss Champion*, the Laird-Turner Racer's final name, began in late 1936. Broke, with no airplane, no backer, and lots of creditors, he determined to build a new airplane in which he could win both the long-distance Bendix and the closed-course Thompson. He wanted it to be so advanced that it would completely outstrip all competitors, enabling him to breeze to victory in races that had been so tough for him to win in the past.

Turner himself conceived the general formula for the new aircraft. It was an elongated Gee Bee racer, with very short, thin wings, powered by the biggest engine available, a 1,000-horsepower Pratt & Whitney radial.

Turner was smart enough to know that he was not an engineer, and he turned to Howard W. Barlow, who had begun with the Glenn L. Martin Company before embarking upon a distinguished academic career, and John D. Akerman, both of the University of Minnesota. Akerman, who had learned to fly in Russia in 1916, worked for an amazing succession of obscure aviation firms (Hamilton, Mohawk, Madaras), as well as for famous ones like Bell and Boeing, and was the designer of the Museum's Akerman Tailless, a Lippisch-like curiosity. The two men turned Roscoe's rough ideas into a sophisticated design; Roscoe himself meanwhile was completely absorbed in making a living from giving endorsements, working with WMAQ Radio in Chicago, and various other projects.

Turner apparently approved of the design that Barlow originated (Akerman had a subor-

dinate role) and turned to the manufacturer of racing planes and aircraft models, Lawrence W. Brown, of Los Angeles, to actually build the airplane. During this entire period Turner had no real capital to finance either the design or the construction, but he did have panache and a dazzling smile. He also had a reputation for being one hell of a pilot, who could probably make some money with a solid new design.

What ensued was so improbable that, while often attempted, the true story has never been told. Brown was a capable man whose most famous design, the lean *Miss Los Angeles* racer, was a lovely airplane but the complete antithesis of Roscoe's proposal. Brown had used a small, low-drag, lightweight airframe powered by a tiny 300-horsepower Menasco in-line engine to achieve a creditable record of first, second, and third places in a variety of races against more powerful competition. The Turner Racer was a brute-force project, different in every way from the work Brown had done in the past.

This basic difference in outlook probably accounted for Turner's dissatisfaction with what Brown had done to modify the original Barlow design. He had lengthened the fuselage, made the tail surfaces larger, and increased the weight; he had retained the short, narrow, original Barlow wing. As Turner studied the aircraft, doubts began to grow, and he called for changes centered on the shape and the area of the wing.

Brown didn't disagree that changes had to be made. He did disagree with most of those that Roscoe proposed, and he became understandably annoyed when it suddenly surfaced that Roscoe didn't have the cash on hand to pay him for his services.

With the race date approaching, Roscoe was getting desperate. He looked to Chicago for aid, and found it in the person of E. M. "Matty" Laird. Laird was a famous figure in the construction of fast airplanes, for Speed Holman had won the 1930 Thompson in a Laird Solution, and Jimmy Doolittle won the 1931 Bendix in the follow-on Super Solution. He made a cost-plus arrangement with Turner to complete the controversial design in time for the 1937 air races, a bargain that would bring him ultimate satisfaction in seeing his

A similar shot taken on August 15, 1939, but showing Turner taxiing out; wing-walkers were essential as the airplane was difficult to see out of in tail-down attitude. Roscoe had insisted on a fixed gear because he did not wish to have to bother with a retraction system during the crucial opening minutes of the racehorse starts of the times. Roscoe quit racing after winning his third Thompson Trophy in 1939; he was forty-three, and decided he had pressed his luck far enough.

product win races, but cost him lots of money in the process.

The two aircraft shipped from the Brown factory proved to be almost equal basket cases. One was Turner's Wedell Williams Racer, the golden Number 25 in which he had won the 1934 Thompson Race, and which he had spread across the New Mexico countryside on his way to the 1936 Bendix. The other was the incomplete, inchoate new airplane, still in parts, now without plans, and worse, without definite ideas for completion.

Fortunately, Matty Laird was (and is) as powerful a personality as Roscoe, and Turner could not doubt his determination to complete the bargain. To do so, however, Laird insisted that Turner keep his hands, voice, and ideas out of the project. As the race date was fast approaching, Roscoe complied.

The National Air Races in Cleveland were less than two weeks away when Laird rolled the sleekly beautiful new racer out of the factory for its first flight. By a miracle of improvisation, the Wedell Williams was also ready

as promised, rebuilt from a ball of metal into the golden beauty that can be seen today in the Frederick C. Crawford Auto-Aviation Museum in Cleveland.

Roscoe was very satisfied with the new airplane, which flew very well and promised the turn of speed he needed to win. But luck was still not with him, for he had a series of gasoline leaks that resulted first in a fire on landing on the concrete runway in Burbank, California. Roscoe was experienced enough to blow the fire out with the propeller blast, and the damage was not too severe; another few moments and it would probably have been a catastrophe.

Then, while the fuel tank was being repaired under conditions that seem dubious even to the crassest layman, an explosion occurred as a welding torch ignited fumes in the tank. The Laird was disqualified, and although the damage to the airplane was repairable, the damage to Roscoe's expectations was disastrous. He had counted on the Bendix winnings to enable him to pay off Laird and his other creditors.

Fate continued to frown on this seemingly happy combination of Turner and his silver racer. He seemed to have the 1937 Thompson well in hand when he erroneously thought that he had missed a pylon in his turn, and circled back to redo it. The loss in time enabled two planes to finish ahead of him, and instead of $9,000 prize money, he netted only $3,000.

Perhaps even worse for Turner's psyche was the fact that his dream of creating an airplane so superior to others in the field that he could just walk away from them in both the Bendix and the Thompson races obviously hadn't materialized. Somewhere along the way, perhaps all along, perhaps between Barlow's drawing board and Larry Brown's shop, and certainly between Turner's changing concepts and Laird's saving grace, changes had been introduced that brought the racer's performance down into a very competitive arena. The Laird Turner, with its fixed gear, was not obviously faster than the older and highly modified Marcoux-Bromberg R-3 or Seversky's racing versions of the P-35 fighter.

Eventually, the rare combination of skills that had gone into the racer began to be rewarded. Roscoe set a U.S. national speed record of 289.908 miles per hour over a 3-kilometer course. Two days later, in the P-35, Jacqueline Cochran served notice that the Turner Racer was indeed not going to walk away from any races by setting a new record over the same distance at 292.271 mph.

Roscoe saw the writing on the wall: it said he would have to win races in the same old way, by flying to the maximum capability of his aircraft and himself. He began making small improvements in streamlining to the airplane, now called the *Ring Free Meteor* in honor of the MacMillan Oil Company which had backed him for so long.

Much to his chagrin, Roscoe was beaten in a warm-up race in Oakland in May 1938 by an old competitor and genuine rival, Earl Ortman. Ortman, who, behind Rudy Kling, had bested Roscoe in the 1937 Thompson, was flying the Marcoux-Bromberg Special. This was an aging warhorse that had been treated to a succession of ever larger engines to make it more competitive. Very advanced at its debut in 1934, with its all-metal construction and retractable landing gear, the airplane was almost always a bridesmaid and a bride only once—in Oakland.

In Cleveland, however, things were different. The Turner Racer, now catchily named the *Pesco Special* in honor of the Pump Engineering Service Corporation of Cleveland sponsorship, romped home in first place with a record-setting speed in excess of 283 miles per hour. Turner flew the race beautifully, and enjoyed winning immensely.

The following year, at a speed just 1 mile per hour slower, Roscoe repeated his triumph, becoming the first and only pilot to win the Thompson three times. He then announced his retirement, feeling at forty-three that he had pressed his luck far enough. He began his business in Indianapolis, and did very well during the war years when there was a sizable pilot-

Not a good photo, but one that clearly shows the brute power and slim lines of the Turner Racer.

After Turner went into business in Indianapolis, he hung *Miss Champion* from the rafters of the ceiling. Later, it went to the Roscoe Turner Museum, and finally came to the Smithsonian, where it was exhibited in the old Exhibition Flight Gallery, along with Gilmore, Roscoe's pet lion.

Gilmore the Lion was always an attractive exhibit, living or stuffed, as shown here at the Exhibition Flight Gallery of the Museum, which was open from 1976 through 1980. Museum visitors liked to pluck Gilmore's whiskers, which had to be constantly replenished from a supply of plastic whisps.

The Turner Racer in Building 24, next to the Beech Staggerwing.

training program going on. Later, Roscoe's business ability did not match his racing skills; this, and his impulsive generosity, kept him from ever becoming more than comfortably well off.

Turner at first hung his silver *Miss Champion* in the rafters of his hangar. Then it became the centerpiece of the Roscoe Turner Museum, along with other mementoes of his career. In 1970, at age seventy-four, Roscoe died of cancer. It was ultimately decided by his heirs that the racer should go to the Smithsonian Institution. It was placed in the gallery entitled Exhibition Flight, in company with Gilmore and Turner's flying regalia. When that gallery closed, it was moved to a prominent display position at Silver Hill.

The Other Side of the Question

During the many times that the history of the Turner Racer has been examined, it has always been assumed that the original Barlow design was a bad one, and that it took many fixes to bring it to *Miss Champion* status. There is another possibility, however, which is that the original design might have had all the capability Turner sought, and if brought to fruition, might have let him achieve the clear superiority over contemporary racers that would have made life—and racing—easier for him.

In a letter to the Museum from one of Howard Barlow's graduate students of the time, a Mr. W. Bird of Pointe Claire, Canada, a good argument is made that the original design had such potential, and that this was lost when non-engineers were given the task of building the aircraft. Mr. Bird indicates that Barlow and company were fully aware they were building an aircraft with a very high wing loading for the time, but that Turner was regarded as having sufficient piloting skill to handle it. The original wing design was quite advanced, with its choice of an NACA symmetrical wing section; and had Barlow had his way, the proposed racer would have been given a retractable landing gear.

Turner vetoed the retractable gear from the outset, saying that he had enough to do just racing without being bothered by tasks that might put his head in the cockpit at a critical time. This was a reasonable attitude, given the crazy racehorse start system of the day, when all the aircraft took off, headed for the first pylon, and often ended up there in a gaggle. It should be noted however, that the retractable landing gear was already a firm part of the racing scene, and his two most formidable rivals gained their competitive margin with its use.

He did somewhat reluctantly allow the use of flaps, as something had to be done to bring landing speeds down to a reasonable level, but these were of the straight trailing edge type, and had the least noticeable effect on flight characteristics. It was not at all unusual that a veteran pilot like Turner would wish the aircraft to be as docile as a racer could be. After twenty laps of high-G gut-wrenching turns close to the ground in near proximity to the propellers of pilots just as poverty-stricken as he was and just as determined to win, nerves had a tendency to fray. Roscoe on more than one occasion told of the genuine terror that gripped him, particularly before and always after a race.

From Bird's letter, one can develop a picture of Roscoe Turner starting out with radical ideas on performance that were not as attractive as he began to consider how they would affect him in a race. He started to alter things here and there, calling for a larger vertical stabilizer and rudder, and different fuel tankage. As the changes were introduced, particularly at the Brown factory, an upward spiral of size and weight began, which was only partially reversed by Laird when he completed the racer.

This is in fact not an unusual story for any kind of aircraft; from concept to first flight, there are usually a vast number of changes as reality rubs against desire. But it is interesting to speculate what Turner could have done with the aircraft if it had been built entirely to Barlow's conception. He might well have walked off with the 1937 Bendix and Thompson races, as well as others; or there might have been a sadder, tragic sequel. We'll never know. But we do know that the plane that did emerge, the silver Turner Racer, was in the end a champion worthy of Roscoe himself.

Ray Brooks's Spad XIII

Lt. Hal Harbird nestled down in the compact cockpit of his Spad° XIII, petting the hard flask that nestled comfortingly at his side, his eyes twin glints of flint as he watched the sharp slant of Fokker fury climbing toward him. Seven D-7s, red nosed and yellow tailed, piloted by the crack vons of Brucker's circus; each had two Spandaus at the ready, lead-hate filled for the single American winging toward Sailly-de-Sec. Harbird shrugged and snarled as he hoiked the Spad into a screaming dive, crackling the Vickers with warming bursts, knowing he would take the Huns and live—or die.
—*Satan's Wings*, June 1934, 10¢

Many of us grew up on tripe like this in *Wings, Daredevil Aces, Flying Aces* (the cream of the crop), *G-8 and His Battle Aces,* and others. It was a potent brew, making instant pilots out of anyone fortunate enough to have a dime to buy the garishly covered pulps and a place to read them where they would not be jerked out of your hands by a concerned parent.

Innocent stuff, in terms of sex and vulgarity, but fully X-rated in terms of violence, the pulps nonetheless provided a picture of the 1914–18 air war that has endured. There was a sense of beauty in the sky, a purity and nobility in the heroes, that rivaled the westerns of the day. Part of this derived from the heritage of reverence with which the contemporary press had treated the actual players at the time. In 1916, there was no sensible way to report that 60,000 young Allied soldiers were killed in one day on the Somme in a battle that accomplished nothing. The press of the time could not recount for home consumption the loss in lives, blood, and dignity of trench warfare, where only the brutality of the system and a naive patriotism could keep tens of millions of men mired in putrid slime for almost five years.

But the air war was different—it was reportable. Battle in the sky seemed to be quick and clean to the ground observer, even if it was not so to the man in the cockpit, and the survivors on the ground enhanced the story by living in a gallant fashion, seeking liquor and women as young men do now and will forever.

The reporters of the Great War had an easy task, no matter what country they were serving. Heroes abounded on all sides. In Germany, Max Immelmann, the Eagle of Lille; Oswald Boelcke, the master tactician; and the truly immortal Baron von Richtofen were all lionized before their deaths in combat. In France, Georges Guynemer was lionized, then cannonized;° his companions-in-arms Charles Nungesser, René Fonck, and others basked in an only slightly less adulatory national glow. Canada produced Billy Bishop, Roy Collishaw, Andy McKeever, and Billy Barker, all master craftsmen who survived the war. In the United States, Raoul Lufberry was the first ace of renown, to be followed by Eddie Rickenbacker, Frank Luke, Douglas Campbell, Bill Thaw, Norman Prince, James Norman Hall, George Vaughn, and more. England was less enthusiastic about trumpeting the role of aces, but could not hide Albert Ball, Edward Mannock, Ira Jones, or James McCudden from the press. Italy had Francesco Baracca, Belgium the still fiesty Willy Coppens de Houthulst; Russia had Alexander Kazakov and Alexander de Seversky, later of fame in America; Austria-Hungary had Godwin Brumowski, Julius Arigi, and Frank Linke-Crawford.

There was something for every country and every reporter. Best of all, so little was known of air combat that the correspondent had merely to tell what *he* understood of what was happening and he had created a masterpiece, even if it was a myth.

It was even easier for fiction writers later, for they could embroider every insubstantial story, puff every evanescent legend, and com-

---

° Technically, the word should be SPAD, from the acronym for the company that made it, the Société pour les Appareils Deperdussin, or, later, the Société pour Aviation et ses Dérives, but Spad became an almost generic term in the literature, and looks better in print.

° The real spelling, of course, is canonized, but Guynemer experimented with a cannon-firing Spad, and it's hard not to throw such a line to the buff.

bine it with the American success formula to make Horatio Algers on wings, creating a genre of fiction that found its way to the silver screen.

For one who had overdosed on pulp magazines, the movies were halfway houses to heaven. *Wings, Hells Angels, Lilac Time, Hell in the Heavens, The Eagle and the Hawk, Ace of Aces*—the recrudescent heroics were evocations of earlier myth. There was usually only a slight touch of romance; drinking was applauded and so was gory, fiery death. The brief battles scenes, in the later films usually outtakes from either of the epics, *Wings* or *Hells Angels,* were enough to sustain otherwise banal plots. It was the air war that counted, where Travel Airs disguised as Fokkers tangled with Stearmans disguised as Nieuports, and the Hollywood idea of a dogfight survives on television to this day. It seemed perfectly natural for fleeing pilots to keep on going straight when attacked, only looking over their shoulders at back-projections of swinish, crooked-goggle Germans or smiling, blond, round-goggle Americans, as the script dictated. Dogfights were generally curving circumfluent interactions, in which the paths of half a dozen planes from each side (Germans were black, Allies were white) would intersect in plan view, but actually be far apart when viewed from above. It was great.

And then there were the documentary stories, with real photos of real heroes taken at "the front." Captain Eddie Rickenbacker dwarfing the Spad he is about to enter; Nieuports being trundled out of Besseneau hangars; Salmsons running up, their observers waving as children wave in home movies. These were the touches that made the froth of fiction real.

In scanning literally thousands of these

The prototypical American hero, Captain Edward Vernon Rickenbacker, beside the classic Allied fighting plane, the Spad XIII. Rickenbacker had liked the Nieuport 28 fighter until he encountered its near-fatal flaw, a failure of the fabric on the leading edge of the upper wing. He survived, and was glad when the much more stoutly built Spad XIIIs arrived to replace the Nieuports. Temperamental, with an engine that was often out of commission, the Spads nevertheless were the best France had to offer. Rickenbacker was America's leading ace, with twenty-six victories compiled in a very short period of time at the front.

photos, one airplane always brought me up short with its uncompromising stance, its absolute insistence on reality. It was the Spad, a sort of U. S. Grant of an airplane—handsome, limited in some respects, but a full-fledged, two-balled fighter with no nonsense about it.

And it was the stuff of legends. I had devoted four decades of admiration and love to the Spad before Jack Bruce, the amiable, erudite Keeper of the Royal Air Force Museum at Hendon, let me and everyone else know the awful truth: the Spad was a bit of a dog, a maintenance nightmare.

The Spad was the creation of a structural engineering genius, Louis Bechereau, who had fathered the swift, lovely Deperdussin monoplanes that had set prewar speed records. Jules Védrines was the first man to exceed 100 mph, and he did it in one of the Deperdussin monoplanes, which would set the next *nine* absolute world speed records.

Despite such a distinguished record, it became necessary to reorganize the company, for the founder, Deperdussin himself, had been found with his hands in the corporate croissant jar to the extent of nearly 30 million francs, and he was packed off to the Bastille with the tough French justice of the time. Louis Blériot took over the firm, renaming it Société pour Aviation et ses Dérives to keep the Spad name.

The first Spads of the war were more hazardous to their crews than to the enemy. In an attempt to solve the problem of firing a machine gun directly forward, the firm had created the Spad A-2, a tractor biplane that looked much like the later Spads from the leading edge of the wing aft, but carried *forward* of the propeller a pulpit-like nacelle in which was seated an apprehensive gunner and a single Lewis gun. It wasn't a bad location for gunnery purposes, but it was an abortion in terms of drag and structure, and made Don Knotts facsimiles out of normally phlegmatic Frenchmen. The arrangement was a death sentence in the event of a nose-over, an all-too-common event in the days of grass fields, no brakes, and pilots with fifteen hours total flying time.

Bechereau retrieved the situation when he was presented with the airframe designer's most ardent wish, a good powerful engine and a means to synchronize the machine gun so that it would fire through the whirling propeller. The 150-horsepower Hispano-Suiza engine, designed by Marc Birkigt, was a very advanced water-cooled engine of relatively light weight and compact size. For it Bechereau created the Spad VII, a sturdy, effective fighter that served from the autumn of 1916 through the end of the war. It proved an almost miraculous reprieve from the agile, fragile Nieuports, being a macho fighter that could dive with power full on and not come apart. Spad VIIs were supplied in quantity to France, England, Belgium, Italy, Russia, and the United States (which purchased 189 examples).

Since the Spad VII was a good thing with its 150-horsepower engine and single Vickers machine gun, a Spad XIII with a 220-horsepower-geared Hispano and two Vickers would, *naturellement,* be even better. And when all was running well, it was. Unfortunately, rarely was all running well.

The geared engine produced in quantity by a number of manufacturers, gave continuous trouble. There were 8,472 Spads built, by nine different manufacturers, using engines from almost as many sources, and quality varied to a great extent. The most desired was a "Spad-Spad, Hispano-Hispano," for if you had a plane built by its parent factory powered by an engine built by the parent factory, you had far fewer problems.

The geared Hispano proved extraordinarily difficult to maintain, and for long periods of time more than 60 percent of all Spad XIIIs at the front were down for engine maintenance. It took mechanics only four hours to overhaul one of the rotary engines used on the earlier Nieuports; it took four days to overhaul the Hispano.

But for the French, the Spad XIII was the only game in town, as the competitive entries in their fighter competitions had all proven to be worse.

The Americans received 893 Spad XIIIs gratefully, for they had nothing of their own, and the Spads were enormous improvements over the Nieuport 28s. The latter were faster, more manueverable, and pleasanter to fly, but had the disconcerting habit of shedding the fabric from the upper wing in a dive. This tended to make the pilots conservative—the one thing a fighter pilot cannot be.

So when young Lieutenant Arthur Raymond Brooks, a pilot then in the 139th Aero Squadron, learned that he was going to fly Spads, he was delighted. As he was not a large man, the Spad's 26-foot 3¾-inch-span wings and 20-foot 4-inch-length fuselage resulted in a package that just suited him. With its small, thin wings, and 1,807 pounds gross weight, the Spad didn't have any gliding angle to speak of and had to be landed power on; but it could be put into outrageous combinations of maneuvers with impunity.

Brooks's first flights over the lines were without guns, there having been a slight inconsistency between armament and aircraft delivery schedules. When the two Vickers were finally fitted, he was understandably happy. He went through a series of Spads and, like other pilots of his time, flew airplanes belonging to other pilots when his own was down for maintenance. He named his own aircraft *Smith I,*

and then, as replacements came, *Smith II, III,* and *IV.* The name derived from his fiancée's college; the Museum has *Smith IV.*

Lieutenant Brooks was an extraordinarily sensitive young man, a well-educated graduate from the Massachusetts Institute of Technology. Far different from the lantern-jawed heroes of the pulps who had only contempt for death, Brooks admits to this day that he was often scared to death and on more than one occasion expected to die on the spot. He recalls that he really didn't expect to live out the war, but was determined to do his duty to the best of his ability.

His logbook and his later conversations reveal a poignant, sometimes pungent, but always penetrating understanding of what air warfare was all about. The first thing that comes through is that Brooks loved flying (and still does, for although he is a little infirm he flies every chance he gets). His descriptions of flight between decks of clouds will ring true with any pilot.

Brooks's logbooks are on file at the Museum.

Captain Arthur Raymond Brooks beside his immortal *Smith IV* at Toul, France, in September 1918. This smiling young man was a sensitive, brave, competent pilot, who unashamedly then as now was fighting for a cause. He frankly did not expect to survive the war, yet was determined to do his best while he served. Somewhat infirm today but still cheerful and witty, he flies whenever he can in anything he can get into, from a Stearman to a twin-engine Cessna.

Let's look at a few excerpts, which reveal much about him and his times:

7/29/18. Machine 2144. *Smith I*. Lt. Putnam and I attacked two Fokker (or Phaltz [sic]) single seaters, and Lt. Putnam's gun jammed. I got the first Boche which went down in a dive and a spin (not confirmed yet,) and when pulling up was attacked by a second Hun. I turned into this fella and down he went in a spin—dont think he was hit, however, don't know he wasn't. Couldn't see crash on account of clouds and business of getting motor working again.

Putnam was Lieutenant David Endicott Putnam, descendant of General Israel Putnam of the Revolutionary War, a member of the Escadrille Lafayette, and a great fighter pilot and leader. The fifth-ranking American fighter pilot, with twelve confirmed victories but perhaps actually twice that many unconfirmed, for much of his fighting was done far behind enemy lines. In one epic engagement he shot down five of the ten Albatros fighters engaging him, the greatest number of victories in one engagement until that time. He himself was shot down, with two bullets in his heart, on September 12, 1918, at Limey, France.

August 11, Machine 1512 (Garris's machine). Patrol with Lt. Putnam. Took Lt. Garris' machine, nothing to report except visibility very poor and German archies very accurate and disconcerting.

August 12, Machine 1512. Overheated motor. Same trouble with all these 220s. Temperature went to 85C, I cooled it to 70 and when I gave it the gun it went to 89; it was 92 after flight back to aerodrome.

September 6, Machine 15229 [*Smith II*]. 10th combat. Was sent up to get a hun balloon, but it wasn't up. So I patrolled and during latter part of time saw a monoplane looking over Lt. Tyndall, Jones & I, then disappeared over Hunland. Twenty minutes later I spotted one of our balloons on ascension, and made in its direction. Saw a Hun attack it. Dove 1,000 feet "tout sweet" but he had fired balloon before we got to him. I pumped 115 incendiaries into his bally fuselage and yet he didn't fire up. I pulled up with a jammed gun, and at that almost ran into him. Fokker monoplace. Tyndall and

Jones pursued. Good Teamwork. I damaged this Hun, too.

Sept 14. Goodbye *Smith II*. Another hot time. 8 huns and me alone. Fokker D.7s. Don't know how I got back, 120 bullets in plane, about 5 within 3 or 4 inches from my person. Some maneuvering I did. Rudder control shot. God was with me. Again. I got two out of the fight. Phil Harringer (sp?) is missing.

These were his fourth and fifth official victories; Brooks had by now survived that critical time at the front when young pilots were claimed from lack of experience. Today, he still recalls this fight with utmost clarity, and says in perfectly straightforward terms that he did not expect to survive it.

October 9th, *Smith IV*. Captain away. I am in charge of patrol. Led patrol of Beane, Clapp, Jones, Tyndall, Crissey, Vernon, Gibson, LaFace, Lowell.*
Saw Huns all around. 1 Fokker above balloon joined by 6 others. 2 biplanes, 2 more biplanes, 5 Fokkers—Fourteen Fokkers. Dove in on one of the first two biplanes. The patrol shot 600 rounds into the Boche— D.F.W. red fuselage, white tail, maneuvered well indeed. Went down, evidently all done. Great Stuff Jonsey. Other Boche had altitude on us, tried to get 'em, but hadn't enough gas.

The quick notes, scrawled at the time into the "Remarks" column of the little red logbooks, reflect the eager, intense excitement of the young Brooks. After the war, he enjoyed just flying, without the fear and thrill of combat. He had a ball flying Breguet 14s (although he didn't like them compared to fighters); Salmsons, the big French observation plane with the water-cooled radial engine; and captured Fokker D. VIIs, which usually had some

* 2nd. Lt. Clinton Jones of San Francisco had eight confirmed victories and won the Distinguished Service Cross. 1st Lt. James D. Beane, Distinguished Service Cross, Croix de Guerre, had six victories; he was killed in action on October 30, twelve days before the war ended. 1st Lt. Remington deB. Vernon, Distinguished Service Cross, had five victories and was killed one day after Beane. Today, Brooks can remember his companions of the 22nd Aero Squadron (to which he had been transferred) with undiluted respect and affection.

maintenance problems to worry about because they were of foreign manufacture, and used some pretty unreliable *ersatz* components.

One last entry from his logbooks, just for contrast:

> April 6, 1919 Fokker D7 4174. Spring day—just had to fly in spite of men's holiday [it was the anniversary of America's entrance into the war] so Sgt. Lib and Cpl Carny revved up for me and I liked hedge-hopping over the country. Dropped a magazine to Johny at Camp Hospital 8. Flew over Jim Wallis' Boche pen at Gradencourt. Played around clouds until mist got too thick.

How idyllic, and how much like the vibrant Arthur Raymond Brooks, who is today just as energetic and forward-looking as he was in 1918. He recently went to Paris for a reunion of World War I fighter aces of all countries, and they drank and reminisced together, even visiting some of his old hangouts, including the Café de la Paix, which had initiated him into the pleasures of Paris. He flew back in the Concorde, and sat in the jump seat during the landing at Kennedy.

Brooks still loves *Smith IV*, the aircraft in which he scored three of his six victories, and which was so badly shot up on one occasion that a new set of wings had to be placed on it. The entire aircraft is covered with little patches with black crosses on them. They mark the passage of German bullets; in its wartime career, *Smith IV* was a party to six victories.

Now it remains the only Spad XIII in the world still in its original fabric. The airplane looks somewhat the worse for wear, for the fabric and the paint have deteriorated over time, and as a result it is the center of furious debate by the buff crowd. On the one hand, some insist that nothing should be done, that *Smith IV* is as original as it ever can be, and that to restore it would detract from verisimili-

The *Smith IV* was one of two Spads chosen to be sent home for exhibit after the war. It is shown here in the old "tin shed" that for many years was the National Air Museum. Note its relatively good condition—a little weather-worn, but the deterioration of age had not yet set in.

Time takes its toll of the organic compounds used in the construction of wood and fabric aircraft. Dope and varnish lose their volatile components, fabric ages, rubber deteriorates, and so on. But, if maintained inside, even if temperature and humidity are not controlled, the essential wood and metal structure survives surprisingly well. The Martin Kitten, from approximately the same time, hangs above the Spad, at an altitude far higher than it ever flew.

Somewhat of a pilot's view, showing the small cockpit. It was a task just to climb into a Spad.

tude. On the other hand, purists of a different sort say that it is a shame not to restore the plane to its factory or at least front-line finish.

The question has become academic, because there is evidence of corrosion of the metal fittings, and the airplane must be placed into the restoration schedule for perhaps two years from now. Some thought is being given to the duplication of the process being used by the French Musée de l'Air in their restoration of the immortal Guynemer's *Vieux Charles*. The fabric of that famous Spad has been removed, the airframe restored and re-covered with a surfacing of ordinary fabric. Over this well-laid foundation, the restored original fabric is being reapplied, in the manner of a tapestry in Venice. It seems to be working well, and it may be the best solution to the problem of restoring while retaining as much original work as possible.

Ray Brooks has strong feelings about it. He wants to see his aircraft restored and in the Museum downtown—and there is every probability that he will.

6
Oddballs and Brave Experiments

Throughout the years in aviation, engineers in all parts of the world have worked methodically to advance the state of the art, building upon past experience, testing carefully, and moving forward only when all the elements of the equation have been analyzed. So you could say that an even progression of sorts, an evolutionary process, takes place in stately manner all over the world.

But there are certain individuals, some engineers and some not, who are not content to work in such a conservative way, and who hope to make a great leap forward by inspired new devices. These inventors fail more often than they succeed. In either success or failure, however, they tend to make life more interesting.

A lot depends upon the circumstances. In times of war, engineers are sometimes driven to radical ideas, trying to compensate for certain shortages in material or numbers by introducing entirely new concepts. Rarely do they succeed, for the same reason that inventors rarely succeed: when one attempts to focus on a particular aspect of an aircraft—the shape of the wing, the type of propulsion—to the exclusion of other elements, one is almost certain to build in trouble.

In this section we'll look at a long series of aircraft that could be described either as oddball or as brave experiments. In every case the people behind the craft were serious, well-intentioned individuals, who wished to gain a

performance advantage in ways that were not yet proven. Some failed abjectly, while others came very close to success.

We'll look first at the Martin Kitten, a darling of an airplane that was featured in photos and advertisements for years and had many good points—plus a host of bad ones.

Then we will compare two wartime aircraft of remarkably similar configuration, the Curtiss XP-55 Ascender and the Japanese Kyushu J7W1 Shinden. Both fighters sought to step ahead of their contemporaries by use of a radical "tail-first" configuration. And although both were conceived entirely independently, for different missions, they were very much alike.

Next, we'll step back in time to investigate the sad tale of the Langley Aerodrome, an airplane whose general potential had been amply demonstrated in model form, but which lacked certain essential elements in full scale. As a parenthetical note, the unfortunate controversy that surrounded the Langley after its display in the Smithsonian will be examined.

The role of the inventor will keynote our look at the Custer Channel Wing, a most unusual aircraft, which in its developed form had a heart-stopping performance and is still a controversial aircraft today.

The next aircraft, the Vought V-173 Flying Pancake, was designed by an engineer-inventor who very nearly saw his idea enter production. A complete departure from all existing aircraft of the time, the V-173 had an almost oval wing of very low aspect ratio, and was a successful testbed for a follow-on fighter. That designer, Charles Zimmerman, endured years of disappointment that were replaced by hope when the Navy ordered an experimental fighter version of his design, the XF5U-1, only to order it demolished because the jet age had arrived and the Zimmerman ideas no longer applied.

In a very similar way, Gerald Herrick experimented with his Convertaplane for years, bringing the unusual rotary-wing aircraft to a fairly successful point, only to have the helicopter supersede it.

And to prove that it happens to engineers as well as inventors, proponents of the autogiro had, after a thirty-year evolutionary process, begun to achieve some real results when they, too, were swept aside by the helicopter tide.

The one characteristic all these varied aircraft share is the intense human interest that brought them to life. These were not "plain vanilla" production-line developments; each had a spark of originality that time has not diminished, and one can only hope that there are other inventor-engineers waiting to delight us in the future.

The J. V. Martin Kitten

J. V. Martin was a genuine aviation pioneer. He was the first man to fly over London, the first to fly in Alaska, the first to fly a twin-float plane in Seattle, and the first to predict, in 1917, the invasion of the United States from Canada. An inveterate inventor, his stream of aeronautical devices—the K-Bar strut, the shock-absorbing combination rudder/tail skid, wing-end ailerons, the double convex airfoil, the list goes on and on—were matched in number only by the suits he filed against the government, other manufacturers, and other inventors. At one time it is estimated that he had a total of $96 million in suits outstanding, and there is no record that he won any of them.

His most famous product, the Martin "Kitten"—variously called, in his best ad-man manner, the "Altitude Scout," the "Blue Bird," and the "K-III"—is hanging from the rafters at Silver Hill, still in its original condition, and embodying many of the inventions that formed the focus of Martin's litigation. Oddly enough, the tiny airplane looks somewhat like the man: small, stoutly built, pugnacious, and perhaps just a little bit bonkers.

There was a strange combination of success and failure in Martin's life that is mirrored in the Kitten, a combination that makes them both very appealing. Martin was a competent, daring pilot with some very advanced ideas; he was also something of a charlatan, who lived as much by the press as by his inventions. In a similar way, the little Kitten, with its less than 18-foot-span wings, was a combination of some advanced ideas, like the first practical retractable landing gear in the United States, and some weird structural and control concepts that could have led only to disaster.

Perhaps strangest of all, there is a direct engineering and romantic link from this tiny biplane to Howard Hughes's huge 320-foot-wingspan HK-1 Flying Boat—a link that was suspected for a long time but was confirmed only after Hughes's death.

Born in Chicago on March 31, 1883, Martin spent his youth in St. Louis before entering the Merchant Marine at age seventeen. In a phenomenally short time for the period (less than ten years) he had gained the coveted Master Mariner certificate and with it the title of Captain that he used unfailingly for the rest of his life.

His years at sea convinced him that he had much to offer the world, and after some time at the University of Virginia, he took some special courses at Harvard, where he founded the Harvard Aeronautical Society. He masterminded the 1910 Harvard-Boston Aero Meet, the largest aviation function yet held in America, and one that attracted many of the world's leading aviators.

Martin had previously supervised the construction of the "Harvard I," a totally creditable effort for a non-flyer. It was a very small biplane, only 200 square feet in wing area, with a 30-horsepower engine—and no tail surfaces whatever. The Harvard I brought with it the mixed emotions that characterized Martin's entire career. He claimed that he had flown the aircraft about 125 yards at a height of 8 to 10 feet, but there were no other witnesses, and the plane was promptly christened "the Ground Hog" by other Harvardites. It was a source of bitter embarrassment to Martin for years.

The Aero Meet was a total success, and Martin realized that if he wanted to fly, he should do it properly. So he enrolled in the Graham-White Flying School at Hendon, England, present site of the magnificent Royal Air Force Museum.

At Hendon, Martin became a star turner, earning rave notices in *Flight* magazine, which on February 11, 1911, stated that Martin in a Graham-White "New Baby" had made "a most excellent flight of twenty minutes. The first four circuits were performed at an average of 400 feet, but he gradually descended and for the last three circuits skimmed the ground. Later he made a splendid right hand turn, banking up well."

In those days when every turn was noted by the press, it did not take long to get a license, and Martin received the Royal Aero Club F.A.I. certificate No. 55 on February 7, 1911, only thirty-eight days after he started training and twenty-four days after his first solo.

The next six months must have seemed like a dream to the ex-sailor. He became an instructor at the school, and one of his pupils was the attractive Lilly Irvine, whom he first taught how to fly and then promptly married. On March 11, 1911, he became the first man to fly over London.

He also nearly crashed, and this led to the earliest of his long, almost interminable, series of inventions. He felt that his near crash was caused by the drag created by the low wing in the turn, and as a remedy proposed interconnecting the ailerons to obtain a differential effect, a control pinciple used to this day. When you consider the bitter nature of the control controversy then raging between the Wrights and Curtiss, his invention was a considerable achievement.

Martin returned to the United States with his wife, and began a fast-paced life that led them across the country, to Alaska and Hawaii, flying at air meets, lecturing, and later, entertaining. Mrs. Martin entered vaudeville as "Lilly Irvine, Queen of the Air in Britain," with a "Specialty Classic Posing Act and Remarkable Motion Pictures of Her Record Breaking Flight from Cedar Point to Euclid Beach."

And Martin kept inventing. His first airplane looked like a Blériot in a Farman suit; built by the Queen Aeroplane Company of Long Island, New York, it was called by the enthusiastic press a "hundred horsepower tractor biplane-monoplane." It had a number of unusual features, including a sheet-metal cowling used to shield bystanders from the oil slung by the whipping Gnôme rotary engine, but which Martin later claimed was the predecessor of the NACA ring cowling. It also had interconnected trailing edge ailerons, and most unusual elevators, which were built in two halves. Operated normally for horizontal control, they separated and operated differentially with the ailerons for lateral control. The plane was very fast for the time, and Martin always claimed it was a fundamental type, the tractor biplane, that completely outclassed contemporary Wright and Curtiss pushers.

The next years of Martin's career are difficult to separate into fact and fiction. If he did all that he claimed to have done, he was an extraordinary man; just reading the things he is known to have done is impressive.

He claimed to have reentered the Merchant Marine upon the U.S. declaration of war in April 1917, commanding the U.S.S *Lake Fray.* He also claimed to have headed the Canadian government's Steffanson rescue expedition, and to have worked with Herbert Hoover in the Russian Relief campaign. This possible embroidery of the genuinely worthwhile career touches upon the basic flaw in Martin's make-up, an ego that was not satisfied with very genuine accomplishments, but had to enhance fact with fancy.

All during this time he was bubbling with ideas, the first of which he demonstrated on a Curtiss JN-4; it won him the Aero Club of America Medal of Merit in 1917. The device was a wing-end aileron, fitted with a vertical surface and a counterweight that operated automatically. The pilot had only to operate the rudder and elevator. Martin claimed it was an automatic lateral-control device, which would "promote safety for flight in fog." He demonstrated the practicability of the device in a flight from Mineola, Long Island, to Princeton, New Jersey.

The invention was later tested at Dayton's McCook Field by the renowned Alexander Klemin, who said that it was impossible to tell whether it was the airfoil or the pendulum that was effective, but in any case control reaction was unpredictable, being as likely to amplify a response as to dampen it out. This was later borne out when it was tested on an H-16 Flying Boat, which went through some wild gyrations before being brought down by a thoroughly shaken pilot.

In early 1917, Martin founded the Martin Aeroplane Company in Elyria, Ohio, where he drew on the talents of a competent engineer, Flavius Loudy, to put into practice the unending stream of his inventions. "Old Pink Whiskers," as he was called, was ready to enter full-scale aircraft production.

Flavius Loudy, the man who translated many of J. V. Martin's ideas into reality, sits in the little Martin Kitten in the Martin factory at Elyria, Ohio. Here it looks entirely plausible. It is a machine of high quality, as the burnished varnished surfaces suggest; it is nicely streamlined for the time, and the wheels are retracted into a very neat well on the side of the fuselage. Note that behind the wheel is a streamlined fairing, exactly like that used on the Seversky P-35 almost twenty years later.

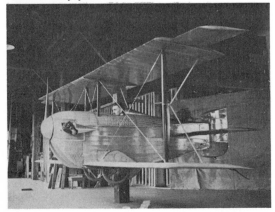

The Kitten was the first product of the factory, and it was pressed upon the War Department for evaluation. With a wingspan of 17 feet 11¾ inches and an empty weight of only 350 pounds, the Kitten was powered by a two-cylinder A.B.C. Gnat engine of 45 doubtful horsepower.

The principal feature of the little scout was its practical retractable landing gear. This device, which formed the basis for the snappy J. V. Martin Company motto: "Every First Class Aircraft Deserves a Retractable Chassis," was a starkly simple mechanism of stout welded-steel channel to which Ackerman "Inner-spring" wheels were solidly attached. The entire structure was manually shifted back so that the struts fitted into recessed grooves in the bottom of the fuselage, while the wheels slid into stylish fender mount–like wells on the fuselage side. Half of the wheel remained exposed, as in many later aircraft like the DC-3; the Kitten could theoretically take off or land with the gear in any position, retracted, intermediate, or full down.

The Kitten also used wing-end ailerons, Martin's method of sidestepping the Wright-Curtiss lateral-control argument. A large biconvex plate was located at each upper wingtip, joined together by a stout torque tube, which ran all the way through the wing. Martin claimed that this control system was more efficient, stronger, and offered less drag than conventional ailerons, although later testing proved this not to be the case.

The aircraft was stoutly built of plywood formers with plywood skinning on the fuselage, and featured several other Martin inventions. The rudder was ruggedly built, and doubled, for no apparent reason, as a tail skid.

One of the most distinctive features was the patented Martin "K-Bar" struts. The doughty little captain claimed great savings in weight and drag, without loss in strength. McCook Field engineers disagreed, saying that any other configuration of struts (parallel, X, I, V, or N) would have been better.

It has to be borne in mind that Martin had become an irritating incubus to the hard-pressed engineering and contracting staff at McCook Field, who were trying to fight a war and didn't need Martin's unasked-for assis-

The Kitten was thrust upon the Air Service at McCook Field by J. V. Martin, who always labeled any interference with his ideas a "conspiracy." Note the Ackerman "Innerspring" wheels, which acted as shock absorbers. The "K-Bar" struts are particularly evident here. The tiny two-cylinder A.B.C. Gnat engine has a streamlined fairing behind it. There is much evidence of good workmanship and attention to detail. (USAF Photo)

The Kitten looking remarkably jaunty, with its wheels fully extended, on the absolutely simple landing gear structure. The channel iron simply slid back when moved by a long-handled worm gear, and had a feature that has not been found on many retractable gear since. It could be moved to any position from full up to full down, and the airplane (theoretically at least) could still land and take off. (USAF Photo)

With wheels retracted, Kitten assumed a more pugnacious stance. Note the wingtip ailerons on the top wings, wingtip skids on the bottom. In practice, the Ackerman wheels proved to be too weak, and had to be considerably reinforced, removing much of their shock-absorbing capability. The handsome, well-dressed flying officer on the right is not identified.

tance. Martin knew how to use the press and Congress to his advantage. He was apparently offering his services to the government at no cost, yet the bureaucracy was ignoring him— or so it was portrayed.

The Air Service for its part was young, born almost yesterday. But it was not buying Martin's claims that the Kitten could reach 25,000 feet altitude, fly at 112 mph, and carry a pilot, heated flying suit, oxygen, two Vickers machine guns, and 2,000 rounds of ammunition.

Still, claims were claims, and while Martin was insisting that his Kitten be taken seriously and was advertising in all the aviation magazines, he managed to secure a $67,000 contract for an even more ambitious project, the twin-engine "Cruising Bomber." This large, well-finished aircraft incorporated all of the Kitten's features except for the retractable landing gear, and added a gear box that transmitted the throbbing horsepower of two Liberty engines to two propellers via a very flimsy drive shaft system.

Through all of this, Martin persisted in his role of patriot battling the nefarious interests of the Aircraft Manufacturers Association, which had been formed to sidestep the issue of the Wright-Martin patent fight, and which amounted to a patent-pooling cross-licensing association. He badgered the Air Service with claims and counterclaims, and even as late as 1924 could with equanimity portray himself to Congress as a major aircraft manufacturer and designer of record-breaking aircraft.

Martin implied then, and throughout his life, that the Kitten had flown, and had achieved its vaunted performance. A full testing program conducted at the Dayton Hill and Dale Community Country Club during the period of July 28 to August 10, 1919, resulted only in sixty short hops. These privately sponsored tests were conducted by the well-known engineer Lieutenant W. F. Gerhard, who would have a distinguished career, but would be best remembered for the films of a collapsing Venetian blind arrangement of wings, his attempt at a human-powered aircraft. Gerhard found that the Kitten was so excessively tail-heavy, he could take off only by moving the retractable landing gear part way to the rear and placing 75 pounds (20 percent of empty weight) of pig iron in the nose. The Gnat engine did not furnish enough power to climb out of what is today called "ground effect," and Gerhard never flew more than 4 feet off the ground. Probably just as well, for he also found a total lack of lateral control—at the maximum speed attainable, he could slap the stick from side to side in the cockpit without any effect.

The Kitten was later donated to the Smithsonian Institution, where it was long exhibited with a label indicating that it had flown, and calling attention to its retractable gear.

To J.V.'s intense pleasure, the Kitten design had a reprise a few years later. There was a contest in 1921 for a submarine-based scout plane, and the Gallaudet Company manufactured three modified examples of the Kitten. The wingspan was increased to 24 feet 2 inches, and conventional ailerons were fitted. The K-Bar struts were retained. The plane flew well enough, but the program died after six similar types built by the Glenn Martin Company were purchased. J. V. Martin derived a great deal of pleasure from the fact that the later floatplane Kitten, known as the K-IV or KF-1, was faster than the contemporary Sperry Messenger, a land plane powered with the same 60-horsepower Lawrance engine.

J.V. lived on, still inventing and still suing. In the late 1930s, he apparently secured the interest of no less a person than the British First Lord of the Admiralty, Winston S. Churchill. Martin convinced Churchill that it would be practical to replace conventional merchant shipping with a huge twin-hulled catamaran "Oceancruiser"—a seven-engine aircraft that would negate the submarine menace by flying over the sea-lanes. Churchill, not surprisingly, was intrigued by the idea, and asked the Admiralty to investigate. The Admiralty contracted Henry Kaiser, who in turn got in touch with Howard Hughes. And Hughes's engineers have told me that the first six months of the ambitious HK-1 ("Spruce Goose" to the uncaring) project were devoted to the creation of a twin-hulled catamaran type.

So between the enormous white HK-1, now at long last in safe anchorage at Long Beach, and the tiny, frail-looking, somewhat tattered Kitten at the Garber Facility, there is a definite link, the inspiration of a man just as eccentric as Howard Hughes but not as rich—J. V. Martin.

Martin died in 1956, an embittered man, never properly recognized in his lifetime for what he did and never really unmasked for claiming what he didn't.

Later in life, J. V. Martin conceived the idea of a twin-hulled ocean cruiser and sent the notion to Winston Churchill, who turned to the Admiralty, who went to Henry Kaiser, who went to Howard Hughes—thus the Kitten is the ancestor of the Hughes Flying Boat. Later, after the war, Martin offered the idea again.

The Kitten as it exists today, wheels tucked up and somehow brave and proud. It would be an interesting project to determine just what minimum changes are needed to render the airplane safely flyable. A project for the homebuilder who has done everything?

Among ultra-light aircraft like this Eagle, the canard surface has become very popular. A canard confers a number of advantages, but one of the most important is that the canard surface will stall first. When it does so, it pitches the aircraft down, and prevents the larger rear surface from reaching a stall. Oddly enough, the configuration of this lightweight vehicle is not too different from the two fighters, the XP-55 and the Shinden. Note pusher propeller, swept wings, wing-mounted vertical surfaces, and canard.

Tail–First into Oblivion

Curtiss was for forty years one of the proudest names in U.S. aviation. Unlike the Wright brothers, who were unable to create a manufacturing company of sustained success after the first flush of their triumphs, Glenn Curtiss established himself before World War I as the preeminent U.S. manufacturer of aircraft and aircraft engines. As late as 1917, the Curtiss firm was the only one in the country actually capable of mass production.

The initial Curtiss success in mass manufacture was based on the famous Curtiss JN-4 Jenny. Although this was only a training plane, it laid the basis for what would become an aviation empire. After the war, Curtiss went on to establish itself as the leading manufacturer of fighters, bombers, observation planes, transports, and with the acquisition of Travel Air, civil aircraft also.

But companies, like people, vary in their adaptation to success and to age. The swift growth and rapid accumulation of wealth of the company seemed to increase its conservatism in proportion; profits and dividends became more important than new products. The Curtiss line of fighters, once the best in the world, became obsolete simply because the firm preferred to try to stretch existing designs rather than create totally new ones.

The firm's management watched as first Boeing and then others began to take away its business. Then, with one last gasp of insight, it brought in a bright young man named Donovan R. Berlin to create a new line of all-metal, low-wing monoplane fighters. He did so, beginning with the Hawk 75 series, which led to the Curtiss P-36 and the immortal (and profitable) Curtiss P-40 of Flying Tiger fame.

The P-40 firmly reestablished Curtiss once again as the manufacturer of the finest fighter aircraft in the United States, even though in the world market the P-40 was regarded as already obsolescent. The timing was perfect. It arrived on the scene exactly when enough money became available to expand production lines, and was soon being turned out in quantity in several plants. Ultimately, more than 14,000 of the type were built, and they served with distinction in every theater of war.

But the welcome flush of success with the P-40 was a temporary cure. Berlin found that the Curtiss management had not really changed, that what has later been termed "corporate senility" was creeping in, and he left.

It was not that the Curtiss management was unaware of what was happening; it knew very well that there had to be a replacement fighter for the P-40, which was basically a 1934 design, modified in 1937 to take the Allison liquid-cooled "pointy nose" engine. The question was how to create one.

The first and most obvious method was to improve the P-40, and numerous efforts were under way. The basic production P-40 had been stretched through a long series of modifications, which began with the P-40A Tomahawks and ran through the P-40N Warhawks. In the process, speed had climbed from about 320 to 340 mph, and there were improvements in range, firepower, and armament. But the airplane was clearly inferior, at every stage, to the North American P-51, the Republic P-47, the Messerschmitt Bf 109, and the Supermarine Spitfire. Something new, different, and better was called for.

Given the need, Curtiss engineers were turned loose, only to find that in the fossilized welter of management, radical improvements were not easy to generate. The first attempt was the Curtiss XP-46, basically a smaller P-40, with some minor improvements based on observations of the Spitfire and the Hawker Hurricane. The XP-46 had heavier armament, inward-retracting landing gear, and a lighter gross weight. The problem with the XP-46 was that it was no better performing than the P-40Ds already in production, and thus not a solution to the problem.

The next attempt was to mate the basic P-40 design with the new laminar flow wing, and the promise of a high-powered Continental inverted-V engine. This hopeful combination was called the XP-53. As a safeguard to the possible unavailability of the Continental en-

gine (and as it turned out, the Continental never materialized in production), the Curtiss XP-60, powered by a Rolls Royce Merlin engine, was planned.

Work proceeded rapidly on this beefed-up version of the best of the P-40 and P-46, and the first flight took place on September 18, 1941.

Curtiss, like all other manufacturers, had problems with the critical finish requirements of the laminar flow wing, which wouldn't work properly without a glassy smooth surface. It also had problems with weight control. The XP-60 got fat instead of faster, and the original Merlin engine installation was canceled in favor of the more readily available Allison turbosupercharged V-1710-15 engine of 1,425 horsepower. The airplane was overweight and underpowered, and Curtiss proposed the installation of a 2,000-horsepower Pratt & Whitney R-2800 engine, which made the plane look like the result of an illicit mating of a Yak-9 and a P-47C.

The endless drill of changes and poor performance went on, while at the same time the P-47s and P-51s were being steadily improved. The XP-60 series was ultimately dropped, including the bulbous XP-60E, which looked as if it had been tailor-made for Hermann Goering.

During this same awful period, Curtiss was trying and failing with the grotesque XP-62, a heavyweight high-altitude fighter that had so many teething problems it rarely got off the ground, and the Curtiss XF14C-2, a Navy fighter not so ugly as the XP-62, but that flew no better.

Small wonder then that Curtiss hopes began to turn on an outrageous-looking airplane conceived at the St. Louis plant in response to the U.S. Army Air Corps Circular Proposal R-40C. R-40C was an attempt by the service, newly rich with undreamed-of appropriations, to gain a jump on the world fighter race by hazarding radical new departures in fighter design.

Circular Proposal R-40C brought forth a whole host of designs, as well as an intelligent method of evaluating which were the best of the proposals. A panel of judges looked at a number of factors, including predicted performance, serviceability, cost, and so on, and

The Curtiss XP-55 was actually not a true canard, which has a fixed forward surface; instead, the XP-55 had a nose-mounted elevator. The wing sweep was pronounced, and would have been a happy complement to the installation of a jet engine rather than the somewhat underpowered 1,275-horsepower Allison that was installed. (USAF Photo)

In flight the XP-55 offered an arrow shape never seen before in America. It looked like a world beater, although its performance never met the standards of the P-51 or the P-47. The propeller was fitted with an explosive charge that would blow it away in the event of an emergency, so that the pilot would be able to bail out. (USAF Photo)

rated them via a weighted system. The winner was a twin boom pusher by Vultee that ultimately proved to be the clunker XP-54 Swoose Goose. Number two was the "tail-first" Curtiss entry that proved to be the clunker XP-55. Number three was the tailless Northrop entry that proved to be the clunker XP-56.

The Curtiss entry was tested in wind-tunnel form by the Army, and turned down because of poor stability and the probability of bad stall characteristics.

With so few arrows remaining in its experimental quiver, Curtiss felt impelled to gamble with the XP-55, and built a full-scale flying mock-up, the Model 24-B. This plywood, steel-tube, and fabric-test airframe was powered by a 275-horsepower Menasco engine and was intended only to prove the feasibility of the configuration—which, with its pusher propeller, lack of empennage, and forward elevator surface, was wildly radical for the time.

The Model 24-B was flown by test pilot J. Harvey Gray on some 169 test flights, the first one only five days before Pearl Harbor.

These showed that the configuration was indeed feasible, and although it had some problems was indeed worthy of development. The U.S. Army Air Force, backed by seemingly inexhaustible funds, ordered three XP-55 prototypes, to be powered not with the Pratt & Whitney X-1800 engine for which it was designed, but by the semi-obsolescent Allison V-1710, the same basic engine that the P-40 used. Thus the advanced new airframe was condemned to the level of performance of an engine that was available, but capable of only about 1,300 horsepower.

Gray was selected to be the primary test pilot for the airplane because of his experience with the Model 24-B, and he made the first flight in the hot-looking new fighter on July 13, 1943. Gray was engaged in an intensive, three-month test program when, on November 15, 1943, he began exploration of the effect of the wing spoilers on pitching characteristics in a stall. He had made two efforts at obtaining a full stall. On the third, the XP-55 pitched forward 180 degrees onto its back and fell into the very same inverted vertical descent that

Curtiss, in a rare spirit of wry humor, suggested the name "Ascender" for the XP-55; the stolid War Department accepted the name as befitting an interceptor, not realizing that it was a *double-entendre* nickname. The shadow gives a better feel for the aircraft's shape than does the picture itself. (USAF Photo)

The XP-55, like all Curtiss products, was exceedingly well finished. Engine installation was superb, perhaps the cleanest ever for a pusher. If the 2,200-horsepower Pratt & Whitney X-1800 engine for which it had originally been designed had been available, it is possible the XP-55 would have had the desired 500-mph performance. (USAF Photo) had been predicted in the original Army wind-tunnel tests. The engine quit, and nothing Gray could do could break the stall or even affect the attitude of the aircraft. After a perfectly stable but nerve-shattering fall of 16,000 feet, Gray bailed out. The aircraft continued straight down, totally destroying itself on impact.

There was an immediate rash of "fixes" to cure the problem. The wingtip had a 2-foot extension added, the elevator travel limits were increased, and an inverted fuel system was installed to permit longer periods of inverted flight, in the hope that the pilot might "power" himself out of the condition.

It really didn't matter. The performance of the aircraft with the Allison engine was mediocre—about 377 mph instead of the 500 mph hoped for in the original design submission. Test pilots were somewhat spooked about the aircraft, and Ben Kelsey talked about the utterly indescribable wild gyrations it went through time and again, as he tried to determine what went wrong when the engine stalled.

There were other problems, too. Russ Schleeh, a famous test pilot of the time, recalls that the XP-55 was terribly unstable, and that if you took your eyes off the horizon even for a moment, even in the landing pattern, the plane would drift wildly off course.

In any event, the thousands of Mustangs and Thunderbolts being turned out were obviously going to be enough to do the job, and by December 1944 all formal interest in the XP-55 was ended.

The XP-55 featured in one more tragic accident, this time no fault of its own. The third example was being flown at Wright Field just after the war by a pilot unfamiliar with its characteristics. He came in low over the field, attempted a barrel roll, and didn't have sufficient altitude to complete it. He crashed into a parking lot, just one more example of the hundreds of totally unnecessary accidents of the time.

The remaining XP-55 was sent to the Park Ridge facility in Chicago, and ultimately to Silver Hill, where it now awaits restoration parked near an equally fascinating airplane with a totally different background but a very similar appearance—the Kyushu J7W1 Shinden.

The XP-55 is in relatively good shape. It will probably be restored for a future Oddballs of Aviation Gallery.

The "Magnificent Lightning" was a far more radical departure for the Japanese than the XP-55 was for the Americans, and there is little doubt that it would have encountered the same sort of teething problems that the Curtiss product did. Note the frail, stalky nose gear, the twin tail-protection wheels under rear fins, and the relatively straight, unswept wing.

The "Magnificent Lightning"

The Japanese began the war with an entirely erroneous reputation as "copiers" of foreign equipment. The popular press was filled with stories of how their aircraft derived from U.S. or German designs, and were, naturally, inferior.

Even long after the war, in which so many Japanese aircraft had demonstrated their quality, it was still fashionable to believe that the Zero was copied either from Howard Hughes's racer or from a Vought design. The Japanese engineers did in fact make use of their knowledge of foreign technology, but so did every engineer in every country.

When the war started, Japanese aircraft were generally conservative in outline but somewhat radical in construction, for their designers had to sacrifice strength, armament, and redundant equipment in order to achieve the specified speed, range, and maneuverability. And, like the United States, the Japanese were further handicapped by the lack of engines equivalent to British or German standards.

This native Japanese ensemble—lightweight aircraft and less powerful engines—was nevertheless formidable at the beginning of the war, when the Zeros cleared the path for the Greater East Asia Co-Prosperity Sphere. By mid-1943, however, the handwriting was clearly on the wall. The prewar Japanese designs were hopelessly dated, totally unable to cope with the B-29; Japan needed a fast, heavily armed interceptor capable of climbing swiftly to high altitudes. To obtain this aircraft, there would not only have to be a radical shift in design concepts for the engineers; there would have to be equally radical changes in testing and procurement procedures so that it would be available in time.

Just as Curtiss experienced internal pressures to do something radical to stay competitive in the rapidly changing fighter arena, so there were pressures on the Japanese. And if the pressures were similar, it is not surprising that the responses to the demand for an unconventional design were also similar. The Curtiss XP-55 came into existence in an at-

The rear view shows the six-bladed contra-rotating propeller, which was driven by a long extension shaft from the equally untried 2,130-horsepower Mitsubishi air-cooled radial engine. The Shinden was envisioned from the start to be a candidate for the installation of a jet engine.

From the front, the Shinden looks remarkably like the XP-55 from the same vantage point. (Richard Seely)

The size of the Shinden is totally amazing for a Japanese product. Its wingspan was not great at a little over 36 feet, but the height was an impressive 12 feet 10 inches, and small-statured Japanese could walk right under aircraft. (Richard Seely)

A remarkable aspect of the conflict with Japan was the discipline with which most of the armed forces accepted surrender. Within a few days of V-J Day, Allied soldiers could walk with impunity amongst crowds of still armed Japanese. Note the American standing just inside the right landing gear, and the total unconcern of the crowd. (Richard Seely)

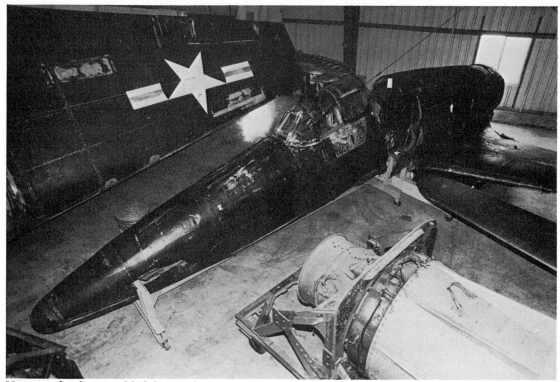
Not completely assembled, but with parts in close enough alignment to be able to see how the aircraft looked, the Shinden waits at Silver Hill for restoration.

tempt to make a great leap forward to surpass domestic and foreign fighter competition. The Japanese engineers, in the exactly same way, but with vastly different resources, produced the very attractive Kyushu J7W1 Shinden. With its swept wing, outboard-mounted rudders, and pusher propeller, the Shinden, or "Magnificent Lightning," looked very much like the XP-55.

While the Curtiss had come into being in 1939–42, the Shinden began its development in late 1942, when Lieutenant Commander Michinori Tsuruno, a member of the Institute of Naval Aeronautical Research Board at Yokosuka, Japan, conceived the idea of a canard-type, high-altitude interceptor. Like the XP-55, wing-tunnel tests revealed some stability problems, and again like the XP-55, a flying scale model was made, in this case the MXY 6 Glider. Flight testing was somewhat limited, but the design showed sufficient promise on paper to warrant selection for production beginning in 1945, with a goal of 1,800 airplanes to be produced in 1946. The firm that produced the aircraft, Kyushu Hikoki, was almost unknown in the United States at the time.

The Shinden was far more radical for the Japanese than the XP-55 was for the Americans, and the decision to go into mass production from the drawing was even more so. The need for high-altitude performance had become so great that a second gamble in the design was attempted. This was the selection of the 2,130-horsepower Mitsubishi Ha 43-42 eighteen-cylinder, air-cooled radial engine, which was itself still unproven. The engine was installed in the fuselage directly behind the pilot's cockpit, driving a six-bladed pusher propeller by means of a long extension shaft.

Armament for the Shinden was exceptionally heavy for a Japanese fighter, in recognition of the difficulty encountered in attempting to bring down the stoutly built Boeing B-29s. Four 30mm cannon were mounted in the nose, and the Japanese hoped that in the Shinden they would at last have an aircraft that could engage the B-29 on an equal footing.

Time was running out, however. On August 3, 1945, the first flight was made, and two other short flights, which brought the total air time to only forty-five minutes, were completed before the war ended.

Despite its brief flying career, the Shinden had indicated some severe problems, including a very strong pull to the right on takeoff and heavy vibration in the propeller drive shaft. Both of these conditions might have been cured, had time permitted, but it was not to be.

In at least one respect, the Shinden was far more advanced than its Curtiss counterpart, for it had been intended from the first for conversion to jet power. The Japanese had planned to use the 1,984-pound thrust Ne 130 turbojet; if it had been installed, the Magnificent Lightning would have had both of its major problems solved along with a tremendous increase in power.

In time the Shinden will be restored, too, and visitors to Silver Hill will be able to compare it with the XP-55, two wayward diversions on the road of aviation progress.

The Langley Aerodrome— Microsuccess and Macrofailure

The Langley Aerodrome's four white wings dominated the main workshops of the Garber Facility like a gigantic, well-meaning dragonfly, a bumbling giant too large to be housed anywhere else conveniently, too important not to be shown, and so filled with the nostalgia of lost battles and family feuds as to be unforgettable.

It is difficult to take the Aerodrome in all at once, and even more difficult to photograph it. Only the wings seem substantial—the rest is a cobweb of silver tubing, wire, and fittings. One of its anomalies is that it has no alighting gear, neither wheels nor floats, so it sits upon a specially constructed stand that mirrors its own plumbing structure.

Few aircraft have had such a promising beginning turn into such an ignominious end. The Aerodrome is a visible product of the old boy network, the aristocratic answer to the problem of flight at the turn of the century. Professor Samuel Pierpont Langley, third secretary of the already venerable Smithsonian Institution, had turned from his traditional scientific pursuits to the desire to fly, and he marshaled his own considerable genius and the resources of the Institution to achieve his aim.

In six years of developmental effort, Langley finally arrived at his original goal of making a heavier-than-air unmanned model that would fly for an appreciable time and distance. The Aerodrome No. 5, in appearance very much like its full-size descendant, made a flight of 3,300 feet, rising perhaps as high as 100 feet in the air before running out of fuel and gliding smoothly to the water on May 6, 1896. It was a signal success, but one that would persuade Langley down an implacable path to disappointment with his full-size Aerodrome A.

The success of this and the next model led Langley into the fatal error of assuming that the models, which had been especially designed to have the minimum weight of airframe and engine combined with the maximum output from the engine, were amenable to scaling up to a full-sized, man-carrying version. He also ignored the requirement to have a three-axis control system, and instead thought that the full-size machine would have the same automatic stability as the models, derived from generous dihedral, though he did install a rudder to provide flat turns and an elevator to control ascent and descent. Worst of all, he did not realize that the materials and construction techniques satisfactory for a structure the size of his models would not be suitable for a full-size aircraft.

Despite Langley's success in obtaining backing from the War Department to the tune of $50,000 and additional amounts from the Smithsonian, the full-size aircraft did not come quickly. The principal delay involved what would ultimately be the only successful part of the entire apparatus, the engine, and it was not until October 1903 that the huge Aerodrome was ready for testing.

As it emerged piece by piece from the two-story laboratory behind the Smithsonian Cas-

The fuselage, if it can be called that, of the Langley Aerodrome in the process of erection. The tubular structure was light and quite strong, reinforced by many wires and turnbuckles, all exquisitely handmade. The water-cooled radial engine was mounted transversely, just as in a modern K car, and drove the propellers through an elegant series of shafts and gears. The canoe-shaped structure was the pilot's compartment, neatly placed where he would be submerged on every landing.

Mounted on the houseboat, the Langley Aerodrome really looked convincing. After all, his models with exactly the same configuration had flown well. Note, however, the position of the center spar in relation to the curvature of the wings, and their apparently fragile mounting to the central structure.

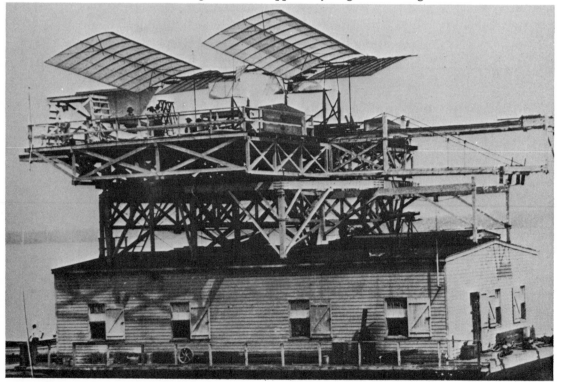

tle, the Aerodrome was an impressive machine. The fuselage structure was made up of steel pipe milled down for lightness, and connected with an elaborate set of handmade fittings, wiring, braces, and gussets. The wings were intricately fashioned of hollow ribs and spars, tapered for lightness, and giving an impression of strength that belied their fragile nature.

The models had been launched from a catapult device, and Langley, with an amazingly simplistic point of view, had an even larger one created for the Aerodrome. Mounted on top of a houseboat, the catapult was intended to accelerate the Aerodrome to flying speed in the space of 70 feet; the strain on what was really a rather weak structure should have been apparent to all involved.

Charles Manly, who had been the principal person responsible for the magnificent engine in the Langley (of which more later), was also to be the pilot, although he had never flown any kind of aircraft. And here we have the permutational certainty of failure: an aircraft that had never flown, powered by an engine that had never flown, was to be launched by a catapult that had never launched an aircraft, and piloted by a man who had never flown. It was an incredible aggregation of uncertainties.*

Langley was an imperious man, sometimes difficult to work with, but a scientist of genius. He could see that flight was within the grasp of mankind, and he believed absolutely that his solid base of experimentation with the models provided the solution.

But in the last months of 1903, he suffered three bitter blows. The first came on October 7, when in the words of a Washington newspaper, the regal-looking Aerodrome slid into the Potomac "like a handful of mortar." The accident was attributed to a launching failure and the Aerodrome was rebuilt for a second attempt, on December 8. This time it collapsed upon launch and turned turtle before falling over again into the chilly Potomac. Fortunately, the young Charles Manly, doubling as

* The Wright brothers had made more than 2,000 gliding flights prior to their attempts in December 1903; they also had taken the trouble to develop a three-axis control system.

A remarkable photograph of the second failure. The wings have failed, the aircraft is pitching down, a man's dreams are being destroyed. Fortunately, Charles A. Manly, the engineer-pilot, was able to survive this second ducking. He apparently never lost faith, for it was he who helped instigate the notorious series of tests by Curtiss in 1914.

engineer, engine builder, and pilot, was able to struggle free, although on the second attempt he very nearly drowned, being trapped first in the wreckage and then under the ice. It was typical of the unevenness of Langley's idiosyncratic genius that he had provided no means of alighting except a few floats suspended well up in the structure. The pilot was sure to be immersed on every flight over water, and if he had to come down on land, probably injured or killed.

The third blow fell on December 17, 1903, when the Wright brothers made their successful flights at Kitty Hawk. Langley found it difficult to accept that others had succeeded where he had failed, and the raillery of the newspapers, the jibes of congressmen, as anxious then as now to take a cheap shot at a prominent figure, brought about a decline in his health that ended only with his death in 1906.

The Smithsonian Institution itself found Langley's failure difficult to digest. It was correct and gentlemanly to attribute the failure to the launching mechanism, but this predisposition to excuse led to a notorious series of events that would cost Langley, the Smithsonian, and the Wright brothers dearly.

In all fairness, it must be remembered that the Wright brothers' triumph was not generally known or believed for several years; the truth of their success was not acknowledged as it should have been until Wilbur's epic flights in Europe in 1908. As a result, it was not too difficult for scientific myopia to occur, and to lead the Smithsonian to exhibit the rebuilt Langley Aerodrome in 1918 with this label:

ORIGINAL LANGLEY
FLYING MACHINE, 1903

The first man-carrying aeroplane in the history of the world capable of sustained free flight. Invented, built and tested over the Potomac River by Samuel Pierpont Langley in 1903. Successfully flown at Hammondsport, N.Y. on June 2, 1914. Dimensions: 55 feet long, 48 feet wide, sustaining wing surface 1,040 square feet.

Even more insidious than the ambiguous wording of the first sentence, which clearly implied that this was the first successful man-carrying aircraft, was the third, which used the phrase "Successfully flown."

Hammondsport was Glenn Curtiss's home base, and the testing of the Langley Aerodrome there was one of the most classic cases of conflict of interest in the history of flying. The original interest in retesting the aircraft

had come from Lincoln Beachey, the famous stunt pilot, via Charles Manly, who had a natural concern about validating a configuration that he had worked so hard on and suffered so much from. A suggestion to do the tests was made by Langley's successor, Dr. Charles D. Walcott, to Curtiss. Curtiss was apparently somewhat embarrassed, for he was locked in a life-or-death legal battle with the Wrights over patent infringments at the time, and a successful testing of the Aerodrome might have a bearing on the case. Nonetheless, he accepted a contract from the Smithsonian to test the airplane. To worsen the situation, Dr. Albert F. Zahm, the recorder of the Langley Aerodynamical Laboratory, and expert witness for Curtiss in the various lawsuits with the Wrights, was there as the official representative for the Smithsonian.

As the original Langley design called for ducking the pilot after every flight, Curtiss decided to put floats of his own design on the Aerodrome. There are claims that hops were made with no other changes, and using the original Manly engine. Later, purportedly to test the tandem configuration of the wings, extensive modifications were made, including the use of a Curtiss engine and propeller,

Vastly modified, fitted with floats worked on by Albert Verville, the Langley made a series of hops, which proved precisely nothing.

The Langley Aerodrome prior to restoration. It had been suspended in the Arts and Industries Building for many years, and while structurally sound was badly corroded. About 2,500 man-hours were required to restore it.

changes in the camber of the wing, in the attachment of flying wires, in the placement of king posts, and even in the aspect ratio. Several short flights were made that didn't add much to aeronautics, but did diminish the reputations of all involved.

Needless to say, Orville Wright was furious (Wilbur had died in 1912), and his ire was rekindled in 1925, when the label on the Aerodrome was changed again, this time emerging even more weasel-worded than before:

LANGLEY AERODROME

The Original Langley
Flying Machine of 1903, Restored.

In the opinion of many competent to judge, this was the first heavier-than-air craft in the history of the world capable of sustained free flight under its own power, carrying a man.

This aircraft slightly antedated the machine designed and built by Wilbur and Orville Wright, which, on December 17, 1903 was the first in the history of the world to accomplish sustained free flight under its own power, carrying a man.

The label went on to say that the Langley houseboat failures had been due to imperfect operation of the catapult, and that the tests at Hammondsport indicated the original ma-

chine would have flown in 1903 if it had been successfully launched.

In actual fact, the Aerodrome was both aerodynamically and structurally unsound. It lacked the essential system of three-axis control devised by the Wrights, lacked a means of landing without damage, and depended upon a far too demanding launching system. Structurally there were many ways it might have failed if it had somehow become airborne; but the gravest defect, and the one that most probably destroyed it on its second "flight," was a fragility that permitted its broad wings to twist up and back until they failed.

Orville had finally had enough. In 1928, he shipped the original Wright Flyer off to the Science Museum in London, where it remained until an older and wiser Smithsonian Institution modified its stance, made many apologies, and agreed to write labels for the Flyer that would clearly indicate its primacy. Peace was restored, and in 1948 the Flyer returned home to the old red brick Arts and Industry Building that was "the Smithsonian" for so many years. It was to stay there until moved to become the centerpiece of the Milestones of Flight Gallery in the National Air and Space Museum.

Ironically, the most successful thing about the Aerodrome was its engine, a startlingly

Once restored, the Aerodrome posed a problem: Where could it be exhibited? It is a large aircraft (Langley did not stint on wing area) and it doesn't have any alighting gear, so it either has to be suspended or placed on a support.

The interim solution was to build a black-pipe support stand and just work around it. Here Karl Heinzel works on a D.H. 4 aileron underneath the shadow of the Aerodrome's rear surface.

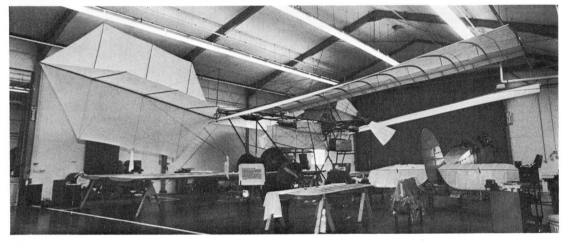

good five-cylinder, water-cooled radial, which Manly himself developed from the aborted attempts of Stephen M. Balzer, a New York automobile-engine builder.

Langley had requested Balzer to build a rotary air-cooled engine (one in which the cylinders rotated about a fixed crankshaft) of 12 horsepower. Balzer tried desperately to succeed, but failed badly. Manly finally took over the engine, converted it to a stationary radial, with water cooling, and tinkered with its valves, timing, ignition, and carburetion until he achieved an amazing 52-horsepower output, which was sustained in three consecutive ten-hour test runs. (The Wrights had their own homemade four-cylinder engine, which developed 16 horsepower for a few seconds before settling down to a steady 12. It was enough for the flights they had intended, but some jesters say that if they had had the Manly engine, they would have flown home to Dayton.)

Manly's engine achieved a low weight-to-horsepower ratio that was not excelled until the Liberty engine of 1918. Yet so great was the debacle of the Aerodrome that the magnificent engine was overlooked.

There is, perhaps, some justice in this world, however delayed. Today, Manly's engine is on exhibit downtown in the National Air and Space Museum, with full credit given to it for its superior performance. The big Aerodrome is out of the limelight at Silver Hill, a replica engine mounted amidships, waiting, as it has waited all its existence, for the next big chance.

The Custer Channel Wing

There are a number of instances where a single-minded man and a single-minded mission become so inextricably woven that it is impossible to tell where the man begins and the mission ends. Examples include Gutzon Borglum and the mammoth sculptures of Mount Rushmore; Sir Edmund Hillary and the assault on Mount Everest; Hitler and the *Drang Nach Osten;* Eiffel and his tower; and, surely, Willard Custer and his Channel Wing.

Willard R. Custer is a figure straight out of American folklore. He is the prototype Yankee inventor, smart, tough, resourceful, unafraid of the machinations of big business, big government, or fate. He is William Henley singing his *Invictus* against the disbelieving engineers who dare to doubt that the Custer Channel Wing will not do all that Willard claims for it.

The Channel Wing, which he has now championed for more than fifty years, has a distinctive shape that appeared on no other aircraft—the channels look like two half-barrels or U-shaped attachments on either side of the fuselage. Custer claimed that the device lowered stall speeds, shortened takeoffs, made short, spot landings easy, and at the same time improved speed and range characteristics.

Curiously, at least half of his claims were justifiable; the others were perhaps pardonable exaggerations for promotional purposes. Most engineers, cynics, and parents know that you don't get something for nothing. If you obtain better performance on the low-speed side of the spectrum, you usually sacrifice something on the high-speed side, and vice versa.

But to a true believer all things are possible, and no true believer could have been more ardent than Willard R. Custer, to whom the Channel Wing and "aerophysics" are not mere words but a religion.

Custer got his faith in an appropriately awe-inspiring way. As a young man, he was taking shelter in a barn during a near hurricane when suddenly the roof soared off. Custer, who had been fascinated with aircraft for a long time, wondered how it was that an airplane was required to move down a runway to gather speed for takeoff, while a roof, a poor airfoil surely, took off from a barn solidly anchored to the Maryland earth.

He soon came upon a distinction that has eluded other investigators, postulating that when air passes over an object, such as the barn roof, that is "speed of air"; but when an air-

A very early promotional effort by Willard Custer, which does point up some interesting details in his design. Note the two sets of ailerons, one outboard for conventional flight—and one inboard in the propeller slipstream for V/STOL (Vertical/Short Take Off Landing) work. (Willard R. Custer)

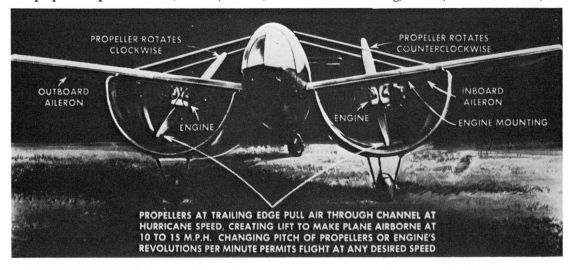

craft flies through the air, that is "air speed." In his own words, "It is the speed of the air and not the speed of the object which counts." The airfoil was designed to obtain a reaction from an air mass *through which it moves.* His own channel was designed to obtain a reaction from the air mass *moving through it.*

The first aircraft to which he applied this principle, after some serious experimentation with models, was the CCW-1, or Custer Channel Wing-1, which now hangs at the Garber Facility. Still surprisingly modern in appearance, it made its first flight on November 12, 1942. It is an unusual combination of futuristic lines and engineering anomalies: the well-made wooden fuselage, with its large Plexiglas-fitted cabin area, is smoothly streamlined, but the wings are appended to the fuselage with two-by-four struts, and the landing gear appears to have been stuck beneath the channels as an afterthought. The channels themselves are the distinctive features—big 6-foot-diameter half-barrels, in which were mounted 75-horsepower Lycoming engines.

The principle of the channel wing is essentially the Bernoulli principle. A circular airfoil is created on either side of the fuselage, and in it is mounted an engine with a propeller that in later models fitted precisely inside the channel rim. When the engine operates, air is sucked through the channel and blown out over the rear of the wing. The faster velocity of the air over the curved channel surface creates an area of lower pressure, just as an airfoil's shape creates a lower pressure above its upper surface as the wing moves through the air.

Proponents of Custer's theory agree to all this, but add a little more. They say that in addition to taking advantage of the Bernoulli principle, the propeller-channel arrangement minimizes losses due to reverse flow around the trailing edge, and then across the ventral surface, which greatly adds to the efficiency of the device. They also say that during the wartime tests of the Channel Wing, there was simply not enough aerodynamic theory available to explain the effect, and consequently the tests were conducted using the wrong means of investigation.

The NACA tests, proponents say, failed to reveal that the principal source of lift is due to the increased velocity in the channels, and that the test should have highlighted the fact that the static lift generated by the early, still undeveloped channels was still greater than the weight of the test vehicle; it was, in fact, capable of vertical flight. This basic fact underlies the most salient advantage of the Custer Channel Wing, which is its simplicity. It is able to operate in a STOL (Short Take-off and Landing) mode without either the expense and maintenance problems of a rotary-wing aircraft or the alternative expensive high-lift devices of other STOL craft.

The initial cost of a Custer Channel Wing aircraft is probably greater than that of a conventional type, but far less than that of one with an equivalent STOL performance obtained by means of flaps, slots, vectored thrust, and so on. The operating costs would also be far lower because of lessened maintenance requirements. In certain applications, where the requirements for vertical ascent or descent were not critical, the Channel Wing could compete on the same basis as helicopters.

In sum, fans of the Channel Wing maintained that the concept provides for an efficient, economic solution in certain situations, not currently met by conventional STOL aircraft like the Helio Courier, or by helicopters.

There is a con side, too. Those who take a negative view of the Custer Channel Wing do so persuasively and authoritatively. Their initial reaction is usually, "Oh no, not the Channel Wing again!", followed by a measured explanation which shows that there is not nor ever has been any emotional or political prejudice against Custer's ideas. If, they say, the Channel Wing had demonstrated merit, there would have been economic and military forces to foster its development.

In more specific terms, the opponents of the Channel Wing say that it has less potential now than when it was introduced because the helicopter has been so greatly improved. Opponents concede that the Channel Wing's lack of flaps results in a simple system, less expensive to build and to operate, and they also admit that the generation of high lift by the configuration is accompanied by a low pitching momentum compared to conventional STOL wing/flap combinations.

Having said that, however, the CCW opponents argue that the following facts prevail:

1. The CCW has higher drag, due to the bulky channels.
2. The very simplicity of the arrangement works against it, for it is optimized for only one mode of flight. The admittedly more complex wing and flap arrangement permits optimum performance in several modes of flight.
3. The requirement to cross shaft engines so as to overcome uncontrollable asymmetric forces in the event of an engine failure offsets the CCW claim for simplicity.
4. Higher landing speeds are required in the event of a power-off landing.
5. The structure is more complex.
6. There still has not been a complete engineering investigation into the problems of stability and control; Custer company tests have been far too simple.
7. Rerouted wing spars mean a heavier structure.

To all of which Custer snorts "Poppycock!"— he knows he is right. Not a pilot, he inadvertently made the first flight in the CCW-1 when, while taxiing it one day, he put on too much power and rose into the air, his initial flight as a pilot and the plane's first time off the ground. He got it back down safely by the simple expedient of chopping the throttle and holding on.

The CCW-1 flew about three hundred hours during the 1942–43 period, almost all of it spent in short, low, straight-ahead hops. A demonstration before the military took place at the Beltsville, Maryland, airport, and Brigadier General W. E. Gilmore, a man famous in the old Air Corps for his gruff temperament, was excited enough to place a personal call to Orville Wright, asking that he come out to witness the Custer phenomenon. Orville was apparently unable to attend, but the aircraft was placed in a military test program.

The results of the tests proved to be typical of all the many government tests Channel Wing aircraft were to receive over the years. Army Air Forces Technical Report No. 5142

The first CCW-1 (Custer Channel Wing-1) featured a very modernistic fuselage, two rather narrow channels, and some exceedingly crude support structures. This photo was taken at the L. H. Crook Laboratory on November 11, 1942 at Hagerstown, Maryland. (Willard R. Custer)

Harold Custer is shown flying a second version of the aircraft. Harold has more Channel Wing time, about 1,000 hours, than anyone else. The stub wings, each 36 inches long, were fitted at the insistence of the Civil Aeronautics Administration, although the plane flew perfectly well without them. (Willard R. Custer)

concluded that the lift generated by the channel was similar to the increment of lift generated by normal slipstream velocity in conventional wing/propeller arrangements, and that the Channel Wing was inferior to the helicopter in generating static lift. The conclusion of the report somewhat surprisingly says that the device does not show sufficient promise of military value to warrant further development by the Army Air Forces. This conclusion, at a time when every conceivable prospect was being explored—from the Cornelius swept-forward wing flying gas tanks to amphibious gliders—seems incomprehensible.

Custer's immediate and customary reaction only helped the controversy along. He hinted darkly that perhaps the test results had been *too good,* and that the helicopter interests were trying to suppress the aircraft. In fact, he had some support in this from other engineers who felt that the idea had merit, and from the results of a later test at Wright Field, which forms the basis for further patents by Custer.

The government's word-waffling was really a disservice to Custer; tests should have been structured that would have proved either the merit or the lack of it in the project. If the evidence was conclusive that the Channel Wing had nowhere to go, Custer could have spent his considerable talents over the next four decades in other areas. If the evidence was conclusive that the idea had some potential, funds could have been obtained from either government or private sources to develop the concept.

But Custer had faith in himself, and a little thing like government bungling was not going to deter him. Over the next forty years he obtained financial backing for a series of aircraft, including the CCW-2 and the CCW-5. The CCW-2 was an engineering testbed that his son, Harold R. Custer, flew for more than 100 hours, developing further insight into the Channel Wing configuration. The Custers found that not only were the size, shape, and finish of the channels crucial, but it was essential to fit the propellers as closely as possible to the lip of the channel, almost forming a seal.

Custer's messianic belief in himself and his invention managed to convince enough investors over the years to bring him to the brink of full production on at least two occasions. In

The CCW-5 was a conversion of a Baumann Brigadier; it flew very well, and received a great deal of favorable attention. At one point it seemed certain that the aircraft would go into full-scale production, with an initial run of 100 aircraft. Note how thick the channels are in relation to the earlier aircraft. (Willard R. Custer)

The number one production CCW-5, just after rollout from the factory. A very proud Willard R. Custer stands ready to enter the cabin. Films of this aircraft in flight are absolutely breathtaking—it turns in steep banks at extremely low rates of speed, jumps off the ground in very little distance, and lands in just a few feet of runway. (Willard R. Custer)

Painted up, with fairings fitted, the production CCW-5 looks very convincing. Unfortunately for Custer, he was never able to obtain the complete financing needed to undertake production. (Willard R. Custer)

Today, the very first Channel Wing aircraft rests jauntily at Silver Hill, where it is sometimes visited by its still persuasive inventor, Willard R. Custer.

1951, he was able to employ the Baumann Aircraft Company to modify one of their handsome pusher Baumann Brigadier executive aircraft to the CCW configuration. The result was the prototype CCW-5, a beautiful airplane by anyone's standards, which was powered by two 275-horsepower Continental engines.

Walker J. Davidson made the first flight in the CCW-5 on July 13, 1953. It was highly successful, according to Custer, who spent the next several years demonstrating the aircraft to civil and military audiences. The demonstrations consisted largely of hair-raising maximum-performance takeoffs, with sharp turns to the right and left, at speeds so slow it seemed obvious that the airplane would fall out of the sky. Motion pictures of these tests are still frightening, for you can see that the airplane should be stalling and spinning in. Instead it keeps on turning, nose high and at 50 or 60 degrees of bank.

Slow flight was naturally a specialty, with forward speeds as low as 22 mph being measured. On August 27, 1954, the CCW-5 actually hovered against an 11-mph wind.

The prototype's performance was good enough to attract additional investors. At one point it seemed that Custer and Noorduyn Aircraft, Ltd., of Canada would join together in a production venture for at least 100 aircraft. On the strength of this proposal, a production version of the CCW-5 was built, roll-ing out on July 4, 1964. Outwardly similar to the converted CCW prototype, the new aircraft had been built from the ground up. This time Custer ran into trouble with the Securities and Exchange Commission, which claimed that the stock had not been issued correctly, and the rug was pulled out from beneath the entire project.

Custer was disheartened at times by the lack of foresight of investors and buyers who couldn't see the evident value of his invention, and perhaps a trifle annoyed by those people who should have known better, the engineers and military men, who surely should have seen the light. Still, he is never discouraged for long.

And there were things that ultimately heartened him. It did not take Custer an instant to see that the experimental Boeing YC-14, a STOL transport, had utilized the principles he had so long espoused. Similarly, he had but to glance at the Fairchild Republic A-10 attack plane to see that again his principles had been misappropriated. Neither Boeing nor Fairchild agreed, of course, and Custer took the matter to court. The initial judgments went against him, but he still has avenues of appeal.

Regardless of the merit of the case, one almost hopes that Custer wins what may very well be his last tilt with the titans. He is overdue for a victory, and it would be within the American tradition for him to close out a valiant career with a satisfying triumph.

Wings, Things, and the Flying Pancake

Throughout the history of flight there has been a tremendous fascination in tinkering with existing practice to gain some slight advantage in speed or range or altitude. No part of an aircraft has escaped this fiddling, and the wings have received most of the attention.

Wilbur and Orville Wright established the first common practice here with their successful biplanes. Two wings, one mounted above the other in reasonable symmetry, provided plenty of wing area in a well-balanced, strong structure.

The conventional practitioners followed them: Voisin, Farman, Sopwith, de Havilland, Curtiss, Martin, Sikorsky, all went to biplanes. There were a few advocates of the monoplane, men like Blériot, Esnault-Peltrie, Levavasseur, and others, who knew intuitively that there was less drag in the design, but did not yet know how to provide adequate strength.

To inventors, however, the wing seemed the easiest point of departure from which to obtain significant improvements. The fuselage (except in the eyes of men like Burnelli and Northrop) was an unavoidable attendant to the requirement to carry bombs or passengers. The empennage was a necessary evil, and engines were far too complex and required too much development time for anyone but a specialist in the field to fool with.

Thus there developed an entire array of wing planforms, chosen by inventors and designers as the best way to make a significant contribution. And it should be noted that it is as a result of the basic study of wings—the airfoils, the relationship of span to chord, the degree of sweep, etc.—that most legitimate contributions to flight have been made.

The number of variations is remarkable. Among the first radical efforts were the "Doughnut" wings of Kitchen and Lee. These were round wings with a large hole in the center, annular efforts that flew, but not well. John William Dunne had far greater success with his arrow-shaped, tailless biplanes, which achieved an amazing stability and would have had far greater influence except for their radical appearance.

Not only were the shapes experimented with; so too were numbers of wings and their placement. A. V. Roe and Tom Sopwith succeeded with triplanes, as did Anthony Fokker; the latter stubbed his toe on the quintaplane, a five-wing fighter that made only a couple of short hops. It was modest compared to the later Johns Multiplane, however. Here was an inventor who felt that one could not have enough wings, and laid on no less than seven. His enthusiasm for wing area overcame such fundamentals as weight and drag, and his Multiplane skipped off the ground and into oblivion.

Another line followed the original Langley wing tandem layout, which had a great deal to recommend it in terms of center-of-gravity travel and stall characteristics. Albessard of France essayed at least four different aircraft, all of which flew well enough, but not better than conventional aircraft. Then de Lanne excited prewar enthusiasts with a series of elegant fighters, tandem-winged and featuring a power-driven multiple gun turret in the tail. Oddly enough, it remained for a homebuilder, Burt Rutan, to achieve final unqualified success for the tandem configuration, in his sensational series of VariViggen, VariEze, Quickie, and Defiant aircraft. It should be noted here and now that Burt Rutan will someday be recognized as the premier genius of the second golden age of flight, and that Cessna, Beech, and Piper will ultimately march to his music.

Another oft-essayed type was the canard, which placed the wing farther aft, and sought to avoid some of the "dreaded stall" problems with a forward-mounted control surface. The Wright brothers began with canards, of course, and most later versions did not succeed so well. The Curtiss XP-55 was not a true canard, but other aircraft, similar in appearance, like the Kyushu Shinden and the Italian S.I.A. S.S.4, were, and promised success that was not achieved until the late 1960s. Then a host of useful solutions emerged, the most prominent of which was the Swedish Saab Viggen fighter. Now a canard is often found on supersonic transport proposals, drawing-board fighters,

The very low aspect ratio aircraft has been one of the most difficult tasks in aviation. No one has come as close to solving the problem as did Charles Zimmerman with his Vought V-173 "Flying Pancake." The basic idea was that at low speeds, the large-diameter propellers would provide sufficient lift to get the aircraft airborne; the relatively low drag shape of the fuselage would also permit higher speeds. Original designs envisioned a prone pilot, and lots of glass area was provided for forward visibility during the high angle of attack (nose-up) operations. (Vought Aircraft)

and, surprisingly, among the new generation of ultra-light aircraft that is swarming like gnats over the landscape.

Still another variation was the extremely long, high-aspect-ratio wing, like the Hurel-Dubois aircraft of the 1950s and the Short Skyvans of today. Here the wing resembles a huge venetian blind slat, supported by large struts, but generating a great deal of lift in relation to its drag. The ultra-long, thin wing has had its greatest success in sailplanes, where the very high aspect ratio wing has been the *sine qua non* of performance.

On the other side of the conceptual spectrum is another wing form that has had far less success: the very low aspect ratio, circular-wing form. Its antecedents go back at least to the Kitchen "Doughnut" in 1911, and its monoplane development in turn to Cedric Lee in 1913, the parabolic Russian Tscheranovsky of 1924, the Miami University "Flying Saucer" of 1934, the Arup of the same time, and the later Lippisch, Horten, and Northrop flying wings.

Of all of these, only the last three achieved a

measure of success, and then only because a wartime environment permitted the luxury of development. The same was true of a lesser-known experiment, Charles H. Zimmerman's "Flying Pancake," the Vought V-173.

Zimmerman was a man with the saddest of all fates. He was a true believer who suffered long in the wilderness before seeing his beliefs confirmed, only to find that his concepts had been overtaken by technology.

The young Zimmerman began taking aerodynamic courses in the 1930s, and then joined NACA, the predecessor of today's NASA. At an early date he conceived of a radical idea for an aircraft: a circular wing that would have good high-speed characteristics, but would also have an advantage in the low-speed modes by virtue of its propeller placement and design.

Fundamental to this concept is the realization that in every conventional aircraft there are large losses in efficiency due to the drag created by disturbed airflow at the wingtips. This was the departure point for Zimmerman's elaboration.

In essence, he was trying to design a STOL aircraft that would almost hover due to its large-diameter articulated propellers, placed at the extreme ends of the circular wing to overcome the tip loss, and which would have an exceptionally high speed due to its low drag profile. Zimmerman succeeded, but his timing was off.

The young engineer had attracted attention to himself at NACA's Langley Field because of the high quality of his work. He had made important contributions to the improvement of NACA's wind tunnels, and his unswerving commitment to the circular airfoil did not detract from the esteem in which he was held. He first served notice of the radical nature of his genius in a design competition for a "people's airplane." His entry did not win (the only mildly radical Stearman-Hammond did), but it caught NACA's eye.

Zimmerman felt that his basic concept of a circular airfoil would have certain characteristics ideal for a carrier-based aircraft. He wanted a plane with fully competitive fighter qualities in terms of speed and maneuverability, but which could be flown slowly and with precision down a glide path to the pitching deck of an aircraft carrier. He built model aircraft, wind-tunnel models, and even a small man-carrying model (which, probably fortunately, never flew) of his concepts, and in demonstrations to the Navy brass inevitably won rave reviews—but no contracts.

NACA liked Zimmerman's work, but also appreciated the fact that it would not be able to subsidize his career while he delved into the unique problems of a circular airfoil. NACA recommended that he go to private industry, so in 1937 he joined the Chance Vought division of United Aircraft.

Vought was an unlikely prospect for radical designs, having a history of gradual evolutionary development over the years. Yet such was Zimmerman's impact that it soon built an elaborate wind-tunnel model of his concept, calling it the V-172. The quarter-scale flying model of the proposed prototype was powered by a huge electric motor.

Test results were sufficiently good to have the Navy agree to furnish enough money to build a full-sized aircraft, the V-173. Powered by two 75-horsepower Continental engines, the V-173 differed from anything Vought or the Navy had done in the past. A proof-of-concept vehicle, it had a circular wing 23 feet 4 inches in diameter with a symmetrical NACA airfoil section. The V-173 weighing 3,050 pounds, was relatively heavy for its 150 total horsepower.

The construction was steel tube and fabric of the simplest sort, for Vought didn't wish to make the design any more complicated than it already was. Two huge three-bladed propellers were mounted at each "tip" of the circular airfoil, blanketing the entire aircraft in their slipstream. At the end of the wing/fuselage was a rather complex empennage, consisting of two normal-looking horizontal stabilizers and elevators, two rudders, and, on the midpoint of the fuselage, two large elevators. The landing gear was a stalky set of struts from which two

Somewhat surprisingly, the V-173 flew very well, once the rather unusual control characteristics were determined by test pilots. (Vought Aircraft)

The V-173 suffered several forced landings, and survived even this turnover with negligible damage.

As you might imagine, the press had a field day with the Flying Pancake, which performed almost exactly as its designer had predicted. Note the combination elevator/aileron surfaces at rear. (Vought Aircraft)

The V-173's performance was good enough to warrant the development of a fighter based on it, the XF5U-1. This aircraft would have had a formidable performance, particularly if turboprop engines had been fitted. As it was, it arrived simultaneously with the jet engine, and was canceled after taxi tests. (Vought Aircraft)

The V-173 sits in rather crowded conditions in Building 7 at the Garber Facility, dusty, but taped up and in good shape. The engine in front of it is from the Japanese "ground-up" kamikaze, the Nakajima Ki-115. At left is a Mosquito fuselage.

long stroke oleos were attached to wheels with low-pressure tires.

The V-173 went through a 139-hour test program, primarily under the guidance of Boone Guyton, whose book *Air Base* was as effective a recruiting device for Navy pilots as Bernie Lay's *I Wanted Wings* was for Army pilots. Guyton made the first flight on November 23, 1942.

He handled the aircraft effectively, even though its flight characteristics and control responses were most unusual. After a sufficient number of flights to get the controls tuned, Guyton found the Flying Pancake, as it was inevitably called, to have some endearing qualities. The aircraft could be flown at very low speeds, almost at a hover, and it could sustain minor damage without danger to the pilot.

The Navy was increasingly concerned about the high approach speeds of fighter airplanes, and felt that the V-173 pointed to one possible solution. As a result, it ordered the construction of the Chance Vought XF5U-1, the last Vought piston-engine fighter. The XF5U-1 was of substantially the same configuration as the V-173, but much more rugged and equipped for service work. It was powered by two Pratt & Whitney R-2000 radial air-cooled engines, mounted inside jet-intake–like nacelle open-

ings. Power from the 1,600-horsepower engines was transmitted to the two four-bladed-propellers by means of heavy transmission gear boxes and some intricate cross shafting.

The XF5U-1, which was predictably dubbed the "Flying Pancake," offered great promise of a high-speed fighter that could still be handled comfortably from existing carrier decks. Unfortunately, the jet fighter was on the horizon, even in Vought's own shops, where the pudgy XF6U Pirate was taking shape. Everything was set to begin flight tests on the XF5U-1 when the order came down from the Navy to halt proceedings. It was not considered worthwhile to test the aircraft in view of the forthcoming shift to jet engines.

Vought, and most especially Zimmerman, were terribly disappointed. It seemed totally wasteful to bring the radical new fighter to completion and then not to test-fly it. The Navy was adamant, however, and had the aircraft destroyed with a wrecking ball.

That might have been the end of Flying Pancakes were it not for farsighted individuals who managed to sequester the V-173 for later museum use. It sits now in a long flat building, dusty but complete, awaiting the day when it will be restored and exhibited, a tribute to the man who designed it.

Rotary Wings—Cierva's Autogiros

Almost by chance, the Garber Facility has the most unusual collection of rotary-wing aircraft in the world, not excepting even the wonderful Army Aviation Museum at Ford Rucker, Alabama. The collection, while not overwhelming in number, is bewildering in its variety, ranging from the very first Pitcairn-Cierva autogiro built in the United States down through tilt wings, tilt props, tilt jets, and into Convertaplanes (the subject of the next section), and, of course, helicopters.

Rotary wings have impressed inventors since the beginning of time, for nature provided hints in the swirling winged seeds of maple and zanonia trees. Leonardo da Vinci began the mechanical concepts with his screw-type helicopter, and inventors continued to experiment through the years, despite a signal lack of success. In every country men tried vainly to achieve vertical ascent by means of rotating airfoils; but it was not until the late 1930s and early 1940s that significant progress was made. Today, there is a bewildering fleet of helicopters of all sizes and shapes, ranging from the tiny one-man bubbles used to scout highway traffic to huge Skycranes to the experimental Piasecki "Heli-Stat," a combination of four helicopters and a Blimp.

The helicopter was so long in attaining success simply because it is so much more complex than a conventional aircraft. The need to ascend vertically from a small area, and to descend safely, perhaps without power, nonetheless had a strong appeal for inventors who recognized the inherent difficulty in creating a helicopter but thought there might be other means. First and foremost among these people was Juan de la Cierva of Spain.

There is a charm and a poignancy about Cierva's life. He was driven to the study of rotary wings by witnessing the crash of a trimotor bomber of his own design in 1919, when he was only twenty-four. The aircraft had crashed in the classic stall–spin style from a low altitude. Cierva was determined to find some way to prevent this all-too-common accident. (Ironically, he was to lose his own life in the

crash of a transport plane at the age of forty-three, when he still had much to contribute to aviation.)

Cierva achieved his great successes by a combination of insight, empirical testing, and the ability to validate the results of his experimentation by retrospective mathematical proof. It was an unusual method, somewhat the reverse of most engineers, and would not have been possible without his intuitive sense.

He had begun his work at sixteen, when with the help of some friends the same age he built two gliders. This was followed a year later, in 1912, by the creation of the first Spanish aircraft to fly.

The shock of the trimotor crash caused Cierva to focus on the problem of safe vertical ascent and descent. He sensed that the safety problem lay in the dependence of the aircraft's wings on the forward motion through the air. So he tried to devise a means by which the wings would move through the air independently of the aircraft's forward motion.

When one looks at a rotary-wing aircraft, autogiro or helicopter, it is easy to assume that the principle of the screw, or of the falling seed pod, or simply that of the propeller, has been extrapolated. Not so, for the rotary wing is just that, an airfoil that not only advances toward the line of flight but, for half of its motion, retreats from it, creating formidable problems of stability and control.

Cierva recognized this, and went through a long series of designs before arriving ultimately at the autogiro. He conceived a paddlewheel arrangement, not too different in principle from those of packet boats, as well as more radical dispositions of multiple wings that rotated around the fuselage like the fingers in a butter churn.

In 1922 and 1923 he built three experimental autogiros, each progressively less complex and more successful than the last. The first two featured coaxial rotors, mounted one above the other above a rotary-engine–powered aircraft fuselage. The two rotors did not behave identically because of the unequal flow conditions

Juan de la Cierva achieved a notable success with his C-8 autogiro, which had an impressive short-field performance. In an autogiro, the rotor is not powered by the engine, although the blades are "pre-rotated" either by a rope starter (in the early days) or by a takeoff drive from the engine. The pre-rotation is not sufficient to lift the autogiro into the air as a helicopter's blades lift a helicopter; instead, it provides a sort of "jump start," which converts rotational energy into lift by a sudden change in the angle of incidence of the blades. The energy is soon dissipated, but the autogiro has by then gained sufficient forward speed for the rotor to begin acting as a wing.

they created, and they exaggerated the already complex problems of stability of the configuration.

Cierva went to a single rotor on his next attempts, which edged him closer to success. The autogiro would now taxi quite readily, but on gathering speed to the point of liftoff would begin to roll over, tilting to one side so that the rotor tip dug into the ground. The rolling effect was determined to be due to the fact that the blades did not produce equal lift as they described the circle: the advancing blade would create far more lift than the retreating blade, creating a dissymmetry that caused the roll.

Experimentation gave Cierva insight into an astoundingly simple invention that made the autogiro practical, and would provide inspiration for later engineers working on helicopters. He simply permitted the blade to rise and fall freely about a hinge at the rotor hub, in response to relative velocity. This equalized the lift, and removed the "tilt force" that had caused the earlier autogiros to roll over as they approached takeoff speed.

On January 9, 1923, at Getafe Airfield near Madrid, Cierva's fourth attempt at an autogiro made its first successful flight. After several tentative attempts, during which he was feeling the aircraft out, the pilot, Lieutenant Alejandro Spencer, applied full power, lifted the autogiro off the ground, and then landed successfully. The flight seemed to herald a whole new era in aviation, but there were long years of development and disappointment ahead.

Cierva had characteristically concentrated on the principal problem of vertical ascent and descent, and his successful autogiro had been adapted from a Hanriot fighter's fuselage, using its original Le Rhône rotary engine. Most later autogiros would be specially designed from the ground up.

In 1925, Cierva was invited to England to demonstrate his invention. The famous long-lived Frank Courtney was test pilot of this hybrid, which used the fuselage of a stock Avro 504K, England's standard primary trainer for many years. This aircraft used four rotor blades instead of the previous aircraft's three, and had a very primitive system for starting the rotor up. A rope was wound around the rotor shaft, then a group of ground crewmen grabbed the rope and ran at top speed to set the rotor spinning. The pilot gunned the engine to gain forward speed and continued the rotation, and the autogiro lifted off the ground. Much later, autogiros would be able mechanically to wind their rotors up to a considerable speed, permitting "jump" takeoffs that came closer to approaching helicopter capability.

Cierva's autogiros demonstrated their value more clearly at the other end of the flight, by making safe landings after an almost vertical descent. Courtney was a master at judging the wind, and was often able to bring the autogiro apparently straight down to a previously marked spot on the airfield.

There was a moderate boom in autogiros in the 1930s, with most major military powers expressing interest. Probably as many as five hundred were made, all over the world; of these only a very few remain.

The aircraft seemed perfect for liaison work and appeared to require only increased power and improved pre-rotation devices to make them completely practical. It is curious, but just about the same relative degree of success

with the autogiro was achieved in England, the United States, Russia, and Japan. In each of these countries, small numbers of autogiros were procured and tested; and in every case, the relatively low speed, limited range, and low load-carrying capability made them impractical for military work. The United States tested autogiros successfully in the 1930s, landing a Navy version on the *Langley*, the United States's first aircraft carrier. The Marines worked with one in Nicaragua in 1931, and the Air Corps procured ten during the mid-1930s.

Perhaps the best military work was done in England, where Cierva C-30s proved to be ideal for use in calibrating radar sites. The young RAF pilots would fly the airplane out to a known point—over an intersection or a cathedral tower—and then by expert piloting hold it firmly in spot against the wind while the radar personnel adjusted their equipment.

Cierva spent the rest of his short life improving his invention. He himself had achieved the most glamorous of all autogiro flights when he made a grand tour of Europe,

The Pitcairn-Cierva C-8 and a Pitcairn Mailwing, side by side. The autogiro so fascinated the Pitcairn firm that it abandoned fixed-wing construction, and pursued autogiros until it finally became evident that the helicopter was going to be the rotary-wing aircraft of the future.

The Pitcairn C-8, the first autogiro in America, was donated to the Smithsonian, and flown to the Mall.

covering 3,000 miles horizontally and almost as many vertically, in demonstration after demonstration.

In 1927, he conceived the idea of hinging the rotors vertically, which permitted the blades to pivot a little, and thus relieved some of the tremendous strain on the structure imparted by the mass of the revolving blades.

In 1928, Harold Pitcairn, a practical businessman whose firm had produced the trim biplane mail carriers that laid the foundation for Eastern Airlines, saw the autogiro as an ideal substitute for the as yet unattainable helicopter. He understood the complex mechanics of the transmissions required for helicopters, and wished to sidestep the issue. He became enamored of the possibilities, and a four-bladed Cierva was brought over, in the start of a long association between the two men.

Pitcairn formed the Pitcairn Autogiro Company, which in turn spawned the Autogiro of America Corporation. The latter licensed the Kellett Aircraft Corporation to build autogiros, and thus accounted for almost all of the American activity in the field.

The autogiro achieved more commercial prominence in the United States than elsewhere, primarily because it was valued more for its publicity worth than for its revenue-generating capability. Various firms, especially newspapers, would lease autogiros for short promotional ventures, garnering a few headlines. The manufacturers sedulously courted the press, never missing an opportunity to appear at an air show, a factory opening, or a military parade. James Ray, Pitcairn's chief pilot, even landed on the White House lawn in celebration of Pitcairn receiving the Collier Trophy for his work.

The rotary-winged novelty lent itself readily to journalistic exploitation; it was easy to imagine it in the class of the Model T, and make it everyman's airplane. It seemed deceptively easy to fly, and according to the tabloids, could land and takeoff in the average backyard. In actual practice, of course, the autogiro required a relatively higher level of piloting skill than the average airplane of the time. Amelia Earhart soon involved herself in record-seeking with the autogiro, and achieved a great deal of publicity in the process.

On July 17, 1931, the very first autogiro that

The C-8 as it exists today. This very important aircraft will be introduced into the restoration cycle soon.

A rare shot of the cockpit of the Pitcairn-Cierva C-8. Note the tachometer for the rotor, measured from 40 to 180 rpm.

Pitcairn had brought over from England was donated to the Smithsonian Institution. In the course of its two and a half years abroad it had acquired several hundred hours in the air, and had been reequipped with an American Wright Whirlwind engine. It went on display for several years, but as time passed it began to deteriorate and was taken to Silver Hill for storage. It is scheduled for restoration in the near future.

During the 1930s, the theory and the mechanics of the heart of the autogiro, the rotor hub, both continued to improve. The direct-control rotor appeared in 1932. In this system, the rotor could be tilted in any direction, resulting in forces that would control the direction of the autogiro accordingly. As a result, the vestigial stub wings and ailerons that had been used for control were dispensed with, and the autogiro moved further away from being merely a hybrid airplane to more definitively its own genre.

The next step was to provide power from the engine directly to the rotor while still avoiding the much more complicated helicopter transmission with all its difficulties. Power from the engine spun the rotor; as speed built up, the pilot would declutch the engine from the rotor and simultaneously change the pitch of the rotor blades. The swiftly spinning blades would then impart a lift that caused the autogiro to leap straight up. Transition to forward flight came about as a result of the propeller's thrust.

Eventually, the synthesis of Spanish, English, and American improvements would lead to a rotor hub system remarkably like that of a modern helicopter. It then remained only for the development of transmission systems and improvement in torque control to make the helicopter possible.

During this period the Pitcairn Company moved steadily from one design to another, sacrificing its interest in fixed-wing aircraft and pursuing the autogiro dream. In 1935, Pitcairn succumbed to the almost universal American desire to somehow combine the airplane with the automobile, and came up with the tiny AC-35, which is now at Silver Hill. Actually a product of the subsidiary Autogiro Company of America, the AC-35 was an attractive departure from previous Pitcairn designs.

The effect of the focal plane shutter of the camera gives a distorted appearance to the rotor and propeller in this shot, but the AC-35 is clearly seen to be a streamlined, smart-looking vehicle.

The Pitcairn AC-35 was perhaps the nearest approach to the really practical autogiro, for it combined folding rotors with a drive mechanism for the rear wheel. The little airplane could be flown almost anywhere, landed on a very small piece of ground, and then driven at 25 mph to its destination.

After a long test period by the Pitcairn Company, the AC-35 was turned over to the Civil Aeronautics Administration for further tests. The engine was mounted behind the cabin, and drove the propeller by means of an extension shaft.

The small size of the AC-35 is evident in comparison to a 1940 Plymouth (at curb) or the 1942 Chevrolet immediately behind it. The streetcar, long since abandoned, would be a welcome sight back on city streets.

Smaller in size than any of the previous efforts, with a rotor diameter of just over 34 feet and a gross weight of less than 2,000 pounds, the AC-35 had two radical features. The first was foldable blades, to facilitate ground transport; the second was direct drive to the single rear wheel, so that it could be driven along city streets.

A seven-cylinder Pobjoy radial engine of 90 horsepower was mounted behind the two passenger seats, and drove the tractor propeller through a drive shaft and a set of reduction gears. The three-bladed rotor was mounted on a streamlined pylon, just over the neatly faired-in cabin.

The aircraft went through a long series of tests, mainly in an effort to improve its somewhat sensitive stability problems. The AC-35 flew very well, and after a variety of fixes was capable of "hands-off" flight for relatively long periods of time. It also offered a surprisingly good road performance, clipping along at a top speed of 25 miles per hour.

The Bureau of Air Commerce obtained the aircraft from Pitcairn on October 1, 1936, and did some additional flight testing before donating it to the Smithsonian Institution.

The performance of the AC-35 was sufficiently good to have a near rebirth in 1961, when the Skyways Engineering Company was formed. Skyways purchased the license rights from Pitcairn and planned to clean up the design and install a 135-horsepower Lycoming engine. The additional 45 horsepower would have considerably improved performance. A new rotor hub was planned—one that would have provided a hydraulic pre-rotation of the blades and a jump-start capability.

As a footnote to this Quixotic tale of Ciervas and Pitcairns, the autogiro was plagued with the nickname "Windmill" throughout its history. It made journalistic sense, of course, particularly in the early days, when the Spanish Cierva's rotors tended to be rather wide-bladed and more than a little reminiscent of the Don's nemesis. But there was a fundamental difference in operation that made the name erroneous. The wind blows the windmill's sails around, striking their undersurface, and pushing. On the autogiro, the blades turn in an op-posite direction to the relative wind, due to their positive angle of incidence. The autogiro blade is much more closely related to the wing of an aircraft than it is to the sails of a windmill.

The helicopter was still a mechanical nightmare, with transmission and control problems that seemed insoluble, just at a time when autogiros began to be looked at seriously all over the world for military liaison purposes. Then, in 1940, Igor Sikorsky produced the VS-300, America's first successful helicopter, and a tidal wave of progress ensued. Within just two or three years the helicopter was seen to possess definite advantages over the autogiro. There was, however, yet another kind of aircraft that would bridge the chronological, if not the technical, gap between the autogiro and helicopter: the convertaplane, which we'll examine next.

The AC-35 under restoration at Building 10 "during the old days." The building was always in a state of helter-skelter disarray. It is amazing that workmanship of such high quality could have been achieved there.

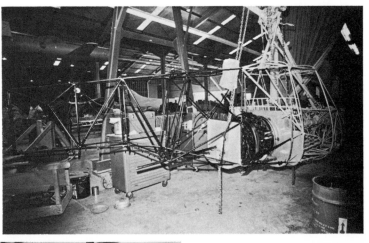

The AC-35 is now in Building 24. At its left is the Bellanca C.F., the first cabin Bellanca. On the wall behind, in glass cases, are the very first aeronautic artifacts of the Smithsonian Institution. They are Chinese kites, presented by the Imperial Chinese government for the 1876 U.S. Centennial.

Hapless Hybrids—The Convertaplanes

Inventors often get so involved in their solutions to a particular problem that they lose sight of the overall requirements. Such was the case of the Herrick Convertaplane, the lifelong dream of Gerald Herrick, a pleasant and dedicated gentleman who spent his life in pursuit of yet another wing planform. Herrick's vision was one that bridged the gap between the autogiro and the helicopter. He had been able to bring his design to fruition just a few years earlier, he might indeed have provided a transitional type that would have had several potential applications. Curiously, although Herrick's particular formula did not succeed, the basic idea of conversion from one mode of flight to another did persist, and is now, in the Bell XV-15, apparently very close to success.

We should note here that Herrick called his own invention by a variety of names—Convertaplane, Vertaplane, Convertiplane, and so on. Later, other aircraft adopted the term "convertaplane" as a generic one.

Herrick had studied and understood Cierva's ideas in the autogiro, whose principles were at once both simple and complex. On the one hand, the autogiro rotor was little more than a cruciform wing, designed to rotate freely as the autogiro was moved forward by its conventional engine and propeller powerplant. The forward movement caused rotation, which imparted lift, and this permitted a relatively high rate of climb compared to the forward distance traveled, as well as a means to descend almost vertically. Still, that was not a satisfactory solution to Herrick. He felt that the rotor caused far too much drag, compromising the autogiro's performance in ordinary flight. He conceived the idea of a convertible aircraft—one whose rotor would permit near-vertical ascent and descent, but that could be fixed in flight, turning the aircraft from an autogiro into a more or less conventional biplane.

The idea was simple, but the execution difficult, for a fixed rotating conventional airfoil would find itself going backward exactly half of the time. This problem, as we saw earlier, was solved in the autogiro and the helicopter by articulating the blades, but such a solution was no help for the rigid Herrick rotary-wing installation. Instead, after much wind-tunnel experimentation, Herrick devised a symmetrical airfoil, mounted on a strong central rotor pylon, which permitted the wing to be adjusted for aerodynamic control.

The Herrick wing was in essence a rigid two-bladed rotor that converted into a single cantilever wing. It could be tilted as it spun, and this, with its symmetrical airfoil, presented the same shape to the relative wind throughout the rotation.

The first Herrick Vertoplane was a rather willowy creation, with a very long upper wing/rotor that must have set up enormous rotational forces. The aircraft flew as a rotor plane, and as a biplane, but crashed on an attempted conversion from biplane to rotor-plane status.

The second example, built several years later, featured a much smaller upper wing/rotor, which could be pre-rotated to assist takeoff. Several in-flight conversions were successfully completed with this aircraft.

The first Herrick aircraft, called a Vertoplane, made its initial flight on November 6, 1931. It was a rather frail-looking aircraft, powered by a tiny three-cylinder Poyer engine of 48 horsepower. The plane was flown as a conventional biplane first, with the long upper rotor fixed in position. Later, it was flown, rather tentatively, as an autogiro. The rotor shaft would have a long rope wrapped about it; a group of men ran with the rope, spinning the rotor much as a lawn-mower motor is started. The aircraft then accelerated, and lifted off as an autogiro would. It made a series of flights in this way.

As happens so often in test programs, disaster struck during the first attempt to convert in flight from its biplane to its autogiro mode. The Vertoplane had taken off as a biplane, and climbed to 4,000 feet. The upper wing was released from its fixed position, so that it could rotate and let the Vertoplane descend. The aircraft immediately began to gyrate wildly, then plunged vertically into the ground, killing the pilot.

Despite the crash, Herrick felt he had proved the principle. So he embarked upon the costly and time-consuming task of securing sufficient capital to build the definitive Vertoplane, one that would have both autogiro and aircraft characteristics.

The intervening years were frustrating, but by 1936 he had built a much more handsome aircraft, the Herrick HV-2A, and started a much more professional flight-test program with it.

The HV-2A was considerably refined over the first effort. The upper wing/rotor was smaller in relation to the lower wing than in the number one aircraft, and it employed an electric drive mechanism in lieu of the rope starter.

Not unexpectedly, there were problems. The gyroscopic forces of rotation tended to cause the HV-2A to veer to one side, but this was controllable. More important was the fact that the drag for the aircraft was unaccountably high, even in the biplane configuration. Complicating the process was the fact that the

The convertaplane might possibly have bridged the gap between aircraft and autogiro if the helicopter had not intervened. This aircraft, registered as 13515, was plagued by excessive drag, which was never satisfactorily explained.

Gerald Herrick's contributions were widely recognized, and even after the war he continued to press his idea forward, on the basis that his convertaplane had a higher range and top-speed potential than contemporary helicopters. This is one of a number of designs offered. None were built.

The Herrick Convertaplane as it hangs in Building 23 today.

Larger companies, like McDonnell, were attracted by the convertaplane concept, for exactly the same reasons Herrick advocated: higher than helicopter performance. Here two XV-1s fly in formation. The XV-1 had a good performance, without standard military equipment, but was too underpowered to undertake the military missions for which it was intended.

first test pilot left something to be desired. Herrick's notes are filled with wistful comments on the fact that instead of discussing the next day's flight plan, the test pilot insisted on drinking and carousing. He owed Herrick money as well, and somehow kept himself from being fired by refusing to pay up—Herrick could recover only through the use of his services. Eventually, Herrick turned to another pilot, and the HV-2A test program speeded up considerably.

With the new pilot, testing proceeded on a much more sensible basis. Even though the reasons for the exceptionally high drag were not found, the airplane was operated in both the Vertoplane and conventional modes, and made several successful in-flight conversions from biplane to autogiro flight. A public demonstration on July 30, 1937, at Boulevard Airport, Philadelphia, gained nationwide publicity for Herrick. The Navy then expressed a mild interest in the aircraft, but could not provide any funds for development.

Undaunted, Herrick carried on his research. Caught up in the war, his efforts resulted in a series of successively more advanced designs, but no hardware. In the meantime, of course, the development of the helicopter dimmed the Convertaplane's chances. Although the Her-

rick itself was never established as a household word in the world of vertical flight, there were other companies, larger and better financed, that followed the difficult path he had charted.

Herrick's long labors had earned him the title "dean of convertible aircraft designers," certainly justified by the fact that for many years he was the only man to build an aircraft that could convert from fixed-wing to rotary-wing flight in the air.

His basic concept of combining the best features of the autogiro and the aircraft was supplanted after the war when others tried to combine the best features of the helicopter and the airplane. There were a surprising number of contenders for this dream, following either tilt-rotor or unloaded-rotor concepts. There was the nicely named Transcendental, of which more later; the pivoting-wing Convertawing; the Kaplan Quadrotor; the Dobson Delta, with its tilting-nose rotor; the double-rotor Gyroliner, with blades that stowed themselves fore and aft for high-speed flight; the ramjet Gyrodyne; and many others. We'll follow two representative types at the Garber Facility that led to what looked like the end of the convertaplane in the 1950s, and then touch briefly on a current type that revives the entire prospect.

Curtiss Wright built and flew the X-100 successfully, although the test program left much to be desired. This is the "newest" Curtiss aircraft that survives, the third last built by the venerable firm.

A very poor photo, taken from a film, of the X-100 in flight. The aircraft had control and stability problems, but was sufficiently successful to warrant production of the last two Curtiss aircraft, the two X-19s.

McDonnell Aircraft Corporation entered the fray when it flew its first XV-1 on July 14, 1954, and went on to a successful, record-breaking test program. The rather attractive, businesslike XV-1 used the unloaded-rotor concept, which meant that the rotating blades used for vertical lift and descent delivered little lift during high-speed flight.

The XV-1 resembled in some ways the later attempts by Herrick, but employed a far more advanced technology. It was powered by a single Continental R-975-19 engine of 550 horsepower, which drove a pusher propeller for forward flight, and in this respect was "conventional" for a convertaplane type. The big difference was that the engine also provided air pressure to the 170-pound-thrust McDonnell pressure jet engines, mounted at the tip of each of the three rotor blades. These engines had been developed on the previous McDonnell XH-20 "Little Henry" helicopter, and were most effective.

But the biggest advantage the XV-1 had over all its predecessors was the ease and safety with which it could switch from one mode of flight to another. The XV-1 reached speeds in excess of 200 mph and was quite maneuverable, requiring no special techniques to be flown effectively. Like all vertical-lift aircraft, however, it consumed inordinate amounts of fuel, and was relatively short-ranged. The program was abandoned in 1957, after many successful flights, primarily because the Continental engine was underpowered for potential military tasks. Like so many of its kind, it could do part of what was asked of it, but could not achieve the heavy demands of a military mission.

In the same building at Silver Hill is another brave attempt, this one somewhat sad in that it was the third to last aircraft to be built by the Curtiss-Wright Company, and was in fact the last of many routes that company would explore in its quest for survival.

It is the X-100 of 1959, a development of the Transcendental aircraft mentioned above, and it was used in a flight-test program to demonstrate the possibilities of a tilting rotor.

In unloaded-rotor examples, like the McDonnell XV-1, two different systems are used: a rotor for vertical ascent and descent, and a propeller or jet for forward motion. In the tilt rotor, a mechanism is built in that allows the rotors to be used for vertical ascent; they are then tilted forward for forward motion. The advantage for the first system is the relative simplicity of its mechanical components; the advantage in the second is the reduction in the number of thrust sources required.

The X-100 was a relatively small plane, using a single Lycoming YT53-L-1 shaft turbine engine of 825 shaft horsepower to power two tilting rotors, with deflected exhaust thrust for pitch and yaw control in hovering flight. During a fourteen-hour test program, the X-100 demonstrated one full conversion

from vertical to conventional flight, but the deflected exhaust thrust proved inadequate for control.

Yet the Air Force, exasperated almost to distraction with the difficulties of dealing with the moribund Curtiss-Wright firm, was persuaded to fund one more project, Curtiss's last true aircraft hurrah, the X-19.

The X-19 was a far more ambitious project, even for 1962, and in typical Curtiss fashion was intended to be even more complex than it was, for the firm hoped to have it powered by Wankel rotary engines. Eventually, and mercifully, it was equipped with two Lycoming T-55 free turbine jet engines, which drove four propellers, cross-shafted fore and aft. Each propeller was 13 feet in diameter, and possessed blades fat enough truly to be termed windmills.

The Curtiss Wright X-19 was a rather handsome aircraft of its type, and was originally intended to have Wankel engines. The propellers tilted from the vertical to the horizontal to make the switch from vertical to normal flight. A crash terminated the program and Curtiss Wright as an aircraft builder.

After more than two decades of experimentation and many hundreds of millions of dollars, Bell's XV-15 seems finally to have achieved Gerald Herrick's dream of a true convertaplane. This tilt-engine aircraft has a sensational performance and is almost certain to succeed where every predecessor has failed.

The Air Force insisted that the aircraft be fitted with ejection seats over Curtiss's vehement objections. The firm's designers knew the power-to-weight ratio to be marginal under all but the best of conditions, and ejection seats were so much dead weight.

During the test program, the X-19 proved to be a troublesome combination of promises and problems. It flew a total of 3.85 hours before a gear case failed from fatigue, a propeller was shed, and the aircraft pitched up and rolled sharply to the left at about 390 feet above the ground. The two pilots ejected, blessing whoever it was that had insisted on ejection seats, and their new, ballistically deployed parachutes opened 230 feet above the ground, where they had just a second to watch the abandoned X-19 auger in. It was August 25, 1965, and I happened to be in the control room with Major General Thomas Jeffries, commander of the Air Force's Aeronautical Systems Division. He heard about the crash and asked if the pilots were okay. When told they were, he sighed, "Thank God that program is over"—a short, heartfelt commentary on what

And if that's not enough, Gerald Herrick, the Piasecki Heli-stat might satisfy you. Four helicopters are attached to a Navy Blimp to form a heavy lift vehicle. Due for first flight in 1982. (Courtesy Harmon Harris, Piasecki Aircraft Corporation)

seemed to be the end of convertaplanes and proved to be the end of Curtiss aircraft.

But concepts have a way of coming back, and the Bell Aircraft Company has been playing with convertaplanes for years. They experimented with the Bell ATV, a tilt-engine prototype that is at Silver Hill, and they worked extensively on the XV-3, a contemporary of the McDonnell XV-1.

The XV-3 appeared in the mid-1950s, and featured three-blade rotors, which were mounted at the tops of the 30-foot-span wing and would rotate through 90 degrees. There was no effective cross-shafting, but the XV-3 employed an emergency device which in the event of engine failure, reverted the rotors to the helicopter position where they could be used for auto-rotation.

Now the XV-15 is on the scene, and seems at last to have achieved the success that helicopters have enjoyed for so many years. A sleek-looking twin-rotor aircraft that can fly at about 140 mph as a helicopter and 350 mph as an airplane, the XV-15 absolutely rocked the crowds at the 1981 Paris Air Show with its brilliant performance. With extra tanks, it can fly as much as 2,000 miles, and can carry loads up to 6,000 pounds. It has a vast potential for expansion; larger versions weighing up to 60,000 pounds are planned.

The success of the XV-15, remarkable as it is, points rather poignantly to the difficulties under which Herrick and others of his time bravely labored. Bell had about five similar projects prior to the XV-3. Over the next twenty years it engaged in no less than sixty major projects leading to the XV-15, none with a much greater relative degree of success than Herrick achieved with his very limited resources. The basic idea was good, however, and Bell was able to persuade the Air Force, the Navy, the Army, and NASA to pump money into the process. Gerald Herrick would undoubtedly be pleased with Bell's success, and would also without doubt enjoy knowing just how well he did with so little. It was a far tougher problem than he knew; but if he had not tried, others might not have followed.

Today, the Herrick Convertaplane hangs at Silver Hill, looking plausible still, awaiting the day when the XV-15 becomes a museum piece to join it.

7

Bombers, from *Gitterschwänze* to Whistling Jets

Man had scarcely flown when the aircraft was seen as a bomber, able to overfly the defenses of London, Paris, or Berlin, and wreak havoc at will. And it was not very long after the Wrights flew that the vision became reality, for on November 1, 1911, 2nd Lieutenant Giulo Gavotti, of the Air Fleet of the Italian Libyan Expedition, dropped 2-kilogram Cipelli bombs on Turkish troops at Ain Zara and the Oasis of Jagiura. The Turks immediately protested that a hospital had been bombed.

This was no mere hit-and-run operation, but a rather well planned and conducted campaign that saw a mobile air unit transported across a large body of water—the Mediterranean—and engaged in systematic operations against the enemy. The weapons were lightweight and the aircraft fragile, incapable of high speeds or long flights, but they did take part in bombing and reconnaissance operations that while doing little material damage, certainly hurt Turkish morale.

The capability of the bomber to render destruction was amazingly low for the next three decades. The German punishment of the English during the 1940 Blitz was severe, but in no way approached the decisive results predicted by Douhet, Mitchell, and others. Not until the joint U.S.-British bomber offensive against Germany and the American devastation of Japan did the bomber come into its own, meting out the punishment that had been feared and forecast for so long. And it was not

until the modern bomber was mated with the nuclear weapon that aerial bombardment was carried to the gross excesses that are with us still.*

During this long period of development, the performance of bombers followed a rather shallow curve, one dictated both by aerodynamics and by economics. The bombers that served well in World War I, the Handley Pages, the Gothas, the Capronis, achieved a level of performance in two years of activity that was not vastly exceeded in the next ten. As an example, the Handley Page 0/400, built in America and powered by two Liberty engines, had a top speed of 94 mph, a service ceiling of 7,400 feet, and a range of 550 miles with 2,000 pounds of bombs. Ten years later, the Keystone LB-5, which followed the same biplane, twin-engine formula, had a top speed of 107 mph, a service ceiling of 8,000 feet, and a range of 435 miles with 2,312 pounds of bombs.

As more powerful engines and improved structures became available, more modern bombers like the Martin B-10 appeared on the scene. The B-10, with its enclosed cockpit, retractable landing gear, and single cantilever wing seemed light-years ahead of the Key-

* In a later chapter we'll deal at length with some of the airplanes that should be added to the collection at Silver Hill, to fill the terrible gaps caused by attrition. This is particularly true of bombers, for we have to move from the World War I de Havilland to the World War II Boeing B-17, simply because we have no examples of the awkward Keystones, the classic B-10s, or such rare types as the Curtiss B-2 or the unique Boeing XB-15.

stones, and in fact performance was vastly improved. The B-10 had a top speed of 207 mph and a service ceiling of 21,000 feet, but the range with 2,260 pounds of bombs was still only 523 miles. Despite its limitations, the B-10 was adopted as the standard service bomber and taught the Army Air Corps a great deal about maintenance, crew training, and bombing, for it was the first aircraft to have the Norden bombsight as standard equipment.

The Martins began to equip bomber squadrons in 1934; their replacement, the Boeing B-17, entered squadron service in 1939 in very modest numbers. Even then, twenty years after the close of World War I, the United States had not yet learned to build real warplanes, with a complete equipment of armor, armament, and the hundred miscellaneous items that would enable them to survive in hostile skies.

From 1939 on, however, the quality of bombing planes improved rapidly all over the world, reaching their wartime peak in the piston-engine B-29 and the jet-engine Arado Ar 234 from Germany. Let's take a look at how it started, and where it led.

It is hard to believe that this assemblage of struts, wires, braces, and assorted parts could have a military mission, yet the Caudron G.4 was a first-line bomber for France, penetrating into German soil in raids against carefully selected targets. The minimum bombload carried was offset by the total novelty of war from the air. The Germans, it is true, bombed England and Paris, but this was totally different—someone was bombing them!

A "more advanced" version with ten-cylinder Anzani radial engines replacing the whirling rotaries of other Caudrons. These engines could be set to run in opposite directions, counteracting torque. (Note how pitch of propellers is opposite each other.) How do you like the airy machine-gun placement? There was no shortage of insignia, either, with five cocardes visible, and probably another three to five on the reverse surfaces. This aircraft belonged to the Royal Naval Air Service, which no doubt considered it an ideal vehicle for long-range patrols over the North Sea.

The Caudron G.4

All of the billions of dollars invested in bombers in the twentieth century can be traced back, step by step, through a genealogy that begins with stick and wire, fabric-covered bombers like the Caudron G.4. There were others of similar type and capability on both sides of the lines, but none of the same improbable configuration. The Caudron G.4 was a singularly unattractive airplane, with seemingly endless 56-foot-span wings sandwiching an incongruously small nacelle and two well-cowled Le Rhône rotary engines of 80 nominal horsepower. A forest of struts connected the wings and the engines. Affixed to this was a wicker framework of bamboo running back to a tailplane that had four vertical surfaces festooned across the horizontal stabilizer. The Germans called it *Gitterschwänz*, or "Lattice tail."

The big wings had no ailerons, relying, like the Wright Flyer, upon warping for lateral control. They were very thin, and featured the attractive scalloped trailing edge so characteristic of the time.

Yet as unlikely as this combination of two wings, three nacelles, four stabilizers, four rudders, two engines, two tail booms, two skids, and assorted parts seems today, it flew very well and was used with audacity by the French, British, Italian, American, and Belgian air services. Furthermore, it was manufactured in three countries—France, England, and Italy. And most striking of all, it was truly one of the world's first strategic bombers.

The G.4 was built just outside Paris, and introduced into service as a reconnaissance bomber in the spring of 1915. Its successful use then encouraged the French Air Force, which

The basic configuration, however weird in appearance, was sound, and was developed into the rather handsome G.6, shown here captured and in German markings.

began a series of long-distance raids with it on the heart of the German armament effort in the Rhineland. In contrast to the later rather feeble efforts made by the French in World War II, when bombing activity over Germany was largely confined to pathetic leaflet raids, there was a systematic effort to pick out key chemical and munitions factories as targets.

The first raids, made in daylight in November 1915, were scarcely opposed except by the ad hoc antiaircraft defenses of the time. The size and quantity of bombs that could be carried was negligible, but there was a widespread effect on morale, the counterpart of the Zeppelin raids on London. As a result, the already short-handed Germans had to assign forces to defend the cities, and to create the usual network of warning stations, communication links, and so on that was required in those non-radar, limited-radio days.

With the development of fighter defenses, the Caudrons, which had an extremely limited defensive capability, were relegated to night bombing or action on quiet sectors of the front. By the end of the war they were in use largely as trainers.

The French tried to improve the ability of the Caudrons to penetrate German opposition by formation flying, but the single machine gun mounted on a Deligny rail in the front cockpit did not provide much firepower. On the floor, beneath the observer-gunner, was a

metal trapdoor that looked for all the world like a portion of a rolltop desk. The observer could ease this back to take photos or to drop three slender bombs that were hung on leather straps in the cockpit, using the *oculair* (eyeball) technique.

The pilot sat well aft, 4 feet or so from the observer, and despite a large cutout in the upper wing had very little visibility, especially on takeoff or landing. He was, however, an ample distance from the whirling twin propellers, while an incautious observer would pick up a nasty wound simply by flailing his arms about in Gallic excitement.

The G.4 had been an obvious and direct development of the single-engine G.3, which it resembled in every way except the use of two engines. Caudron's next aircraft were, by contrast, extremely handsome, and gave very good performance. They included the R.4, G.6, and R.11, which with a top speed of 114 mph probably did not have any German or English counterpart.

The thought of a squadron of G.4s taking off together, their twin rotaries whining and kicking up two columns of dust, the wires singing and bamboo creaking, the wind whistling over the fabric, is truly inspiring. The gyroscopic reaction of the two rotary engines operating in the same direction must have been formidable, although with four large rudders one would assume that there was adequate control available. Some G.4s had 110-horsepower, ten-cylinder Anzani radial engines installed, and with these the aircraft reputedly topped 95 mph. The Anzanis were unusual in that they could be made to run in either direction, and on a twin-engine aircraft could be so set up as to eliminate torque—a not inconsiderable advantage, given the inexperience of the pilots of the time.

The G.4 came to the Smithsonian in 1918, as part of a continuing exhibit of war material. It came without engines or propellers, these presumably being in short supply at the home base, and Paul Garber had to locate them later, after the war, purchasing a set of two for $25 each. Later, when the aircraft was suspended from the old Arts and Industries Building, the engines were gutted of their pistons and cranks to save weight. It hangs now at Silver Hill over a sleek North American F-86 Saber, which provides a thoughtful contrast.

Still in original condition, the Caudron hangs above the F-86 at Silver Hill.

Note the "leopard spots" on the propellers. As the varnish used in the World War I period dries, it coalesces into hard spots, giving this characteristic dotted appearance. Note the open "bomb bay door" under the nacelle, and the close proximity of the arc of the propellers to the observer.

The Voisin Type 8 was a very straightforward-looking airplane, which was in almost no danger at all of nosing over. The baby-carriage landing gear made takeoffs and landings on rough fields fairly safe, but added its bit to weight and drag. Rear wheels had both shock absorbers and brakes, advanced features for the time. Note the huge ailerons, inter-aileron strut, and mammoth-size aileron horns. There must have been a blacksmith in the Voisin fuel supply. (National Archives)

The Voisin Type 8

The Caudron's bombing buddy, the Voisin Type 8, came to the Museum at about the same time, also without an engine. It is a huge airplane by any standards, with great wide chord wings of 61-foot 8-inch span, and weighing a hefty 4,103 pounds.

It seems both more attractive and more formidable than the Caudron, a very practical approach to the multiple problems of the time. Powered by a Peugeot 220-horsepower engine, the Voisin had a top speed of only 75 mph, but it was rugged, and the gunner had a relatively free field of fire to the front.

The first Voisins entered service with Groupe de Bombardement 1 at the end of 1916, and was operated primarily as night bombers. Over 1,100 were built, and eight were purchased for use by the Americans. Even as late as August 1918, fifty-one of the type were still in use. One can only wonder what the jaded crews must have thought as they staggered out to the prehistoric-looking Voisins for yet another night mission. Like the Caudrons, the Voisins were committed to action far behind the lines, penetrating to the Rhineland with their load of 396 pounds of

bombs. A significant attack was made on the poison-gas factory in Ludwigshafen in 1918—one that caused consternation to the authorities because of their inability to deal with the local contamination.

The Voisin featured almost as many drag-inducing fixtures as the Caudron. The landing gear resembled that of an avant-garde Conestoga wagon, but it provided protection from nose-over on the rough fields upon which night landings had to be made. Four wheels sprouted from an assemblage of struts. The rear wheels had both shock absorbers and brakes, a rarity of the period.

The brave French crews were housed in a flat-sided bathtub nacelle that allowed them good visibility and better breezes. A few aircraft were fitted with a 37mm Hotchkiss cannon, but the resulting weight and drag further penalized performance, and the Voisin could shoot only at something that inadvertently crossed its path, for it had no hope of running anyone down.

The aircraft was laid out with a straight edge, possessing almost no curves except for its cylindrical gas tanks slung from the first bay of struts. It was strongly made of steel tubing, and of course was fabric-covered. For all its faults, it had the virtues of simplicity and strength. Some luckless French aircrews probably spent the war in the airplane, starting off with gallant daytime raids over the Rhineland, and ending up dropping anonymous bombs in the night behind the front lines. *C'est la guerre.*

The Voisin was rendered either formidable or impotent by the installation of the 37mm Hotchkiss quick-firing cannon, depending upon whether you were a hapless German pilot who wandered into the gunner's sights or an alert German pilot who saw the Voisin coming. Already slow, the addition of the heavy cannon made the Voisin virtually immobile. The sleek, cylindrical fuel tanks are an incongruous attempt at streamlining in an otherwise barn-door approach.

The U.S. Air Service bought eight of the Type 8s, and used them for training. They would certainly have been adequate for the entire rigger's corps. Note in this aircraft the odd slant of the outboard struts, which are either a rigging or photographic anomaly. Unfortunately, the Museum's Voisin is disassembled and in such a position as to be virtually unphotographable. Some restoration efforts were made at an earlier date, but much work remains to be done. Like the Caudron, it was shipped to the Museum sans engine.

De Havilland D.H. 4—
The (What Else?) Flaming Coffin

Aircraft are not spared the great American process, applied to folk heroes, of deification, debunking, and rehabilitation. Just as Elvis Presley went from stardom to martyrdom to a ghoulish dissection of his eating, bathing, and bedding habits, and President Eisenhower from the perfect American President and father figure to a befuddled man who may or may not have done some fiddling around in England, to now, thankfully, a growing reappreciation, so it was with the de Havilland D.H. 4. It started out as a war-winning, sky-darkening weapon that would prove the genius of American industrial capability, only to end the war as a flaming coffin that consumed billions of American dollars in shabby deals. Lately it has at last been reevaluated to receive its dues.

The D.H. 4 was a product of young Captain (later Sir Geoffrey) de Havilland's combination of design and piloting ability. De Havilland had started life as a "motor engineer," finding a place in England's burgeoning auto industry, but he soon became fascinated by airplanes. He designed, built, flew, and crashed in his first aircraft; his second served him better by teaching him to fly. As pilot-designers were still relatively rare, this self-taught genius joined the British Army Balloon (later Royal Aircraft) Factory at Farnborough, England, and there in 1912–13 developed the frail but immortal F.E. 1, F.E. 2, B.E. 1, and B.E. 2 designs. Of these aircraft, so imposing when they arose almost overnight from the de Havilland drafting board to creaking flights over Salisbury Plain, two had important careers that ranged from formidable to pathetic. When the F.E. 2 and B.E. 2 were first pressed into production, they were equivalent to anything in the field, and the British, with their myopic procurement practices, decided immediately to "standardize" the type to ensure volume production. (The Brits had had a bad experience during the Boer War with non-standard wagons, and they weren't going to make *that* mistake again.)

The procurement procedure didn't take into account the rapid development of efficient air opposition on the front, and the valiant men who flew the wood and fabric biplanes soon fell victim to Fokker Eindeckers and the later Halberstadt and Albatros scouts. Nor was their obsolescence the only problem, for the "attack, always attack" philosophy of "Boom" Trenchard, immortal architect of the Royal Flying Corps and Royal Air Force strategy, turned them into deathtraps. The young pilots were condemned to fly them as late as 1918 against superior German equipment.

De Havilland left the Royal Aircraft Factory to escape the bureaucracy, joining the independent Aircraft Manufacturing Company, Ltd., in June 1914. It was the start of a career that would be a catalogue of immense personal triumphs and numbing personal tragedies. In World War I, his name was attached to more than one third of all British aircraft produced; de Havilland became a household word between the wars with such triumphs as the Puss Moth, Tiger Moth (de Havilland himself was a student of lepidopterae), and the first Comet, which won the London to Melbourne Race in 1934. Between 1939 and 1945, another 23,000 de Havilland warplanes were produced, including the fabled D.H. 98 Mosquito. As sharp, bitter contrasts to this success, de Havilland had to bear the loss of two of his sons test-flying his aircraft, and then, late in his life, the excruciating failure of the de Havilland Comet, the first jet airliner to enter service.

His fourth design for Airco, however, was an unlimited success. It was the D.H. 4 (Airco having given him the unusual privilege of appending his name to his designs, much as Focke-Wulf did for Kurt Tank in World War II) and it was the first aircraft designed to a specific military request for a day bomber.

Thoroughly conventional in appearance and construction, as most de Havilland aircraft were, the D.H. 4 was a biplane of simple clean lines, high-aspect-ratio wings, and the unwitting good fortune to receive a first-class engine, the Rolls Royce Eagle of 275 horsepower. Originally designed for a Beardmore-Halford-Pullinger B.H.P. engine of 230 horsepower, the D.H. 4 might never have achieved success if the powerplant had not run into development difficulties and the switch been made to the Rolls Royce. The combination of two high-quality products, the Rolls engine and the D.H. 4 airframe, was truly fortunate. It went to France with No. 55 Squadron, Royal Flying Corps, on March 6, 1917, and immediately established a reputation for high speed and fighting capability. It cut a swathe against German fighters until the end of the war, for it was usually faster than they were, and had both forward-firing Vickers and rear-firing Lewis guns for defense.

There were flaws in the design, however, and in these lay the basis for the later complaints against it. The pilot and observer were separated by a considerable distance, the interval between them being occupied by the main fuel tank. In combat, coordination was difficult, and once engaged, the D.H. 4 was considered relatively easy to shoot down. The gas tank was not fastened sufficiently well to the fuselage structure, and in the event of a crash would usually break loose and move forward, crushing the pilot against the hot engine with a rush of gasoline.

For these and other reasons the British Air Ministry decided to replace the D.H. 4 with an improved version, the D.H. 9, in which these defects were remedied by improved structure and relocation of the cockpits aft of the tank. Inexplicably, however—or perhaps inevitably in the case of the Air Ministry, which had an absolutely zero batting average on engine-installation decisions—the D.H. 9 was to be powered with the Siddeley Puma, the improved production version of the original B.H.P. engine. This was basically the same engine that had been originally envisaged for the D.H. 4, and for which the Rolls had been so cleverly substituted. The Rolls, incidentally, was ultimately developed to produce 375 horsepower, which turned the D.H. 4 into a hummer with a 143-mph top speed capability.

The result was that the D.H. 9 had a markedly inferior performance to the D.H. 4, and worse, absolutely rotten reliability. Engine failures were so common that squadrons of twelve sent out to bomb the Germans often crossed the lines with eight or nine, and the reduced firepower then resulted in more losses in combat. And so remarkable is the blindness of bureaucracy, military or civil, that units which had "good" D.H. 4s were often stripped of them and reequipped with "bad" D.H. 9s, just to achieve conformity. (Eventually, the D.H. 9 was modified to accept the American Liberty engine, often on a bootleg basis, when enterprising British squadrons would trade D.H. 9 airframes for Liberty engines to American squadrons operating D.H. 4s.)

At almost precisely the same time that the D.H. 9 was being selected as future equipment for the Royal Flying Corps, the Bolling Commission was in Europe trying to determine what airplanes the United States should manufacture. The D.H. 4 was selected (along with some others, none of which achieved a similar production status) primarily on the basis that more complete sets of drawings were available. The drawings and a sample airframe were sent to the newly formed Dayton-Wright Aircraft Company in Dayton, Ohio, and there the saga of the Museum's aircraft began.

The Liberty Plane

It is hard now to reconstruct the incredible patriotic fervor with which the United States entered World War I. After years of social protest, during which draft dodging, flag burning, and media-altered news have assaulted the American *amour propre*, it's difficult to imagine that Kaiser Bill was so hated, that dachshunds had to become Liberty Dogs, sauerkraut Liberty Cabbage, and presumably, Beethoven Liberty Ludwig. But so it was in the late spring of 1917, when an America totally unprepared for aerial warfare received, on May 26, a stirring call from the premier of France. Alexandre Ribot, in a few short sen-

The very first American mission over the lines in an American-built aircraft, with an American-built engine, August 9, 1918. There is a lot of controversy over this mission, some placing it on August 7, and so on, but most people agree that it was pretty much of a washout in terms of making war. There was a heavy cloud cover, and most of the aircraft did not get across the front lines. But it made wonderful newspaper copy.

Mass production at the Dayton-Wright plant, where the rate rose from 108 D.H. 4s to over 12,000 annually. The Dayton area was simply a huge pool of skilled talent, waiting to be tapped by the aviation industry. It still is.

As the factory got into the swing of things, public-relations efforts increased to match the production tempo. Each benchmark was closely watched, and if the 1,000th D.H. 4 got a big sendoff, then why not the 1,001st?

tences, asked the United States to furnish a flood of warplanes; the country and the Congress showed an insatiable desire to respond.

Unfortunately, a flood of airplanes was difficult to conjure up in the country that had created the airplane, for in the years from 1903 to 1917, Congress had ignored the aircraft as a means of defense. While Germany, Russia, France, Italy, and even smaller countries had spent millions on the development of their air services, the United States piddled along, appropriating nothing one year, perhaps $125,000 the next, and firmly refusing to subsidize in any way the development of airpower. By 1916, just months before the declaration of war, a total of fifty-nine aircraft had been procured in the entire thirteen-year period.

There was only one company in the United States that could be said to be manufacturing aircraft on any scale, and that was the Curtiss Aeroplane and Motor Company, which was engaged in building the famous Jennies. All over the United States, though, eager businessmen realized there was a gap, both patriotic and profitable, to be filled, and they set about filling it. In Dayton, Ohio, a group of very capable, intelligent, and well-financed men formed the Dayton-Wright Airplane Company. Some of those associated with the firm in one capacity or another were the

Harold Talbots, Jr. and Sr., Orville Wright, Charles "Boss" Kettering, and Colonel E. A. Deeds.

Dayton-Wright received an order for the manufacture of four hundred Standard J-1 trainers, and this began the process of establishing an aircraft-manufacturing industry in Dayton, where before this time the Wright aircraft, never developed much beyond the 1905 Flyer, had been built in very limited quantities.

The order for the trainers was soon followed by a series of orders for the de Havilland D.H. 4, to be powered by the Liberty engine. The Liberty engine story is an epic in itself; suffice to say that it was designed in classic American storybook fashion in a hotel room (the Willard in Washington, D.C.) in an incredibly short period of time. The basis for the design sprang from a wealth of previous experience on the part of Jessie Vincent, J. A. Hall, and others, and it incorporated as much modern practice as was possible for a new design intended for immediate mass manufacture.

The D.H. 4 drawings arrived from England, preceded by an engineless example of the airframe. The whole Dayton-Wright complex sprang to work to redo the English drawings to American production standards, and to create the massive subcontracting network necessary to build the thousands of individual components that made up the airplane. These ranged from the basic spruce, linen, and dope required to build the airframes to special turnbuckles, compasses, airspeed indicators, radiators, bungee cords, wheel spokes, gun mounts, and so on.

In a demonstration of the immense labor skills and enormous goodwill available in Dayton, the first American-built Liberty plane flew on October 29, 1917. For many years after the war it was assumed that this *had* to have been the British manufacturing example simply refitted with the Liberty; but the restoration of that aircraft by the Museum proved once and for all that this was definitely not the case. The metal fittings, fasteners, screws, etc., and the woodworking techniques are all of American origin. There are numerous other bits of documentary evidence, which conclusively prove that this was indeed the first "pre-production" aircraft.

Procedures were primitive in those days, and this very first aircraft on its very first flight was put through a hair-raising series of aerobatics by its veteran pilot, Howard Rinehart. Today, an airplane of similar importance would get a gingerly liftoff, or perhaps a quick trip around the pattern; but the very enthusiasm that had brought the plane into being so quickly was manifested in a flamboyant first flight.

After the first Liberty plane had flown, a scramble ensued to sort out changes and begin mass production. There were almost unimaginable difficulties. An army of 13,000 men had to be sent to the Western forests to select, cut, and process the necessary spruce, over the wild objections of the I.W.W. and the native obstinacy of the lumbermen themselves. Factories had to be built to produce the necessary castor oil and dope; fields had to be planted to grow the castor beans; seed supplies had to be found to supply the farmers who were planting the fields. There were also the expected bureaucratic problems. For a long time no decision could be obtained as to what armament was to be installed in the D.H. 4, for at times it was to be the Vickers and at times it was to be the Marlin machine guns. For these and other production difficulties, "Boss" Kettering often proved his genius and his nickname by simply deciding for himself and telling Washington what he was going to do.

As these myriad factors were sorted out, a huge complex emerged at Dayton. In February 1918, Liberty planes were being produced at the rate of 108 per year; by November 1918, they were being produced in excess of 12,000 per year.

The first American-built D.H. 4 reached France in May 1918 and was flown on the 17th. The first flight over the lines took place (it was sort of a comic tour de force) on August 9. For the remaining ninety-two days of the war, the Liberty planes were operated in increasing numbers and with increasing effectiveness. By the end of the war, out of 1,213 delivered to France, 696 were in the Zone of the Advance, and 196 were at the front.

In battle, the D.H. 4 distinguished itself as it had for the British, exhibiting the same virtues and the same faults. As an observation plane it excelled, and its swift, 125-mph speed placed it out of reach of most German fighters. As a bomber, encumbered with bomb racks, bombsight, and bombs, it was not nearly as effective and much more vulnerable. It was not all that much more susceptible to fire than any of its contemporaries, but those that fell in flames earned it the journalistic title of "flaming coffin," a nickname it never lost.

The Air Service had developed a rather sophisticated system of noting and correcting faults in the D.H. 4, and there were plans, by the fall of 1918, to replace it in production with the D.H. 4B, which would have had the same corrective measures applied to it as were applied to the D.H. 9, rectifying the cockpit placement and fuel-tank structure.

The original Liberty plane, *old Yellow,* as it was called, had in the meantime soldiered on as a test plane, amassing more than 1,000 hours of flying time. This was an unprecedented amount for the time, when a front-line squadron expected to have a complete change of aircraft every month, and when even planes in stateside service rarely lasted longer than two or three months before being claimed by an accident or the wear and tear of weather.

The first D.H. 4 served in all sorts of capacities, ranging from test flights to VIP passenger-carrying to movie-ship work. It was differ-

ent from the final standard production version in a number of small ways, including the placement of a radiator tank in the upper wing; but it had done invaluable service over the thirteen months of its wartime existence.

At the end of the war, it was decided to ship it to the Smithsonian, and in what was an excess of zeal from a curatorial point of view, the Dayton-Wright Company refurbished the aircraft to "front-line" standards, repainting it in current service colors and bolting on every item of equipment available. This included bomb racks, bombs, machine guns, Wimperis bombsight, camera, radios, oxygen, electrical-generating equipment, lighting equipment, ammunition drum holder, flare holder, and so on. In today's automotive parlance, it was "stacked." It was then flown to Washington. The original engine, the number four production Liberty, was shipped by rail, and then reinstalled after the airplane's arrival.

The plane was exhibited for a long time in the Arts and Industries Building as well as in the old "tin shed," and eventually was shipped out to Park Ridge for storage. After its return from Park Ridge it was loaned to the Air Force for a temporary exhibit, for which the Air Force prepared it with a bogus paint job. It languished thereafter at Silver Hill until 1980, when it was brought in for restoration.

The restoration task was not too difficult with the D.H. 4 because all the parts were there and in good condition. Still, as in most restoration assemblies, it takes a big hammer applied with a skilled hand to make the final fits—Joe Fichera is a world-renowned big-hammer man.

Looking for all the world like two Ping-Pong players at the world's smallest table with the world's stickiest paddles, Rich Horigan and Karl Heinzel intently watch the doping process.

A Piece of Cake

Rich Horigan and Karl Heinzel found the restoration effort one of the easiest they had ever attempted, for the airplane was complete and in good shape. Only a few sections of fuel- and oil-soaked plywood had to be replaced; most of the rest of the aircraft, particularly its

The finished—almost—product, in front of newly painted Building 10. The aircraft is completely equipped with guns, sights, camera, radio, electrical system, oxygen, and so on.

The finished product—beautiful. Note how the right star insignia is applied slightly incorrectly, just as it was on the original. What an achievement for the Garber Facility!

main structural members, was perfect, needing only cleaning, varnishing, and a new fabric covering.

The original number four Liberty was torn down and reassembled. It, too, was found to be in excellent condition. It was carefully preserved internally, and the exterior was repainted and blued to achieve a like-new appearance. The aircraft would be flyable with only a minimum amount of extra time spent on it, mainly devoted to replacing the electrical wiring.

It was then decided to finish the Liberty plane as it was when it first flew, with a yellow-cream fuselage, topped with a brownish-olive drab, and clear doped wings. Under the bottom wings (but not on top of the upper wing) are located the early U.S. star insignia. It's interesting to note that one of these stars was applied correctly, with the center point going straight forward, while the other was put on at a slight angle. This endearing anomaly was repeated by the restorers.

All of the equipment provided with the airplane was also refurbished and installed, and this represents a curatorial liberty (no pun intended). The plane never flew in the colors in which it was finished with all of the equipment with which it was now loaded. Yet the equipment is so interesting in itself that it would be a shame to leave it off. Thus a compromise, to be detailed in the labels that accompany the aircraft, will give the best of both worlds.

While the first American D.H. 4 had a splendid war and postwar career as a test plane and was an exhibit, the thousands of its successors went on to become a part of American folklore: 3,106 of its type were manufactured by Dayton-Wright, with the Fisher Body Company and the Standard Aircraft Company building 1,600 and 400 more respectively.

At the end of the war, some of the contracts were altered so that the improved D.H. 4B aircraft could be built. In these, the pilot and observer's seats were moved closer together for better crew coordination, and the fuel tank was increased in size, moved forward, and fastened more securely. The landing gear also was moved forward a few inches, which greatly reduced the number of nose-over accidents. The airframe was strengthened by covering the fuselage entirely with plywood, and numerous equipment changes were made.

These aircraft were then continually modified over the years—sixty different special versions have been accounted for, and there were undoubtedly many more field conversions that have not been noted—and they comprised for years the principal equipment of the pitifully few U.S. Army Air Service units. Further modifications, in the form of steel-tube fuselage versions, were ordered from a number of companies. These solved at last the nasty habit the wooden longerons had of skewering unfortunate pilots in the case of a crash.

During the war, D.H. 4s had been used as fighters, bombers, reconnaissance planes, antisubmarine patrol planes, anti-zeppelin interceptors, propaganda leaflet droppers, and as supply planes for units trapped behind enemy lines. After the war, they were experimental vehicles, patiently enduring the installation of all sorts of weird engines, as crop dusters, mail carriers, parachute droppers, "honeymoon expresses," and at long last, as ground targets for tactical tests. Virtually every general officer of the U.S. Army Air Forces in World War II had D.H. 4 experience at some point in his career, and they were equally valuable in training ground-crew personnel during the long, austere, interwar period.

What Were They Like to Fly?

When the D.H. 4s were first introduced, they were regarded as remarkably light on the controls, very fast, and well protected from the elements (as well protected as open cockpit planes can be). As the years passed the pilots gained experience with more modern types, they came to be regarded as difficult to trim, tiring to handle, and of mediocre performance. They had the great virtue of availability: often D.H. 4s were the only game in town, and the crew members were prepared to put up with such outrageous techniques as requiring the observer to leave the cockpit, slide back on the fuselage, and sit by the rudder during a landing approach, so that the tail would go down on

A British D.H. 4 being bombed up, with a Nieuport fighter in the background. These were warplanes that a pilot could become intimate with.

D.H. 4s were used for experimentation, also. Here one is used to loft a target glider in a primitive McCook Field foreshadowing of the 747-Space Shuttle combination. (USAF Photo)

touchdown and the airplane would not nose over. I mean to say!

And what of the "Flaming Coffin" nickname? Postwar analysis revealed that of the 289 official U.S. aircraft losses in World War I, 33 had been Liberty planes, of these, 8 had gone down in flames. Out of a total of thirty-three flamers of all types, eight had been D.H. 4s, seven had been Spads, six Salmsons, and five Breguets. In simple truth, any aircraft flying in combat with an enemy employing tracer bullets, and carrying a non-self-sealing gas tank, was a candidate for incineration.

Thus, in retrospect, it seems that far from a flaming coffin, the D.H. 4 was really more of an earth mother, capable of nourishing entire generations of pilots and mechanics, breeding tradition, legends, and esprit long after it had earned a noble retirement.

The Swoose

Literally thousands of aircraft have been named for wives, mothers, sweethearts, daughters, or movie stars. There is Chuck Yeager's *Glamorous Glennis*, the orange Bell X-1 in which he broke the sound barrier, and Colonel Gerald Johnson's P-51 *Little Annie*. In all the air forces of the world, pilots have traditionally named their aircraft for a beloved woman. The only woman I know, however, that was named for an airplane is Swoosie Kurtz, a Tony-winning Broadway star who was named for her father's airplane, the oldest B-17 extant, the Museum's famed *The Swoose*.

It's probably a moot point whether Ms. Kurtz became an actress because of or in spite of her name. Her father, Colonel Frank Kurtz, U.S.A.F., Retired, was a tremendous overachiever all of his life, and he undoubtedly passed along his own capability and drive with the name. He has had a lifelong romance with the airplane, having flown it in combat with distinction and then saved it from two ignoble deaths in a scrapyard. Of this, more later.

This particular B-17D, serial number 40-3097, began life as the 140th of the 12,731 B-17s that were ultimately constructed by Boeing, Lockheed, and Douglas. The graceful shape, which had seemed so revolutionary in 1935, so formidable in 1939, and so familiar by 1945, was an especially welcome one when it was flown to the Philippines in October 1941 as a part of the last-minute reinforcement of those threatened islands.

The Swoose (the explanation for which comes later) is one of the rare aircraft in the Museum that has multiple reasons for being there. It possesses a distinguished combat history; it is unique in that it is the only remaining one of its type; perhaps more important, it represents an important technological benchmark, that of the first effective modern four-engine bomber. Finally, and much less obviously, it represents an industrial phenomenon—a company that refused to grow old.

In the discussion of the Curtiss XP-55, we noted how the Curtiss Aeroplane and Motor Company seemed to grow as old-fashioned as its name, to slide into a corporate senility that led it into design disasters and financial failure. Curtiss, following this downward path, went out of the business of manufacturing aircraft, abandoning a field in which it had once been premier. Boeing, which began business in 1915 and was thus only a few years younger than Curtiss, had a slower start. Curtiss's swift early growth was most evident through the war years, but by the late 1920s, both firms were certainly comparable in terms of product, if not of size. The next fifteen years, however, saw the complete eclipse of Curtiss, and the ascent of Boeing to the first rung of an aviation ladder that led to its dominance today of commercial air transportation.

The difference was that the leaders at Boeing never forgot for a moment that airplanes were their bread and butter, and that while profits were important, you could not make any in the long run unless you built the best airplanes. Curtiss, on the other hand, became tied up in diversifications, in the concept of stretching existing designs rather than committing capital to the development of new ideas, and, in general, in playing it safe.

Boeing was like a confident young gambler, standing up to the crap table of competition and betting its entire resources on the roll of its latest design. It did so with the 747, the 737, the 727, the 707, the B-29, and perhaps first and best, with the B-17. In these gambles, Boeing has typically made a practice of designing not what the customer thinks it wants, but what Boeing knows it needs. Customer thinking, airline and air force, is often too conservative, bound by the limits of conventional competitive effort. Designers at Boeing look always to the future, stretching concepts and materials to the limit, and literally forcing others in the field—engine manufacturers, system suppliers, etc.—to join them in their advanced thinking or be left behind. In looking to the future, though, the Seattle firm has always worked with a strong foundation from the past, building bit by bit on solid engineering and proven performance.

So it was that in the early 1930s Boeing

fielded four aircraft which are little known today except to buffs, but which formed the gene pool for the B-17. The first was the Monomail, a mail and cargo carrier that was a complete departure from the previous Boeing Model 40 and 80 biplane designs. Boeing made the transition from steel-tube fuselage and fabric covering to an all-metal stress-skinned monocoque construction easily. It embellished the design with a cantilever metal monoplane wing, ring cowling, and retractable landing gear—a heady combination for 1930—which resulted in a creditable 158-mph top speed.

The Monomail didn't go into production. Only two were built; but it did provide the technical basis for the next step. This was the Model 214, a twin-engine bomber that became the YB-9 "Death Angel" (there will always be an ad-man) in service. Virtually a larger twin-engine Monomail, the YB-9 was superior to any other bomber previously tested by the Air Corps, but it, too, was destined not to enter production. Although faster than current biplane fighters, it had been scooped by the even more advanced Martin B-10, which received the quantity production orders. Only seven of the Death Angels (an almost comic misnomer) were produced, including the two prototypes built on speculation.

The third of the series was the slightly better-known type, the Boeing 247 transport. The first all-metal, cantilever-wing monoplane transport with retractable landing gear, de-icing equipment, and other modern features, the 247 completely revolutionized air transportation when it was introduced in 1933. Carrying ten passengers, and 50 to 70 mph faster than the Fokkers and Fords it replaced, the Boeing seemed certain to become the predominant American transport—until it was caught up in a not untypical example of corporate greed. At that time Boeing, United Air Lines, Pratt & Whitney, Hamilton Standard, and other companies formed a consortium that intended to dominate air travel. A decision was made to reserve the first sixty of the new 247s for United Air Lines, which would give it an unprecedented measure of superiority over all of its competitors.

The group underestimated the resilience and tenacity of other airlines and manufactur-ers, however, and it came as a surprise when Jack Frye, then president of TWA, went to Donald Douglas and asked for an aircraft bigger and better than the 247. The result was first the DC-1, and then, in rapid succession, the DC-2 and DC-3. The latter two aircraft were as far in advance of the Boeing as the Boeing had been of the Ford, and the next ten years became the DC-3 decade.

The fourth factor in the series of aircraft leading to the B-17 was a giant, the XB-15. This airplane was designed to meet Army needs for a super-large, super-long-range aircraft, and although it did not fly until long after the first B-17, it made important contributions to the latter's design philosophy. The largest and heaviest aircraft built in the United States until that time, the XB-15 had a 149-foot wingspan and weighed over 70,000 pounds. Like so many other large aircraft of the period, it was terribly underpowered, for instead of the four 2,300-horsepower engines originally planned for it, it had to make do with four of only 1,000 horsepower. It proved to be more of an exercise in building large aircraft than a real production possibility, but it was important for the future.

From all of these four, and particularly from the 247 and XB-15, came a reservoir of knowledge and technology that was peculiarly Boeing's, and that stood the firm in good stead when it came to meeting the new requirements of an Army Air Corps competition for a "multi-engine" bomber.

Boeing had competitors for the potential contracts. Douglas had used its basic DC-2/DC-3 designs to come up with the DB-1 (later B-18) bomber, and Martin had massaged its B-10 formula one more time with the Model 146. In Seattle, the engineers reasoned that given comparable quality engineering, there was no way to establish a decisive edge over either Douglas or Martin with a twin-engine aircraft. It was simply beyond the state of the art to achieve much more weight-carrying ability, range, or speed without a massive increase in horsepower. With no radical new engines in sight, this meant going to four powerplants instead of two.

The problem, of course, was that in standard Army Air Corps parlance, "multi-engine" really meant twin-engine, and a four-engine approach by Boeing might be disqualified. In addition, a four-engine aircraft was certain to cost more, and the Congress usually saw things on a bottom-line basis, often more willing to sacrifice quality to quantity.

Once again assuming that Boeing knew best, and backing this up with some careful questioning of the procurement types of Wright Field, Boeing decided upon a four-engine aircraft, the Model 299.

Fortunately for Boeing, the new aircraft appeared at a time when certain other essential technological breakthroughs were occurring. One important one was the advent of constant-speed propellers, which permitted variation of propeller pitch to suit flight conditions. Another was the turbosupercharger, which had been toyed with since 1917, but which was only now reaching a point where it could be applied to production aircraft with some assurance of reliability. A final "advance" that proved to be totally inadequate in practice was the provision of multiple "blisters," streamlined bay windows through which single machine guns could be aimed.

In September 1934, Boeing had allocated the then massive sum of $275,000 for the Model 299 project, an amount so great that if unrecovered it could have driven the company into bankruptcy. By the July 17, 1935, rollout date, more than $500,000 had been invested, and while this seems small in comparison to today's $25 million unit cost fighters, it was enough at the time to make everyone at Boeing

realize their future was riding squarely in the B-17's cockpit.

First flight was on July 28, and the sleek silver aircraft immediately captivated press and public. Larger than any airplane they had ever seen, and apparently bristling with machine guns, the reporters instantly dubbed it a "Flying Fortress." The name was not yet appropriate, but would become so in just a few years in the fury over Europe.

After a very short test program—seven flights of about two hours each—the Model 299 was flown to Wright Field on August 29, 1935. It sailed across the country for 2,100 miles at an average speed of 233 mph, setting a Seattle-Dayton record, and completely ending any misapprehension the Army Air Corps may have had about "multi-" not meaning "four."

A quick look at the Boeing beside its Martin and Douglas competitors revealed the method in Boeing's madness over four engines. The Model 299 seemed to be only slightly bigger than the competition, but it had twice the horsepower. It was 10 to 20 miles per hour faster, but carried the same amount of bombs twice as far, or twice the amount of bombs for the same distance. In short, it was a step nearer the true strategic bomber the Air Corps had always lusted after.

But fate has a way of intervening, and a small innovation destroyed the prototype Model 299. Control locks were essential on an aircraft of its size, and the Model 299 employed a relatively new type, which was controlled from within the cockpit rather than

This is a Boeing B-17D snapped at the Oakland airport in August 1941 by the generous, prolific aviation historian and photographer Peter M. Bowers. I would like to think that some element of this aircraft ultimately wound up as part of *The Swoose,* for it would make a good "before and after" component. (Peter M. Bowers)

being installed manually on the exterior surfaces. They were overlooked when Boeing test pilot Les Tower and Air Corps Major Ployer Hill made a takeoff on October 30, 1935. The aircraft rose into the air, nose pitching up to the horror of the onlookers, who knew the frantic activity that was going on in the cockpit. The Model 299 stalled, pitched forward, crashed, and burned. Hill and Tower were killed, and Boeing's hopes of walking away with a major contract were ruined.

The results of the contest, in which Douglas received orders for 133 of its smaller, less expensive B-18s and Boeing received only a service test order for thirteen YB/Y1B-17s, suited Congress right down to the "T," and drove the Boeing Company very close to disaster.

The Army Air Corps, however, was sold on the airplane, and made wonderful public-relations use of the thirteen test aircraft, including a tour of South America and the spectacular interception of the Italian luxury liner *Rex* off the Atlantic coast.

But far more important than any publicity efforts was the growing certainty of war in Europe. Congress could not ignore the danger, and token orders were placed for thirty-nine B-17Bs, thirty-eight B-17Cs, and forty-two B-17Ds. There was some foreign interest, too, and twenty B-17Cs went to England, where they became Fortress Is, valued more for their confirmation of the British belief in night area bombing than they were for combat.

And the early B-17s were in fact not the machines they would come to be in the B-17F and G models. The D line, of which *The Swoose* was the thirty-ninth example, did have self-sealing tanks, but lacked adequate armor and armament and did not even have a tail gun. It was not an airplane in which to go to war.

The Yet-to-Be Assembled *Swoose* Goes to War

As war approached faster than anyone knew in late 1941, the young American pilots assigned to fly the B-17s had no idea of the plane's inadequacies; they were convinced that they had the finest bombers in the world, flown, naturally enough, by the finest crews. The potential enemies, particularly the Japanese, were not believed to have anything to compare to it.

One such pilot was Lieutenant Frank Kurtz, an almost sterotypical motion-picture hero of the period. Born in the Midwest, he had made a living selling newspapers until he decided, at age fourteen, to move to California to become not a movie star but an Olympic diving champion. He went through Hollywood High and the University of Southern California (remem-

Many crews flew *The Swoose*, and General Brett was always concerned that they should also receive credit. Unfortunately, the press is cruel, and while it will faithfully record for one story the events in the life of one crew, it will not duplicate its efforts on a similar story for another. From left are Lieutenant Marvin McAdams, Captain Harry Schreiber, Major Frank Kurtz, Sergeant Harold Varner, and Sergeant Aubrey Fox. (Boeing Photo)

Lieutenant General George H. Brett, who commanded the Allied Air Forces in the Southwest Pacific, selected *The Swoose* as a personal transport after more modern versions of the B-17 arrived. He often flew the aircraft himself, a prerogative senior officers exercise to this day. (Boeing Photo)

ber, this was in the smog-free orange-scented days when Southern California was a paradise) and ultimately became, three times, a member of the champion American Olympic diving teams.

He learned to fly as a civilian, and had a distinguished career before entering Air Corps flight training at Randolph Field in 1937. He graduated and went to bombers, where he would rendezvous eventually with *The Swoose*.

After years of what proved to be malignant neglect, the United States decided in the summer of 1941 to reinforce the Philippine Islands and to oppose the Japanese attack that was becoming even more probable. In September, nine B-17s were dispatched via Midway, Wake, New Guinea, and Australia, and in October a further twenty-six were sent; among these were the aircraft whose components would ultimately make up *The Swoose*.

The B-17s were assigned to the 19th Bombardment Group, commanded by Lieutenant Colonel Eugene L. Eubank, and were in place on Clark Field by November 6. Sixteen of the aircraft were later deployed to Del Monte Field, on Mindanao, but the others were still at Clark, presenting an attractive target when the Japanese struck.

Unaccountably, the airplanes were still vulnerable eight hours after the Japanese had bombed Pearl Harbor. The high-level bombers and strafing fighters worked Clark Field over thoroughly, and not one bomber was left serviceable. From these dregs, a few operational aircraft were put together, and in conjunction with the aircraft at Del Monte, carried on the war for a while.

During this heroic time, for which archival records are inadequate, and for which personal recollections are too fragile, the B-17s were employed boldly against Japanese ships, airfields, and infantry. Eventually, as their numbers were reduced and the area left under American control diminished, they were forced down the chain of islands to Australia.

In Australia, over a long agonizing period, reinforcements finally came. As later B-17E models arrived, Lieutenant General George H. Brett, Commanding Officer, Allied Air Forces in Australia, decided that he could afford to appropriate an older model Fortress as his personal transport. He selected what proved to be the sole surviving D model as his personal plane, with Frank Kurtz, by then a captain, as its pilot.

"Sole surviving D model" is perhaps slightly inaccurate, for it was the sum of many parts cannibalized from other aircraft rather than a single aircraft that had emerged shining from the Seattle factory. So mixed was its ancestry that it seemed appropriate to name the plane after a popular song of the time. Marion Holmes, a now-forgotten singer with Art Kassel's orchestra, had helped make popular "Alexander the Swoose," a song in which a poor unfortunate fowl was half-swan, half-goose, and had to suffer some discrimination before realizing its own worth. The B-17D intended for use as Brett's transport was just such a hybrid, and the name and symbol was painted on the side.

The Swoose (which had a somewhat doubtful "It Flys" inscribed under its name) proceeded to average 150 hours flying time per

When it began life, *The Swoose* was a shiny specimen like this. The most distinguishing feature of the aircraft externally was the addition of cowl flaps; internally, self-sealing fuel tanks had been added. (Boeing Photo)

The Swoose added a coat of olive-drab paint prior to its departure for the Pacific. There it eventually assumed a personality of its own as it was successively mated with parts from other aircraft, and then, later, modified in various ways to serve as an executive transport. The wear and tear of operational use shows clearly here. (Boeing Photo)

Wherever *The Swoose* went in the later part of its career, its age (D's were very rare by 1944) and wonderful collection of flags made it an object of interest. (Boeing Photo)

month as Kurtz kept Brett ricocheting around the South Pacific. Among its many distinguished passengers was Congressman Lyndon B. Johnson, then serving as a Navy lieutenant commander, who turned a forced landing in the outback of Australia into a personal political rally. In time, as the air war cooled, the plane was stripped of much of its offensive armament and set up with a rather Spartan executive interior.

In 1942, *The Swoose* set an Australia to United States record, and then went on a celebratory tour in the United States. Subsequently, it was dispatched to South America for routine flying; and finally, at the war's end, was the only B-17D in the world, with more than 4,000 hours accumulated flying time.

Despite its celebrity status, *The Swoose* was assigned to the War Assets Administration disposal site at Kingman, Arizona. It was saved from becoming aluminum ingots once again by the action of Los Angeles Mayor Fletcher Brown, who raised the wherewithal to obtain it from the government and have it flown by Kurtz to Los Angeles to serve as a war memorial.

Unfortunately, airplanes don't make good war memorials, for they deteriorate quickly from their proud operational status to grimy, tattered hulks; in 1949, Los Angeles presented the aircraft with some relief to the National Air Museum. Kurtz, now a colonel, again acted as pilot, this time to Park Ridge, Chicago.

The Swoose would make two further trips before finally reaching its resting place at Silver Hill. It was transferred from Park Ridge to Peyote Air Force Base, Texas, for temporary storage, and then to Andrews Air Force Base, where it was disassembled for transport to Silver Hill.

Once at Silver Hill, *The Swoose* became the target of other stories almost as virulent as the Japanese Zeros that had attacked it during the war. Periodically one reads that this rare airplane is stored outside, a prey to the elements, or that it has been sold for junk. The practical fact of the matter is that *The Swoose* is *disassembled,* treated with preservatives, and stored indoors on sturdy stands. It is not currently scheduled for restoration because it would require the entire resources of Silver

Hill for about three years, and when completed, there would be no place to exhibit it. We hope that someone—the Air Force, or Boeing perhaps—will see the need to restore and exhibit this historic aircraft, which was a part of the five fleets of B-17s that led to Boeing's next famous design, the B-29.

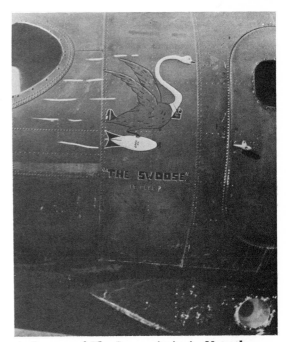

A close-up of *The Swoose* insignia. Note the questioning "It Flys?" at the bottom, a reference to all the damage inflicted on the airplane and to the assemblage of parts from miscellaneous sources that kept it going.

The Swoose today is indoors, mounted on stands that make it easy to move around, and protected from the environment. Behind it is an old enemy, the nose section of a Japanese Betty.

The *Enola Gay* returning from the mission to Hiroshima, a mission that changed the world. The photographer taking the picture knew that something momentous had occurred, but like everyone else—including the crew—was unaware of the full dimensions of the day. (USAF Photo)

The B-29 program was second only to the Manhattan Project in degree of importance or the resources devoted to it. It was also the second biggest gamble of the war, for in it Boeing had placed many innovations that had to be proved together. There was literally no bomber in the world that could compare to it; the Russians were so impressed they made exact copies of it long after the war as a means of catapulting themselves into the age of the modern bomber. (USAF Photo)

The American facility for mass production of sophisticated aircraft reached a wartime peak with the B-29s. These photos, public-relations releases at the time, should have been enough to convince both German and Japanese leaders that they had backed into the wrong buzz saw. By this time, the U.S. was producing aircraft at the rate of about 90,000 per year and was just getting warmed up; in 1939, the rate had been about 5,000 per year, of much smaller types. (Boeing Photo)

Airpower Incarnate—The *Enola Gay*

One airplane stands at the center of the Garber Facility collection like an enormous icon or infamous incubus, depending upon your point of view. To some, it represents the acme of U.S. industrial capability during World War II, an expression of aeronautical engineering genius, of bravery, and of two industrial efforts that dwarfed everything else in America's war production. To others, it is a symbol of a new sort of human suffering, of the beginning of an age still with us, of the first and perhaps final concentration in mankind's hand of the power for his destruction.

The airplane is the *Enola Gay*. Forty-two years after its design was initiated, forty-one years after its design was approved, forty years after its first flight, and thirty-seven years after its rendezvous with history over Hiroshima, it can still command feature-story attention in newspapers all over the world.

As an artifact, it has immense historical importance. It represents a level of aircraft technology never previously achieved and not attained by any of the other warring powers during World War II; a type of aircraft that was tremendously important in warfare, and might be said for the first time to have defeated a country from the air. It also represents a historical occasion so important, so well documented, and so earth-shattering in the only true sense of the phrase that it transcends more popular events like Charles Lindbergh's flight across the ocean or even Alan Shepard's first venture into space.

More than this, it was the union of two diverse technologies, aviation and weaponry, into a terrible single force, which for the first time permitted the aerial delivery of a nuclear weapon—an event that would alter the future for all nations and all mankind.

As a political symbol, the B-29 is controversial beyond belief. Forty years after the war, when fighter aces of all nations still get together, when the 8th Army Desert Rats have reunions with Rommel's Afrika Korps veterans, when all the alliances have been turned topsy turvy, the *Enola Gay* has lost none of its impact.

There are many schools of thought about this formidable airplane, and they range from one extreme to another. There are sincere groups who believe that it is an affront to human dignity to maintain the aircraft in existence in a national museum. They believe that such an infamous symbol of man's inhumanity to man should be destroyed, its pictures expunged from the public record, and the only history shown should be that of the suffering it caused and the potential suffering that may follow from it.

At the other extreme are those who believe that the aircraft should be given a place of honor at the Museum downtown, depicted as a war-winning weapon that saved millions of lives, Japanese and American, by making an invasion of the Island Empire palpably unnecessary, and who consider the Smithsonian to be excluding an important exhibit because of undue sensitivity.

There are even those who insist that it should be given to volunteer groups, restored to flying condition, and that its remaining original crew members should be allowed to fly it again.

The National Air and Space Museum's philosophy about the *Enola Gay* is exactly like its philosophy for any other artifacts. The huge B-29 is a true element of history; no judgment is made as to the wisdom or the morality of its employment. The fact remains that there was a war that began with Pearl Harbor (or with Manchuria, or with the oil sanctions, or any other source that you prefer) and that it was concluded with massive bombing raids, far more destructive than their European counterparts. There is no denying that these raids were made in large part by the B-29 fleet, nor that the *Enola Gay* made a relatively small but infinitely dramatic contribution to the effort. These things happened, and it is a duty of a museum to represent the facts, objectively, without political or philosophical comment.

Perhaps the most difficult person to deal with is the ardent B-29ophile, who, like the P-47ophile, the B-17ophile, or the Gotha Go 229ophile, is absolutely insulted that the plane

Not only did the B-29s require a mammoth expenditure of industrial effort; they required a level of training never attained before. The aircraft commander of this crew is making a point during the pre-flight equipment inspection. (Boeing Photo)

Boeing publicity photos always make great use of clouds and mountains, and impart a serenity to their products that is not always justified by the state of development. When this photo was taken, the B-29 was still beset with engine problems. This is the third prototype, used for aerodynamic and systems tests. (Boeing Photo)

of his choice does not have a place of honor next to the Wright Flyer downtown. Members of this group are generally not politically oriented. They want it displayed not because it dropped an atom bomb, but rather because it represents an airplane they love for its own sake. The true and standard answer is that the 141-foot wingspan of the airplane precludes it being installed in any of the 110-foot-wide galleries of the Museum downtown, and that even if only a portion of it were displayed, it would be so large as to inhibit the use of the gallery for other purposes. This is widely regarded as specious and cowardly reasoning by the true believers, even though it is accurate.

To satisfy this element, it would be desirable someday for the National Air and Space Museum to have a facility large enough to display not only the B-29 but other aircraft like the 747 and the Space Shuttle in a hangar-like setting on an airfield.

Although the general history of the B-29 and the *Enola Gay* in particular had been covered well in the past, it is only fair to investigate both of these subjects in some detail in relation to its present controversial position at Silver Hill.

B-29: *The Origins*

America has always been infatuated with the big bomber, even in the days when the big bomber was inevitably an inefficient, wasteful, and cumbersome way to deliver weaponry, and when such weaponry was of little impact. From the very first, the national psyche responded to the siren call of bombers that could win wars away from the American continent. The first group of outsize bombing aircraft included such notable losers as the Barling, with six engines, three wings, and the inability to get from Dayton, Ohio to Washington, D.C., because of the intervening Allegheny mountains. Another was the LWF Owl, a huge biplane with long tail booms that was intended to deliver either bombs or mail, but with three Liberty engines was too underpowered to do either.

Later giants, like the Boeing XB-15 and the Douglas XB-19, were also underpowered, and incapable of achieving the relatively modest goals of range and bombload desired. Even the famous B-17 Flying Fortress and Consolidated B-24 Liberator were at first incapable of their task; only years of wartime development and their employment in numbers previously undreamed of made them into effective weapons.

The failure of these bombers to achieve all that was expected of them stemmed from two factors, engines and weapons. Bombers were power-limited throughout their development, up to the point of the jet engine. More critical was the fact that no one had any idea of the limited destructive capability of even large bombs (1,000, 2,000, and 4,000 pounds) against industrial and urban targets, nor of the incredible inefficiency of bombing and navigation systems.

Most of the destruction of World War II in Europe was really random. British analysts found that something like 4 percent of all bombs intended for targets were actually hitting them. The German experience was not much better, although the Germans had the advantage of much more potent explosives. American daylight bombing, the mythical "into the pickle barrel from 20,000 feet," required far more training and development than had been dreamed necessary to become effective.

The bitter fact is that the Navy had been correct for years about the ineffectiveness of the heavy bomber. But, from about 1943 onward, the effectiveness of the bomber grew at a very rapid rate.

There were vast improvements in bomb-aiming equipment and techniques, and the introduction of radar and other electronic aids meant that weather and smoke screens could no longer frustrate the bombardier. More important were the use of innovative techniques like Pathfinder squadrons, which would pinpoint areas for less skilled formations to drop on. And most important of all, the commanders began to understand the degree of training and discipline required to become effective, and thereafter devoted the necessary resources to reach their goals.

While these changes in tactical perceptions were taking place, the fruit of many years of experience in building aircraft was emerging.

The B-29 that resulted from all this experience had its beginning in Boeing Airplane Company proposals to create a follow-on aircraft to the B-17, which would meet Army demands for a truly long-range weapons carrier. The B-17 had represented the peak of an earlier design and manufacturing technology. As we have seen, it was the distillation of the experience gained in a variety of important aircraft—an expertly designed and built example of early 1930 technology, suitably modified by the experience of war. It provided the engineering, intellectual, and manufacturing basis for the B-29.

The B-29 was a radical departure in every sense, and resembled the B-17 only in some details of outline, in mission, and in the faithful integrity of the company.

The biggest change was *not* in size, although the B-29 was almost twice as heavy and had almost twice the horsepower. The difference was in manufacturing methods and the requirement for vastly greater precision than ever before. Where the B-17 had a standard monocoque-riveted, stressed-skin fuselage, the B-29 had a flush-riveted super-strong shell carrying pressurized compartments for the crew. The wing, instead of the thick airfoil, aluminum-truss construction of its metal Boeing predecessors, was an extremely thin, long surface with a very high wing loading. The B-29's wing area was 1,738 square feet, compared to the B-17's 1,420 square feet, yet it had to lift a load as much as 70,000 pounds greater.

The performance of the B-29 was vastly superior to any competitor. The B-29A series had a maximum gross weight of 141,000 pounds, a top speed of 358 mph at 25,000 feet, and a range of 4,100 miles. Bombload varied with the mission, but could reach 20,000 pounds. The aircraft had a tremendous defensive capability with ten .50 caliber machine guns and a 20mm cannon, but so remarkable was its offensive capability that later in the war it was able to discard its guns to achieve greater range and speed, the Japanese fighter defenses having been rendered impotent.

As a brief comparison, the Avro Lancaster made its first flight twenty months before the B-29, had a top speed of 287 mph at 11,500 feet, and a range of 1,660 miles with 14,000 pounds of bombs. The infamous German Heinkel He 177 Greif (Griffon) had a maximum speed of 303 mph at about 20,000 feet and a range of 3,417 miles. Normal bombload was about 4,500 pounds.

The Production Effort

It took considerable courage for the U.S. Army Air Forces to embark with Boeing upon a program that had such a high risk of failure, and to which such a considerable portion of the nation's resources were going to be devoted. The B-29 was breaking new ground in a number of areas, particularly in the high wing loading, nearly 80 pounds per square foot, and was to employ the new Curtiss-Wright R-3350 engine, also an unproved factor.

The Army was so concerned about the high wing loading that it made several attempts to get Boeing to redesign the aircraft with a much larger wing. Part of this concern stemmed from the bad experience with the Martin B-26, whose initial small wing had led to performance problems and numerous accidents, and which ultimately had to be replaced by a wing of larger area. But Boeing had done its homework and was convinced it was right. Instead of modifying the B-29 proposal, it undertook a study of the B-26, and found that there were numerous design deficiencies besides the small wing—deficiencies that the B-29 would not have.

Yet the Army was determined to have back-up programs in case these were a colossal failure with the B-29. Consolidated Aircraft received contracts for the B-32 Dominator ("Terminator" to some of the irreverent) and the aircraft was ordered into production. The Sperry fire-control system was funded at the level of $75 million, purely as a back-up for the preferred General Electric system. The one area where no back-up was available was in powerplants.

The test program was agonizing. Engine failures and fires were a literally daily occurrence. There was a series of ominous near misses, combinations of engine failures, engine fires, and propeller failures that were overcome only by the competence of the test crews. Then, on February 18, 1943, Boeing and the world lost a magnificent test pilot and crew when the number two XB-29 burned and crashed near the Seattle waterfront, killing the immensely talented Eddie Allen and his crew, plus nineteen civilians on the ground. It was an enormous setback, for the crew members held an irreplaceable body of information.

The disasters that stud a program like this are sometimes more difficult for a commander than leading a raid on Berlin. In a bomber mission, he would know what to expect, know what his alternatives were, and be able to control most of the events of battle. In a huge production program, there are literally millions of imponderables that cannot be controlled but must be overcome. Through the months and years of anxiety of the B-29 program, the Army Air Forces perserved; General H. H. Arnold retained his faith in the overall B-29 program coordinator, Brigadier General K. B. Wolfe, and in the Boeing company.

Simultaneously with this gargantuan effort, and unknown to almost everyone at Boeing or the Army Air Forces, the Manhattan Project was also under way. It was in fact the only program in the U.S. war effort with a higher priority than the B-29. Facing even greater technical and manufacturing problems, calling upon even more resources, it followed a path that would coincide with the B-29 over Hiroshima.

The intensity of effort on the B-29 program at last began to prevail in 1943. The principal danger remained the powerful new Wright R-3350 engines, which had a fine power-to-weight ratio, but presented many problems that would not be completely solved until years after the war. The engines were difficult to cool, especially in the sleek B-29 nacelles, and were extremely prone to fire. One possibly apocryphal Air Force story runs as follows:

B-29 TO TOWER: Mayday, Mayday, Tower, this is B-29 1546. I'm coming in with two engines burning and two engines turning. I'm declaring an emergency landing for Runway 18.

TOWER TO B-29: 1546, pull up and blow up. I've got two burning on the runway and one burning on final right now.

In short order, however, the B-29s were manufactured, the crews trained, and deployment began to the Pacific. Four groups of the 58th Bombardment Wing went to India in the spring of 1944. The initial B-29 raid was on Bangkok, Thailand, on June 5, 1944, and was led by Brigadier General K. B. Wolfe, perhaps his most satisfying reward for years of endeavor. The second raid took place on June 15 against the Japanese mainland. The attack was made on a steel plant at Yawata, and while it was impressive enough, with sixty-eight aircraft taking part, it was but a whisper of the storm to come.

The fire-control system on the B-29 was an entirely new development, one that worked well. If the General Electric system had not worked, however, there was a back-up system under development—such was the Army Air Forces' commitment to the B-29s' success.

The crew of the *Enola Gay*. Kneeling: Sergeant Joseph Stiborik, Sergeant George Caron, Sergeant Richard Nelson, Sergeant Robert Shumard, Sergeant Wyatt Duzenbury. Standing: Colonel Porter (ground officer, not in crew), Captain Theodore Van Kirk, Major Thomas Ferebee, Colonel Paul Tibbets, Captain Robert Lewis, Lieutenant Jacob Besser. Missing from photo: Navy Captain William Parsons and Lieutenant Morris Jeppson.

Mel Erickson, Boeing, and Colonel Paul Tibbets stand next to the most famous bomber in the world. (Boeing Photo)

One year later, the B-29s had virtually laid waste to Japan, to such an extent that it was no longer easy to choose worthwhile targets. Initial difficulties in getting sufficient bombs on target were overcome by new tactics that brought the B-29s in low, unarmed, and loaded with both incendiary and high-explosive bombs. Tokyo, Nagoya, Osaka, Yokohama, all suffered extremely severe damage due to the combination of buildings that were highly vulnerable to fire and totally inadequate in fire-control systems, and the inexorable nature of the B-29 attacks.

Yet, despite the intensity of these raids and the inability of the Japanese military to cope with them, despite the endless loss of conquered territory to the south and the virtual eradication of naval and merchant shipping capability, the Japanese were resolved to fight on, as their contemporary slogan had it, "Even if 100,000,000 die."

Extensive plans to repell the invasion, all based on the bitter experience gained at Iwo Jima, Okinawa, Tarawa, and elsewhere,

Even at rest, the *Enola Gay* has a dignity and a presence that is impossible to dismiss.

Today, the *Enola Gay* waits at Silver Hill for the time when there will be room and occasion for her exhibition. (She has been made more accessible for viewing since this photo was taken.) McDonnell F-4 Sageburner at left, Heinkel He 219 Owl at right.

turned the Island Empire into a fortress. Aircraft and ships were husbanded for a final convulsive kamikaze effort. It seemed apparent to both sides that an invasion must take place, and that there would be millions of casualties.

The Enola Gay:
The Program Within the Programs

The B-29 production lines were rolling at four major factories—Boeing in Seattle and Wichita, Martin at Omaha, and Bell in Atlanta—and ultimately 3,974 bombers would be built at an average cost of about $640,000. A particular aircraft, B-29-45-MO (the -45 is the production block of B-29s, the MO means built by Martin, at Omaha) USAAF serial number 44-86292 would be singled out for history. It was part of a group of Martin-built airplanes that had been stripped of all armament but the tail-gun position, and fitted with better engines, reversible-pitch propellers, and additional fuel.

In a corresponding manner, a particular squadron, the 393rd, was chosen to become part of a new and secret unit, the 509th Composite Group, stationed at Wendover Field, Utah. Graced with the highest priority in the Army Air Forces, and commanded by the brilliant Colonel Paul Tibbets, the 509th embarked upon the most rigorous bombardment training program ever conducted—one that would at last bring to fruition the foreseen but hazy concepts of Douhet, Mitchell, and all the other early apostles of war-winning bombing.

The two separate programs, B-29 and Manhattan, moved closer together as the 509th trained. The special crews began dropping 5-ton bombs, painted a bright orange for tracking purposes. As far as the crew knew, they were simply going to drop super-heavy bombs of some kind of new explosive, although they may have begun to guess that something else was involved. Training went on under combat conditions, flying out of Tinian, and simulating the ultimate attack that would be made when all the necessary factors—training, weather, and the availability of the weapon—came together.

In late July, the results of the Potsdam Conference were made known to Japan. The demand was for complete, unconditional surrender, yet there was sentiment on both sides for some sort of face-saving solution. The Japanese reply was apparently intended to convey their interest, but was lodged in terms that could only be understood by the West as a complete refusal.

On August 5, 1945, the primary product of the B-29 program, the *Enola Gay*, was loaded with the primary product of the Manhattan Project, a 10,000-pound bomb so slender that it was code-named "Little Boy," in comparison to the rotund "Fat Man" bomb that would later be dropped on Nagasaki. On August 6, Tibbets took off with the *Enola Gay* and "Little Boy" in a mission routine in every way except for its unprecedented historical importance. The weapon was released over Hiroshima at 9:15 A.M. local time.

The final results are as yet unknown. The immediate results were that the Japanese were shocked into a sense of realism that was reinforced by the August 9 drop of "Fat Man" on Nagasaki. The death and destruction, while less than that incurred in conventional firebomb raids on Tokyo, were so sudden, so mysterious, and so ominous that the Japanese acknowledged that saving face was no longer important.

The Enola Gay *After the War*

In the immediate postwar period there was no mixture of sentiments about the *Enola Gay*, its crew, or its weapon. Like the battleship *Missouri*, General MacArthur, and the jeep, Tibbets, his plane, his crew, and his bomb were all approved of.

The *Enola Gay* received a normal amount of publicity, and was of course earmarked for the National Air Museum. It was brought to Andrews Air Force Base in 1951 and waited in open storage there until it was disassembled and brought to Silver Hill. It now rests, disassembled, in Building 22, awaiting a time when there will be an adequate facility in which to display it, and, just possibly, an adequate understanding with which to view it.

The world's first operational jet bomber, the Arado Ar 234B. A very sleek aircraft for the time, as the shadow on the ground indicates. (USAF Photo).

The Blitz Bomber

Some warplanes are so inherently beautiful that you wonder what might have come about if the talents employed in their creation had been applied to some more constructive effort. The Arado Ar 234, the Blitz bomber, is certainly one of these. It was the world's first operational jet bomber, employed by the Germans in 1944 and 1945 when it could have no possible effect on the outcome of the war, but was capable of such outstanding performance that it became an object of vital interest to the Allies.

Its sculptural beauty derived from necessity, as beauty often does. Work had begun on the airplane in 1941, long before it was apparent that jet engines were the wave of the future, and certainly long before it was obvious that Germany would soon be in desperate straits. The engines projected for the bomber in 1941 were not yet developed in practice, and even the theory behind them was so nebulous that it could not accurately be predicted how powerful they would prove nor how much fuel they would consume.

The German Air Ministry had originally called for a reconnaissance plane of great range and speed, and the Arado engineers, Blume, Rebeski, Eckstein, and Wenzel, were driven to create an aircraft of relatively low weight and extremely low frontal area, so that drag could be kept to a minimum.

To achieve these goals, some very remarkable design decisions were made. The fuselage was given such a narrow cross section, and the wing such a thin airfoil, that no conventional landing gear could be installed. Instead, the Arado jet was designed to take off on a jettisonable trolley and land on a skid, much as the Messerschmitt Me 163 rocket fighter did. The long, slim, tubular fuselage was unmarred by any break for a cockpit window, for the pilot/observer/bombardier/gunner duties were all done by one man in the single seat of the smoothly glazed nose. The Arado Ar 234 had lovely simple lines, and promised a previously unreachable performance.

When the first Ar 234 flew on June 15, 1943, the power delivered by its Junkers Jumo 004 turbine engines (the same engines that powered the more famous Messerschmitt Me 262 fighter) imparted a capability beyond all expectations. It was clear that a more advanced version of the aircraft could fly at speeds of 450 mph, and that it would be virtually immune to attack.

Development proceeded rapidly, for in the interval between conception and birth the war situation had deteriorated disastrously for Ger-

The Arado Ar 234 was so sleek that bombs had to be carried externally, either under the fuselage, as shown here, or under the engine nacelles. By the stage of the war in which they were employed, the jet was far more valuable as a reconnaissance aircraft than as a bomber.

The airfields in Germany were littered with abandoned aircraft of the next generation; note the generous flap area and large tires, which permitted operation from unimproved airfields.
(Courtesy Roy Brown)

many. When the possibility of the Ar 234 was first conceived, German troops stood from Kirkenes near the Finnish border in an arc that extended through Hendaye, France, on the Spanish border, down through the Mediterranean where the Afrika Korps threatened Cairo; across the Eastern Front, it seemed that Leningrad, Moscow, and all of the Caucasus would fall. By the time its first flight had occurred, there was disaster on the Eastern Front, the Mediterranean was fast becoming an Allied sea, Italy was reeling toward its next betrayal, and the RAF/USAAF bomber offensive was beginning to intensify. Where once the Ar 234 had been a luxurious embellishment of an already lavishly equipped Luftwaffe, it was now a small bright light in an otherwise gloom-filled prospect.

The jet engines had proved to be more efficient than planned, and it was decided to initiate a second series of slightly larger 234s, which would have conventional landing gear. It had been known from the start that the system of taking off on a trolley and landing on a skid would present enormous handling problems on the airfields, but this had been accepted at a time when Allied air superiority was not fully established. By late 1943, it was evident that the Luftwaffe could not afford to have a field littered with Ar 234s awaiting recovery by special handling equipment, for flights of marauding Mustangs, Thunderbolts, and Typhoons would have found them easy game.

By March 1944, the first of the Arado Ar 234Bs had flown. These were much improved by the introduction of cabin pressurization, an ejection seat, and other niceties, including provision for bombs and external tanks. Best of all, there was a stout tricycle landing gear neatly nestled in the fuselage.

Unlike many of the experimental aircraft of the day, the Arado jets were very pleasant to fly. At very high speeds there were some instability problems that the wind-tunnel work had not forecast, but in general the pilots enjoyed flying them. Even if they had been more intractable, they would have been appreciated, for a pilot's life in a Messerschmitt Bf 109, Focke-Wulf Fw 190, or Heinkel He 111 was no longer either fun or long. Allied air superiority

was becoming crushing in both quality and quantity, and the German pilot was never safe, not even in his own landing pattern, not even in his own bed. Ironically, a German pilot was probably safer aloft in an experimental jet, at altitude and at speed, than he was anywhere else in Germany.

On June 6, 1944, the Allies invaded Europe, their task having been made easier by the fact that German reconnaissance flights over England had been almost entirely suppressed. The Allied radar system and fighter air defense had become so expert that only an occasional German aircraft could get through. The entire long charade of an invasion fleet and army poised to strike at the Pas-de-Calais, a hoax that had successfully tied up the German Fifteenth Army while the Allies chewed up Normandy, might have been exposed if reconnaissance had been possible.

But it was not until late September 1944 that the key to recce flight over England was made possible by the use of the Arado Blitz. From then on, until the end of the war, the Arado, supplemented later by Me 262 reconnaissance versions, was the only effective means the Germans had of aerial observation over France, England, or Italy.

Fortunately for the Allies, production of the Ar 234s was relatively low and the rate of attrition due to both combat and accidents was high. The airplane that could elude all attackers at altitude was vulnerable as it made its descent to land on its home fields, and nothing brought more joy to an Allied fighter pilot's heart than to find the twin black trails of jet smoke leading to a Blitz on final approach, flaps and gear down, totally helpless to evade.

The men who flew the Arados had their hands full. Takeoffs were from fields pockmarked with hastily filled craters; climbout was through patrols of roving Allied fighters; cruise at altitude was relatively serene, except for the concern with fuel consumption, target acquisition, engine performance, and the flight home. The pressure of duties increased as the target was approached. The pilot put the plane on autopilot, and stowed the control column. He would wriggle forward to operate the bombsight and make the bomb run. Once the bombs were away (or in the case of a photo

The small size of this aircraft is evident in comparison to the sentry guarding it. That large protuberance ahead of the cockpit hatch is a periscope unit. Three of the aircraft were captured in Norway.

mission, the pictures taken), he would resume control of the aircraft. At intervals he would check in the rear-view mirror periscope to see if he was being tracked by Allied fighters. If he was, he'd use the periscope to aim and fire the rear-facing 20mm cannon. All and all, he could not complain of underemployment.

Later in the war, the Arados were used in diving attacks that permitted the pilot to continue to fly the airplane, aiming through the periscope rather than using a bombsight.

Just as the pilots and ground crewmen began to gain facility with the aircraft, the war slowed to a close as the front compressed both in the East and in the West. Fewer and fewer aircraft were able to get airborne because of battle damage, maintenance difficulties, and the general prevailing climate of shortage. Only a few more than two hundred Arado Ar 234Bs had been built, and probably no more than twenty or so were ever operational at any one time. They were far more effective than

their numbers might indicate because they were flown with dash by pilots who felt that they had received the one stroke of good fortune remaining to the Luftwaffe, a plane that could compete qualitatively with the endless hordes of Mustangs. Many of the tactical flights of the Arados had been flown almost directly from the test fields or the factories; it was simple enough and good enough to be effective even when still unproven and when flown by pilots who had had only a few hours of time with it.

At the end of the war, the Arado jets became a target for the British, Americans, and Russians to recover. The Russians had overrun the factories where the aircraft had been built, and presumably captured the plans, tooling, and flyable examples. Most of the surviving operational models fell into British and American hands, and were extensively tested after the war. There was almost universal approval by the test pilots, who marveled that such an airplane could have been produced at a time of severe material shortages in Germany.

There was no desire, nor need, to copy the aircraft, for it was a design dead end, reflecting as it did the desperate efforts of the Germans to wring maximum performance from brand-new jet engines. All three of the Allies would soon create bigger, better jet engines and bigger, better jet aircraft; but for its time, the Arado Ar 234 was supreme.

The Museum's Arado Ar 234B came into the hands of the United States by a ploy on the part of a dashing young colonel, Harold M. Watson, who had been given a special assignment, "Operation Lusty." It was Watson's task to sweep through Europe behind the advancing Allied armies and pick up flyable examples of the latest German aircraft. He had a handpicked team of young hotshot pilots and all of the charm—and gall—required. Besides being a first-class pilot and officer, he was a trained engineer who knew what to look for, and an able organizer and administrator who knew how to get what he wanted.

Watson had managed to secure examples of just about everything he wanted by one of several modes of operation. In some cases, he blustered and bullied the Germans into giving what he needed; in others, he charmed and bribed them. The German sense of bureaucracy was such that when they turned over the aircraft, they asked for a receipt, which Watson dutifully made out to them. But one aircraft eluded him—the Arado Ar 234.

He learned that there were several examples in British hands in Norway. Acting entirely on his own, without regard for the complicated niceties that immediately began to characterize postwar Allied cooperation, he flew to Norway, landing at the Arado-stocked airfield with some impressive-looking but entirely bogus papers that seemed to entitle him to three aircraft. He talked the British right out of some prime examples. Then, concerned that his little fabrication might be checked up on, made all haste, with one American and a captured German pilot, to fly them back to American territory.

As war progressed, the Germans used less and less insignia on their aircraft. There was more safety in being assumed to be Allied than in being identified as German.

The Arado Ar 234 is presently disassembled, but will soon be moved to a new building where it will be exhibited in assembled but unrestored condition. Over its head is the only Japanese jet aircraft of the war, the Nakajima Kikka. Beneath the Kikka, looking for all the world like a giant Frisbee, is the only real flying saucer, a joint product of the U.S. and Canadian Air Forces.

The flight out of Norway was uneventful. But the intended landing spot, a small field in Denmark that had the required fuel but no navigational aids, was completely covered with cloud. The Americans flew time and distance, the German on their wing nervously regarded first his fuel counters and then the socked-in landscape below. At the pre-determined time, Watson, the flight leader shrugged, made his descent, and broke out of the clouds right over the intended airport. After they landed, the German walked over to Watson and said: "After seeing navigation like that, I know now why you won the war." Watson didn't say anything.

The airplanes were subsequently flown to France, and then two were shipped to the United States for testing. One went to the U.S. Navy at Patuxent River Naval Air Station, where it was flown and, its usefulness apparently exhausted, was reportedly used for landfill for a runway extension. The other was tested by the Army Air Forces, then sent first to Park Ridge and then to Silver Hill, where it now awaits restoration and exhibit. It should be assembled in the near future, and will be placed on temporary display, pending incorporation into the restoration schedule. Even though it is a little tattered, its paint worn and Plexiglas unpolished, it still has an air of capable beauty that stamps it as an all-time classic warplane.

As a footnote, the Blitz's truly remarkable performance figures should be noted. It had a top speed of 461 mph at about 20,000 feet, and a range of just over 1,000 miles. Service ceiling was relatively low, about 32,000 feet, but this was due to the low wing area and the inefficiency of the early Junkers Jumo 004 engines at altitudes much above 25,000 feet. A four-engine development, the Arado Ar 234C, could reach almost 500 mph, and there were further developments, swept-wing and rocket-powered proposed versions, that promised even better performance.

The Mixmaster

The U.S. counterpart to the Arado stands very near it in Building 22 at the Garber Facility. It is the Douglas XB-43, the first U.S. jet bomber, and its history, configuration, and general appearance is as different from the Blitz as John Belushi was from Bo Derek. It is much larger, stands on an enormous, stalky landing gear, and has a foreshortened yet bulbous nose, which is surmounted by two "bug-eye" canopies, imparting an insectomorphic appearance.

Unlike its German opposite number, this version didn't even start life as a jet. Instead, the basic configuration originated in a Douglas proposal to build an airplane that would do the job of the Boeing B-29 at far lower initial, operating, crew, and fuel costs. This was the radical XB-42 "Mixmaster"—an airplane utterly unlike anything Douglas had done before. (To a generation brought up on Cuisinarts and

Concordes, it should be explained that Mixmaster was a trade name for a high-speed mixing bowl very popular as a wedding gift at the time, and was a reference to the twin pusher propellers that whirled at the rear extremity of the fuselage.)

As different as the configuration was, and despite the fact that conditions mitigated against its success, Douglas was enamored of it, and the postwar years saw elements reappear in the little-known Cloudster, a pusher private aircraft, the first DC-8 project, which used the same engine propeller set up as the XB-42, and in the gigantic C-74 transport, which most incongruously had the twin bug-eye canopies.

All of Douglas's previous planes had been masterpieces of evolution, from the very first Cloudster down to the sleek A-20 Havocs, A-26 Invaders, and C-54 Skymasters that were pouring off production lines. The Douglas style

The sleek Douglas XB-42, the famous Long Beach–based company's answer as a replacement for the B-29. The concept was to create a small, low-drag aircraft of exceptional range and bomb-carrying capability. Its double-bubble bug-eye canopy looked great in theory, but was a bother to the pilots. (Douglas Photo)

had been to make attractive-looking aircraft, with great performance and reliability; it always avoided the extreme.

While the Arado had its origins in 1941, with the first bare glimmering of the jet engines of the future, Douglas did not get underway on the piston-powered Mixmaster until May 1943. Douglas engineers wished to build an airplane of such aerodynamic efficiency and power that they could achieve a drastic reduction in aircraft size for a given range or bombload. In effect, they wished to reduce the ancient and implacable formula that for each additional pound of weight, you required additional pounds of fuel and structure, which in turn required additional fuel and structure. It was an upward spiral that all manufacturers faced, and their experience with the huge 219-foot-wingspan Douglas XB-19 had not given them any reason to believe there was a conventional way out. Douglas in fact was beginning to believe that the current state of the art put an upper limit on the size of the aircraft, and it was time to strive for efficiency. As

a footnote to this philosophy, Douglas dropped out of the competition that ultimately led to the gigantic Convair B-36.

Restated, then, Douglas wished to create a very clean aircraft with a relatively small crew, which would require less fuel to achieve the desired speed, range, and bombload goals. Because good flying characteristics were required, "center-line thrust" was decided upon. The engines would be buried within the fuselage, driving twin propellers at the rear, so that if an engine failure occurred, there would not be asymmetric trim problems that would only be offset by a large vertical surface area.

The aircraft that emerged from these criteria was a slender, midwing pusher aircraft, with two Allison V-1710 engines mounted amidships, driving the twin counter-rotating propellers through five Bell P-39 drive shafts.

Even with this minimal concept, the plane was not small; the span was 70 feet 6 inches, and the gross weight 35,000 pounds. Compared to the 141-foot-span, 140,000-pound gross weight B-29, it was reduced in size;

The second version of the aircraft had a more conventional cockpit. This one crashed outside Washington, D.C., after a record-breaking cross-country flight. (Douglas Photo)

The time had passed for piston-engine bombers when the XB-42 was ready for production, so a static test model was adapted to take jet engines. This produced an even sleeker package, but one that derived from piston-engine aerodynamics and thus had no chance for large-scale postwar production. (Douglas Photo)

compared to the Arado Ar 234's near 47-foot-span and 21,000-pound fully loaded weight, it was enormous.

But it was the B-29's mission that the Douglas engineers sought, not the Arado's, and they had every reason to feel that they were right on track. Even America could not sustain B-29 production at the levels that might be required if it were necessary to employ them in both Europe and Japan, and even in 1943 there were considerations of cost and fuel consumption that made sense.

The radical appearance of the aircraft was accentuated by the way its crew was situated. The bombardier had a conventional position in the nose of the aircraft, but the pilots were seated side by side in individual blister canopies. In theory this was fine, for it reduced drag and provided a splendid all around view for the pilots. In practice it was hazardous, because the pilots had a natural tendency to duck down below the level of the canopy sill to talk to each other face to face, particularly in an emergency situation.

Douglas became increasingly enthusiastic about the aircraft as testing began, even though it encountered normal testing problems, including stability difficulties and vibration. The latter was exceptionally severe when the new "snap-open" bomb doors were operated. Yet the brochures that flooded the Pentagon on the aircraft really offered the sky.

The Mixmaster was portrayed as a long-range bomber that could carry 2,000 pounds of bombs at 470 mph over a distance of 5,333 miles. In its reconnaissance version, it had a range of 6,000 miles; in an attack version, it had a range of 2,100 miles, and was armed with six .50 caliber machine guns and a 75mm cannon.

There was genuine validity in the Douglas claim for aerodynamic efficiency. The XB-42 was projected to have a three-man crew nestled within its "precision gauged body-sealed streamlined fuselage"; its laminar flow wings were unencumbered by nacelles or other protrusions. It could carry a bombload of 2,000 pounds over 5,333 miles for an expenditure of

An in-flight photo shows how sleek this airplane really was. The XB-43 engineers approached the problems of designing intake and exhaust for a jet with the aplomb that comes only from being unaware of the degree of the problem. Had they known what they learned later, it is probable that they might not have attempted such a straightforward conversion.

only 2,085 gallons of fuel; the B-29 required 7,000 gallons to do the same. When the cost of supplying the fuel in terms of ships, manhours, and so on, was computed, the XB-42 seemed like an even better choice.

The twin pusher propellers, both reversible and counter-rotating, reduced drag over a conventional wing-mounted nacelle installation by 30 percent. The clean wing had new vane-type flaps installed, which permitted reasonable landing speeds. The small size of the airplane relative to the B-29 was also claimed by Douglas to ensure less vulnerability to damage. But perhaps most telling of all in the long run was the fact that a B-29 cost an estimated 60,000 man-hours to build, while the XB-42 would cost only 20,000.

In a similar way, aircrews were cut from twelve for a B-29 to three for the Mixmaster, and direct ground-crew maintenance requirements were cut from fifteen to seven.

The arguments seemed inexhaustible, but implacable factors still favored the B-29. It was

proved, it was in production, and it was laying waste to Japan. As desirable as the XB-42 was on paper, it simply wasn't going to be needed.

Douglas amassed 150 hours of flight-test time on the first XB-42 before turning it over to the Air Force, where it became a personal test project for Captain Glenn W. Edwards, for whom Edwards Air Force Base is named. Only a few flights were conducted before an engine failure grounded the aircraft, and the decision was made to modify it to XB-42A status by adding a Westinghouse 19XB-2A jet under each wing.

The second prototype made headlines early in December 1945, when Lieutenant Colonel (later Major General) Fred J. Ascani flew it from Long Beach, California, to Washington, D.C., in 5 hours and 17 minutes, averaging 433.6 mph, and setting a new transcontinental record. On the 16th of the month, Ascani and two other men were returning on a routine flight from Bolling Field when they experienced a gear extension problem. In the way that accidents have, the problems compounded, and the left engine failed about 5 miles from the field. Ascani shut it down and boosted power on the remaining engine, which promptly quit, the proverbial third link in the chain. All three men bailed out, Ascani leaving the suddenly quiet aircraft at only 400 feet altitude.

Long before, in October of 1943, the Army Air Forces had requested that Douglas consider jet engines for the Mixmaster, and it was decided to take the static test example of the XB-42 and convert it to the prototype XB-43, to be powered by two General Electric J35 engines. A second aircraft was to be built from the ground up.

The adaptation was surprisingly easy, as the two jets were installed directly in the space vacated by the Allison piston engines. It was so early in the jet business that the problem of ducting the hot exhaust gases to the tail was not of great concern; in later aircraft this was always a tremendous headache and resulted in jet engines being mounted as far to the rear as possible, or else mounted in the wings where the jet efflux could be exhausted immediately aft of the trailing edge.

Douglas was now trapped into the invidious position of building a hybrid; as advanced as the XB-42 was as a piston-engine type, the XB-43 could not be so advanced as those now on the drawing boards at Convair, Boeing, North American, and elsewhere.

Still, despite its inadvertent access to jet bomber building, Douglas had not lost its facility with brochures. By April 1945 they were rolling off the Long Beach printing presses, claiming a remarkable performance for a totally new attack plane, the XB-43. High speed was claimed to be 460 mph, with an 8,000

Today, old *Versatile II* sits at Silver Hill underneath an early surface-effect vehicle and in front of a North American 0-47 observation plane. The plywood nose was substituted when the Plexiglas window failed.

pound bombload. *Sixteen* fixed forward-firing .50 caliber machine guns were to be fitted, along with twin fifties in a tail turret. Thirty-six rockets were planned to be carried under the wings.

The plane as it emerged proved to be much better than might have been expected under the circumstances. It made its first flight on May 17, 1946, skimming the surface above Muroc Dry Lake. In the year that followed, the test program was frustrated by difficulties in pressurization, which led to the replacement of the clear Plexiglas nose with a very rough-looking plywood cone. When it was operating, however, it performed extremely well, and a high speed of 515 mph was attained.

By now it was obvious to all that there was neither an urgent need for jet bombers in general nor for the XB-43 in particular. It made far more sense to use the XB-43s as flying testbeds, and to let other companies bring more advanced designs to fruition. It would not be long until 1947 would bring the first flights of the North American XB-45, the Convair XB-46, the Martin XB-48, and, most successful of all, the radical Boeing XB-47.

So, instead of darkening the skies over Tokyo with a flood of efficient Douglas XB-42s and XB-43s, the prototypes were to soldier on alone. It is nice to record that in the test programs the hybrid XB-43s were very well liked by crews, and were extremely adaptable to all sorts of test installations. In fact, the second XB-43, *Versatile II,* which came to Silver Hill, carries with it an obvious tribute to its flexibility. Its tail features the exhaust pipes of two totally different engines, one fully 20 percent larger than the other.

8
Beautiful Biplanes

iplanes seem to fascinate airplane lovers more than any other single configuration. Perhaps it stems from the fact that the Wright brothers defined the airplane as a biplane; or that the heroes of the Great War fought in them; or that the golden age of flight began with an immensely varied series of biplanes, military and civil. On the other hand, it may stem from simple aesthetics. Biplanes are typically well-proportioned, handy-looking aircraft, of overall smaller dimensions than monoplanes of the corresponding wing area.

In any event, biplanes persisted long after there was any real design requirement for their existence. New sport planes, designed by the legion of Experimental Aircraft Association true believers, are often as not biplanes simply because they "look good." Similarly, a class of biplane racers has developed, a purely romantic regression, that has inspired some of the fanciest new designs in America.

There is probably some more basic source of appeal, some Freudian significance to the biplane configuration, that escapes observation but accounts for its persistent popularity. It doesn't matter, for the airplanes we'll be talking about here, the Beech Staggerwing, Verville Sportsman, and the Wacos, stand on their own merits. They have an aesthetic beauty that would win them places in an art museum, and they have an efficiency that has won them places in aviation history.

The Beech Staggerwing

There is really no aviation counterpart to the Beech Aircraft Corporation's ability to create a basic design that from the start outstrips all of its competition, and then is capable of maintaining itself in the forefront of the industry not for years but decades. They did it first with the Staggerwing, then with the twin-engine Model 18 (the C-45 "Bugsmasher"), and then with the Bonanza. They may very well be doing it now with their extraordinary line of twin-engine executive aircraft, although not enough time has passed yet to be sure.

And despite the modern beauty of their current products, there is really no basis for comparison with the degree of the triumph of Walter Beech's first design for his newly formed Beech Aircraft Company in 1932. Today's turboprops rest on a solid financial base, have an extensive engineering background, and far from appearing unconventional actually so dominate the industry that they *are* the norm. Not so in 1932, when the wildly radical Model 17R appeared, amid the gloom of a tremendous depression, and was

The Beech Model 17 Staggerwing is regarded by many enthusiasts as the most beautiful of all biplanes. It looks equally fast on the ground or in the air.

quite accidentally given a nickname, "Staggerwing," that would prove to suit it so well.

Walter Beech had soloed in another biplane on July 11, 1914; it was a Curtiss pusher, and it provided him with the background to become, three years later, a flight instructor in the burgeoning U.S. Army Air Service. He followed the traditional barnstorming path after the war until he joined the Swallow Aircraft Company in Wichita, Kansas, in 1923, as a test pilot, designer, and salesman. He entered and won numerous races, including such well-known events as the Admiral Fullam Derby and the Aviation Town and Country Club of Detroit Efficiency Contest, and within two years was general manager of the company. It should be pointed out that this was no small feat, for the other principals involved in the Swallow Aircraft Company were men of merit and substance, including such important figures as the crusty curmudgeon Jack Moellendick and the hardworking, innovative E. M. "Matty" Laird. Lloyd Stearman was later chief designer, and was himself another towering figure of the time.

One of the characteristics of such early companies was that while they served to concentrate talent, they also were hothouses of opinion, and usually resulted in new and different companies being formed. Stearman and Beech had strong ideas about the value of the steel-tubing fuselage replacing the wooden fuselage of the past, and when Moellendick wouldn't go along with them, they simply formed their own company. For financial backing, they picked a Kansas farmer who happened to agree with them about steel tubing and a number of other ideas. His name was Clyde V. Cessna.

The new firm was called the Travel Air Manufacturing Company, and its first product was the Travel Air 1000, a steel-tube fuselage aircraft otherwise not too different from the Swallows Stearman and Beech had built in the past.

Amazingly, the new firm sold nineteen aircraft in 1925, catapulting it from a wistful dream into the first rank of American builders. The airplane—virtually undistinguishable externally from the Swallow, or from half a dozen other biplanes of the time—achieved remarkable success in the 1925 Ford Reliability Tour, the first event of its kind, and an extremely auspicious place to start breaking records.

The Ford Tours ran from 1925 to 1931, becoming increasingly sophisticated each year. In 1925, the rules were still not yet fully formed, but seventeen aircraft of widely varying type competed, including the familiar-looking Swallow, a huge trimotor Fokker F. VII, a Junkers F 13L, and a variety of Waco, Curtiss, and Martin types. Three Travel Airs achieved perfect scores, and the heady publicity boosted sales the next year to forty-six.

The cell division typical of the times went on; in 1926, Stearman left to form his own company, and in 1927, Cessna did the same. In the meantime Beech guided the company from one strength to the next, selling airplanes, winning contests, and improving the breed. He did so well, in fact, that the company became a candidate for acquisition by the mammoth Curtiss-Wright Aeronautical Corporation. Attracted by sales that had reached 527 per year, Curtiss saw that they could not only acquire a profitable company; they could obtain the services of Walter Beech himself.

One of the projects attractive to Curtiss was the Travel Air Mystery S, a low-wing aircraft specially designed for the National Air Races. It set the aviation world in turmoil in 1929 when it walked away with the Nationals, beating the highly touted Army and Navy entrants with an average speed of 194 mph. It was the first time that a civil racer had bested military entries, and it pointed the way for the Lairds, Gee Bees, and Wedell-Williams racers that were to follow.

Despite Travel Air's built-in success, and despite the Mystery Ship's promise (it was tagged Mystery Ship because of the close secrecy with which it had been shrouded prior to the races), the Depression caused Curtiss-Wright to retrench, and Walter Beech decided, once again, to strike out on his own.

In a gesture of friendship that would persevere over the years of rivalry ahead, Clyde Cessna let Beech have a small portion of the Cessna factory to begin business in. Ted Wells, a gifted designer, had prepared plans for a very different-looking four-place cabin biplane, and Beechcraft was determined to build it. At a time when every major manufacturer was lurching in the opposite direction, trying to find a market by building smaller, more economical airplanes, Beech was set on producing

an expensive, high-quality product with a performance in excess of everything else in the field. Times were as bad in the aviation industry as they were everywhere else; prices of used aircraft had dropped to record lows, and aircraft in inventory were being offered at below cost. Further, in 1932 there was no real way to make money flying commercially. The people who flew private aircraft did it from love, for except in a few special applications, such as pipeline patrol or high-level executive transport, there was no way that the aircraft of the time could compete with the magnificent U.S. rail service, which ran day or night, rain or shine.

The determined young manufacturer put stringent requirements on his proposed new product. He wanted a top speed of 200 mph, and a landing speed of 60 or less, at a time when first-line Army pursuits, Boeing P-12Bs, were capable of only 168 mph. To achieve this performance, he specified a 425-horsepower Wright engine (huge for the time), a very modern Smith controllable-pitch propeller, and spatted landing gear which resembled the current Northrop practice, but incorporated a slight retraction of the wheels within the streamlined coverings.

Beech himself was an excellent pilot, and he didn't intend the airplane for the masses. It was going to require a good pilot to fly it, and for that reason he was very careful about inquiries for purchase. The last thing the firm needed was a spectacular accident, for immediately upon debut the Beechcraft was tagged as being "hot to handle."

The first flight of an airplane that would found a dynasty took place on November 4, 1932, and within a few hours flying time it confirmed that Beech had achieved all of his aims.

The degree of a small Beech team's achievement can be measured by a few comparisons. A development of his best comparable previous effort, the Curtiss Wright Travel Air Sedan, could carry six people, but only at a maximum speed of 144 mph, even when it was fully gussied up with ring cowling and wheel pants. Range at the more reasonable 115-mph cruise was an unremarkable 575 miles. A late model Lockheed Vega, one of the cleanest de-

The very unusual "negative stagger" of the wings gave the aircraft a distinctive look that in part explains its lasting hold on the American aviation public. There were very good reasons for the arrangement: it provided biplane pilots with a degree of visibility that they had never enjoyed before. As incidental benefits, the placement of the wings improved stall characteristics, for they were so designed that the lower wing would stall first, and thus pitch down, warning the pilot before a full stall occurred. The lower wing was also in a position where it could be adapted to a retractable landing gear mechanism. (Courtesy EAA)

signs of the day, could haul six passengers at a top speed of 180. At its respectable cruise of 155 mph, it had a range of 620 miles. The Waco series of aircraft, the most popular in the country, could scarcely top 130 mph, and, being of the open cockpit type, was not really a competitor.

It was fortunate that Beech hadn't specified that his tigerish new airplane be perfect for the student pilot to fly. It wasn't; the combination of high power, narrow-tread landing gear, and the unsophisticated fields of the time made landing it a definite challenge. But in the air, it was everything anyone could desire.

The attainment of enjoyable flying characteristics in those days was often a hit-or-miss matter. Not much was known about or attention paid to the harmonization of controls, nor to the relief of pilot fatigue through stable flight characteristics. In truth, pilots did not demand these traits often or loudly enough; it wasn't macho (although the term wasn't known at the time) to complain about flight-handling characteristics. If the plane flew fast, that was enough, and a "good" pilot made up the difference with his physical strength.

The new Beech flew as if it were on rails. The comparison to a luxury automobile is apt, although only in reference to a modern Rolls rather than a 1932 Pierce Arrow. Even today,

the Beech biplane flies with a solidity of feel and a precision of maneuver that few contemporary planes can match.

But as spectacular as the performance was, it was the radical yet beautiful appearance of the plane that gained it instant recognition and immortality. In a departure from all current practice, Beech had let Wells design the airplane with the upper wing mounted aft of the cabin, with its leading edge behind, rather than ahead of the leading edge of the lower wing. This configuration had been seen before, most notably in the de Havilland D.H. 5 and Sopwith Dolphin fighters of World War I, but it had not been used on commercial aircraft.

The reason was simple. The visibility from the conventional biplane, which had its upper wing staggered forward from the lower wing, was wretched, particularly in the landing pattern, where the upper wing would completely blank out the pilot's view in a turn. Beech had solved this problem and at the same time imparted rakish, distinctive good looks to the airplane that would immediately imprint itself on anyone who saw it.

The prototype's fixed landing gear was a less desirable solution and would soon be improved upon in production models by a very neat retractable gear that further enhanced both appearance and performance. One other feature, dropped in all subsequent aircraft, was a split trailing edge rudder, which opened to form an airbrake upon landing.

The airframe itself was a jeweler's joy, an intricate mass of tubular steel surmounted by beautifully crafted wood fairings that smoothed the entire shape of the plane into a harmonious whole. It was relatively lightweight but so immensely strong that it could accommodate engines ranging from 220 to 650 horsepower. Performance varied with the engine, of course, ranging from 166 mph top speed for the small engines to 240 for the large.

Walter Beech knew promotion as well as or even better than aircraft design. He didn't want to sell it to just anybody, and the special people he wanted to buy it, people like Lindbergh, Frank Hawks, or Wiley Post, simply didn't come forward to do so. So he entered it in a variety of races, including the 1933 Texaco Trophy Race in the All American Air Maneuvers in Miami. Here legend has it that the announcer commented: "Look at that negative staggerwing Beech go," and a perfect nickname was born. (It's odd to think that hundreds of thousands of dollars were lavished on a contest to come up with the name Edsel. The difference, of course, is that the Beech looked right and the name fit, while the car didn't and its name didn't either.)

Beech followed up the race publicity with some very well executed advertisements, and he established immediately the idea that the Model 17 (his last Travel Air had been Model 16) was the most desirable biplane in the industry. For many it remains so to this day.

Production did not really begin until 1934, when eighteen were built, and Beech defied not only the engineers but also the economists. In 1935 the run was doubled, to thirty-six, and the Beech Aircraft Company was permanently established in business.

In 1936, he followed the advice of his wife, Olive Ann (who has run the company with extreme competence since Walter's death in 1950), and permitted two prominent women flyers, Louise Thaden and Blanche Noyes, to enter the Staggerwing in the prestigious Bendix Air Race. The little Beech, modified only to the extent that it carried extra fuel tanks, won the race, to the delight of Beech lovers and feminists, then and now. It was in many respects a ladies' race, for Laura Ingalls was second, and Amelia Earhart fifth. Another woman, Maxine Howard, was injured with her famous husband Benny when they crashed in the previous year's race winner, *Mr. Mulligan.*

Beech biplanes are among the most desired by that small band of affluent people who restore antique aircraft. At the annual Oshkosh Fly-in you'll find anywhere from six to twelve of the lovely airplanes. (Courtesy EAA)

As a side note, the sturdiness of Beech aircraft was demonstrated at air shows around the country by shutting off its engine at 2,000 feet, positioning the prop to a horizontal position, and making a deliberate wheels-up belly landing in front of the grandstand. The aircraft would be jacked up, the wheels lowered, and then immediately taxied away for another performance. It was convincing.

Beech, unlike so many of his contemporaries, had managed not only to produce a brilliant aircraft but to keep in business until the upswing in aviation production occurred in the late 1930s, in anticipation of the war in Europe.

Production of the Staggerwing continued at an accelerated rate, and ultimately 781 were built, including those intended for military duties as executive transports. Today, an affluent fan club keeps track of all existing aircraft, restores them to better than new condition, flies them to air shows, and even has created a special museum for them. In Tullahoma, Tennessee, one may visit the Staggerwing Museum and find a memorial to the airplane, to the men and women who flew it, and to the man who caused it to come into being, Walter H. Beech.

Or, if you're near Silver Hill, you can drop in to see the Museum's example, which embodies the loving care with which most of the 781 aircraft were treated during their life, and which accounts for the large number that are still in active, if coddled, service.

The Museum's Staggerwing came off the production line as a C17B—the series of designations eventually ran from the very first seventeen through G17, with twenty-six sub-variants that denoted the differences in engines, use of floats, and so on. There were also sixteen military designations, generally something like UC-43A for the Army and GB-2 for the Navy. The C17B designation was changed to C17L when the engine was replaced by a different model Jacobs in 1947.

The NASM Staggerwing was the ninety-third Staggerwing to be built. The Beech Air Sales Company of New York delivered it to E. E. Aldrin on July 8, 1936; for $9,250, about the price of a contemporary Rolls Royce. Aldrin was a distinguished ex-Air Corps officer who was among the first few pilots who had a strong engineering background. He had served Standard Oil in a variety of engineering, management, and pilot capacities. He was, in other words, exactly the sort of professional pilot-executive for whom Walter Beech intended the Staggerwing. He was also the father of the second astronaut to set foot on the moon, Edwin Eugene Aldrin, Jr.

The Beech, registered under serial number 15840, was specially prepared for its new owner in the custom of the time, with numerous luxurious touches and a customized paint scheme. In the days before terrorist attacks made it necessary for all executive aircraft to be painted in anonymous colors, the word "STANAVO" ("Standard Aviation Oil") was placed in bold aluminum block print on the red fuselage.

Again in the custom of Staggerwing Beechcrafts, and other expensive executive toys as well, the airplane went through a long series of owners, nineteen in all, most of whom put relatively little flying time on the aircraft (today,

The Museum's Beechcraft as it came from the factory. It may be repainted in its original colors for real authenticity at some future time.

Jim Cusack, a man of great skill and patience, looks reflectively at the Staggerwing; the Museum had wanted one for a long time, and so has Jim. Behind is the huge aluminum box in which pressure suits and space suits are stored in temperature- and humidity-controlled conditions.

forty-five years later, it has only about 1,500 hours total time). The last individual registration is to Glenna and Ralph Martin, of Spring Valley, California; the last private owner was Desert Air Parts, of Tucson, Arizona. The airplane was delivered to Washington in January 1980, where it was gratefully received by the National Air and Space Museum, which had lusted after one for a long time.

The Staggerwing joins a Bonanza and a twin-engine Model 18 in the Museum's collection—a representation of which Beech can surely be proud.

The Verville Sportsman

The next aircraft represents both an airplane and an individual whom the fates treated far less kindly than they treated Walter Beech. Alfred Victor Verville was a man of uncommon grace and charm, beloved by all who knew him. He was a brilliant engineer and designer, who tried on several occasions to launch a business that would have given the name Verville the same association of success that Douglas, Martin, or Beech acquired, but each time he failed. The cause of the failure was never in the aircraft, for Verville's designs were uniformly handsome and efficient. Instead, it was most often a question of timing, of partners, and of financing, three shoals that have scuttled many an engineer.

It's a truism that great aviation engineers are often poor businessmen and great aviation businessmen are rarely good engineers. In this all-too-common equation, there is a subtle dif-ference. A great aviation engineer can not always "hire" the capital necessary to bring his dreams to fruition, while a great businessman hardly ever has a problem in hiring good engineers. Thus Pipers succeed where Taylors fail.

The field of aviation is studded with the phenomenon. Time after time good aircraft have been designed and built, hailed with a joyous fanfare by the ever benevolent, always positive, and sometimes gullible aviation press. Time after time the rigors of business have proved to be too much of a challenge, and the design sinks into obscurity. Oddly enough, the aircraft are often excellent, and with the right promotion or backing, might have succeeded; instead, they pass away, their names—Cox-Klemin, Bourdon, Kruetzer, Stout—a mere garland of history.

Yet a man who might have been expected to overcome this jinx was surely Alfred Verville.

The Sperry Messenger was designed by Alfred Verville. Clarence Pangborn is at left, and it is believed to be General Billy Mitchell—or a look-alike—at the right.

Almost no engineer of the World War I period had as varied a background or so long a string of successes as he did. He began with Curtiss in 1914, at the age of twenty-four, and participated in the most significant projects of the period as a design draftsman. He got his hands on the Curtiss Model F Flying Boat, the Wanamaker trans-atlantic hopeful from which stemmed most Allied wartime and postwar U.S. Navy flying boats. He worked on the original Curtiss JN trainer, and even helped with the pontoons that were placed on the Langley Aerodrome during its rigged flights at Hammondsport.

In 1915, he left to join Thomas Morse at Ithaca, New York, and then went on to become chief designer and general manager of the first of many General Aeroplane companies. The pressure of war and his natural talents swept him upward to be, at twenty-seven, executive engineer for the airplane division of the Fisher Body Company, where he worked on the American versions of the de Havilland D.H. 4 and D.H. 9.

His major successes, however, came from that great font of engineers and industrialists, McCook Field, at Dayton, Ohio. In the early 1920s, McCook Field performed the functions that Wright-Patterson and Edwards Air Force bases and the Langley, Ames, and Arnold research centers do today, and within its heady boundaries flourished the leaders of both American's future air forces and its future aircraft manufacturers. Among the leading engineers at McCook Field were Jean Roche, father of the American lightplane; V. E. Clark, designer of the Clark "Y" series of airfoils and many aircraft; Alexander Klemin, the distinguished "Sergeant-Professor"; and many other even better-known names like Donald Douglas, Reuben Fleet, Don Berlin, Dutch Kindelberger, Jimmy Doolittle—it was a glorious band, not of brothers, for rivalries were intense, but of achievers.

And among this group, Verville ranked high. He was responsible for some of the most advanced and attractive fighters and racers of the time, whose features found their way into the biplane fighters that formed the bulk of U.S. pursuit aviation until the mid-1930s. Verville was responsible for developing the tunnel radiators and tapered wings that appeared on the Boeing PW-9 and Curtiss PW-8 fighters, and his own VCP-1 fighter was modified into the Verville Packard R-1 racer, which won the first Pulitzer Speed Trophy at Mitchel Field, Long Island, in November 1920 at a speed of 178 mph.

One of the most famous of his efforts doesn't bear his name officially—it was the Sperry Messenger, a tiny biplane proposed by none other than Brigadier General Billy Mitchell himself, as a liaison aircraft. It had a 20-foot wingspan, weighed only 862 pounds, and was powered by a three-cylinder 60-horsepower air-cooled Lawrance engine, the father of the Wright Whirlwind and in truth the primordial ancestor of all American radial engines, and a lot of foreign ones, too. It had a few flaws—master bearing difficulties, carburetors that backfired and burned, and ignition problems—but it was adequate for the Messenger.

Verville's airplane was itself very well liked, handling easily and having good stall characteristics. It was demonstrated around the country, taking off and landing in front of the White House, buzzing the Washington Monument, and so on, and was used in a whole host of experiments, including hook-ons to lighter-than-air ships and radio-control work. Lawrence Sperry, who took Verville's design and modified it for the production of the thirty-two Messengers that were built, tragically lost his life in one in the English Channel. One original Messenger exists today, on loan from NASM to the great Air Force Museum at Wright-Patterson AFB, Ohio.

In 1922, Verville created what many think to be one of the most important aircraft of the 1920s, for it contained advanced features that would be standard on World War II fighters. The Verville Sperry R-3 was a low-wing cantilever monoplane with a retractable landing gear that almost always worked perfectly and clean lines that would not look out of place in 1939. Three of the racers were built, an enormous effort that was largely frustrated by two complex factors out of Verville's control. The first was political infighting by the Curtiss Company, which did not want him to have the Curtiss D-12 engine, Curtiss Reed metal propeller, and wing-skin radiators that he had specified in the design, and for which he had to substitute the vibration-prone Wright H-3 engine, a big club of a wooden propeller, and drag-inducing Lamblin "barrel" radiators. The second was the unrealistic engineering approach of the time, which didn't take into account the fact that long months of fine tuning were necessary to make a high-performance aircraft really come together. In those charming, primitive days, a hotshot test pilot could take up an aircraft that had thousands of dollars invested in it, fly it around the pattern, and if he didn't like it virtually condemn it on the spot. The requirement for incremental testing and constant tweaking had not yet become apparent.

Thus it was with the sleek R-3. Virtually rolled from the factory to the starting line, it finished fifth in the 1922 Pulitzer and did not complete the race in 1923. In 1924, at last equipped with the Curtiss engine-propeller combination and wing-skin radiators, it won the Pulitzer—and then faded into oblivion. If the Air Service had realized its potential and developed it intensively, the attractive Verville racer might have given the service a ten-year march on foreign competition.

By 1925, flush with all the honors the U.S. Army Air Service could press upon him (honors that could not by law include a decent salary), Verville was caught up in the cheery optimism of the mid-1920s, when it seemed

The Verville R-3 racer was at least ten years ahead of its time, with its retractable landing gear, cantilever monoplane low wing, and generally clean streamlining. If the temper of the times had permitted it, this aircraft could have been developed into a front-line fighter by 1928 or 1929. (USAF Photo)

The closest brush with production success came with the Verville XPT-914, which was purchased as the YP-10, and which, a few years later, might have become a part of the vast Air Corps expansion. As it was, only four were purchased. (USAF Photo)

The sole remaining Verville in the world today—the tidy little Verville Sportsman.

that everyone not only could, but should, make a fortune. He left the government to form his own firm, the Buhl-Verville Aircraft Company of Detroit, Michigan. Then he created the B-V Airster biplane, which had his usual list of innovative features, including folding wings that were interchangeable. The rudders and elevators were also interchangeable, for production ease, and there were many other advanced ideas. This classy-looking airplane received the very first Approved Type Certificate of the newly formed Aeronautics Branch of the Department of Commerce. Unfortunately, less than twenty were sold in the two short years of its production, and Verville quietly left the firm.

A year later, in 1928, he organized his own firm, the Verville Aircraft Company, and created a startling good-looking cabin monoplane, the Verville Air Coach. Lean of line and with a superb finish, the Air Coach sold for $10,500. But any airplane introduced in 1929 was almost bound to fail with Wall Street, and so it was with the Air Coach, of which ten to sixteen were built, depending upon your source of information. The most interesting of

these, in the light of today's fuel situation, was the single diesel-powered 104 P model.

The interest in the diesel stemmed not so much from its economy as from reasons of safety, the diesel fuel being much less volatile than gasoline, and thus safer in the event of an accident. The 104 P was powered by a nine-cylinder Packard DR-980 diesel engine that ran well but smelled just terrible, the stench of diesel fuel permeating the aircraft and the passengers' clothes at all times. The aircraft was ultimately lost in a thunderstorm.

The final Verville design to reach production was a classic approach to biplane design: a two-place clean-limned aircraft designated the Verville AT Sportsman in civil guise and the YPT-10 as a military trainer for the Army Air Corps. Once again it was a question of timing. Had Verville been able to propose exactly the same design five years later, he would have caught the same sort of military upsurge in procurement that carried Meyers forward with the OTW, St. Louis with their YPT-15, and other established builders like Vultee, Ryan, and Waco far beyond their civil production peaks.

The Air Corps in 1931 was able to purchase only four of the YPT-10s, but tested them with five different engines, so that there are YPT-10 through YPT-10D designations. It was probably an ideal military trainer, very much on the lines of the German Bücker Jungmeisters, light enough to be inexpensive and rugged enough to stand the abuse of ham-handed cadets. It was too soon, just as the Air Coach had been too late, however, and the Stearman and Waco companies eventually dominated the biplane trainer market.

The very handsome civil Sportsman was built in slightly greater quantities, perhaps as many as sixteen according to unofficial records. It was conventional in all but its elegant simplicity. The structure of the aircraft is a virtual instruction manual on how to design with great strength and economy a steel-tube fuselage and wooden-wing aircraft. Verville managed to reduce the basic structure to a series of straight lines, which then, with a minimum of formers and fairings, was shaped to produce an elegant appearance. The 165-horsepower Continental radial engine could push it to a top speed of 120 mph, not sensational, but well within the biplane ballpark of the time and more than adequate for flight training.

Verville's career was thus an ironic combination of real achievement, real acknowledgment by his peers, and bittersweet disappointment that none of his lovely creations was ever manufactured in quantity, nor did his name become a household word. Some of his most advanced ideas unfortunately never saw the light of day. He had anticipated the configuration of the world speed record-setting Macchi Castoldi M-72 of 1934, with its tandem engines, in his 1923 proposal for an enlarged R-3 racer with exactly the same fore and aft engine arrangement. In the late 1920s, he proposed a whole series of monoplane fighters with retractable landing gear and heavy armament, clearly presaging the Hurricanes and the Spitfires of five years later. None of these received backing, so that his fame today rests primarily on the Messenger and his racers. The handsome Sportsman hanging from the rafters of Building 20 at the Garber Facility is, however, a worthy memorial.

Wonderful Wacos

Waco biplanes were and are as beloved as Beechcrafts. They have their own varied beauty, their own clubs, and probably some day will have their own museum. If the Waco never had the overpowering mystique of the Staggerwing Beech, it had a much more diverse following, for in the more than twenty years that the firm was actively building civil aircraft, it made a great variety of airplanes, all of them trim, good performers, an excellent value for the money, and backed by a company of impeccable reputation.

Waco began in the early 1920s as the Weaver Aircraft Company of Lorraine, Ohio. Its acronym, WACO, was pronounced "Wayco" by the uninformed and "Wah-co" by the cognoscenti. This company was relatively short-lived, and produced only a few aircraft. But it was the nucleus for the concentration of some marvelous aviation talent, most notably Clayton J. Brukner and Elwood Junkin. These two formed the Advance Aircraft Company of Troy, Ohio, in 1925, which became one of the most intelligently run firms in the sometimes wacky, always risky, aviation business of the 1920s.

Brukner and Junkin started slowly, building a small series of unspectacular aircraft, the first of which was somewhat unglamorously called "The Cootie." The firm gained a good reputation, but only limited sales. They began the practice, however, of noting both what the public wanted and what it needed, which were not always the same, and then designing aircraft that would come close to satisfying both of these demands. They stayed always well within the state of the art, using an optimum combination of modern methods and economical production techniques. Parenthetically, it is amazing how many aircraft were designed then, and to a lesser extent now, based on the fascination of the designer with a

The Waco 9 was used not only as a sport plane and trainer, but even as an airliner. Tourist and first-class passengers rode side by side in this early narrow-body transport—a Waco 9 used by Pennsylvania Air Lines for the first Pittsburgh to Cleveland air-mail service. (Ken Sumney Photo)

The Waco 10 was an improved, more streamlined version of the 9, and gained a wide acceptance.

The Waco 10 in flight was a lovely sight; the simple, trim lines are a continuing delight even in the jet age. (Warren Bodie Collection)

particular technique, material, or even plan-form. An enthusiastic designer of the 1920s could always convince investors that he had a remarkable airplane (and sometimes he did), but no one ever seemed to take the trouble to see if there was a market for its sale. This was a mistake that Waco rarely made before the war—and made only once afterwards.

War-surplus Jennies and Standards had filled almost the entire American aviation requirement before the war, being available for a song and capable of doing most of what the fledgling pilots of the period required. Mercifully for would-be aircraft manufacturers, the supply of the two types was finite, and the rate of attrition from crashes and weather was high.*

By 1925, then, the market had begun to quicken, and the Advance Aircraft Company was ready with its Waco 9. This aircraft was considerably smaller than the Jenny, with a 31-foot 7-inch upper wingspan and a gross weight of 2,100 pounds. Using engines similar to those in the Jenny, either the 90-horsepower Curtiss OX-5 or the 150-horsepower Wright-Hispano, it naturally had a much better performance. It was so attractive that there was a veritable flurry of sales—47 in 1925, 164 in 1926, and a further 65 in 1927, when the Model 10 had been introduced. Its three-place capacity even made it attractive to a few small airlines; but its principal use was as a trainer and a sport plane.

Waco, as the firm came inevitably to be called, had demonstrated its keen appreciation of publicity by entering the Model 9 in the first Ford Air Tour in 1925. There, like Walter Beech's Travel Air, it achieved a perfect score. The Ford Air Tour and other lesser but similar competitions were the swiftest route to national acclaim.

With an almost unexpected degree of success thrust upon them, Brukner and his colleagues produced an improved version, the Waco 10, in 1927, and quickly rose to a production rate of better than one plane per day. The "Ten" was really much more sophisti-

cated than the "Nine," in terms of pilot comfort, streamlining, and so on, but possessed the same easy handling, low maintenance, and rugged strength. It achieved national prominence by winning a class in the 1927 Air Derby, a well-organized, well-handicapped race from New York to Spokane, Washington.

With this basic foundation, the Waco firm began to move from strength to strength in terms of design, accommodating itself to new engines, new requirements, and new markets. At the same time that Waco was prospering, dozens of other firms, building aircraft not very different in appearance, price, or performance, would come onto the aviation scene, blossom for a while, and then drift from sight. Famous names like Travel Air, New Standard, Command-Aire, American Eagle, Alexander, and Laird all ultimately faded from the picture, as did the lesser-known types like Butler, Bourdon, Brunner-Winkle, and Crown. Most were destroyed by the Depression and its aftermath. But their destruction was made easier by the fact that they had not done their marketing homework as well as Waco had done.

The Depression hurt Waco, too, yet the firm was so resilient and produced such a never-ending series of good designs that it survived. The introduction of the higher-powered Waco "Taperwing" in 1928 illustrates just how clever the firm really was. Basically a standard Waco 10, the airplane was adapted to take the new Wright Whirlwind radial engine of 220 horsepower and fitted with wings of a new tapered shape and airfoil reminiscent of that being introduced on the new Army and Navy fighters. The result was a really "hot" airplane for the time, with a 135-mph top speed that made it competitive in cross-country derbies, closed-course air racing, and aerobatic demonstrations. Even today, "Taperwings" are among the most desirable of restored biplanes, and there is an organization in Florida run by a Wacophile named Jack Jiruska that is devoted solely to the type.

By 1929, more than 1,900 Wacos had been manufactured, and it was the undisputed leader in its field. Aircraft had been sold to foreign countries—a market previously untapped by manufacturers of small civil biplanes—and a bewildering variety of engines had been

---

* Life expectancy for a Jenny at a wartime training field was about three months; it would be interesting to have figures developed on what it was in civil hands after the war.

Fastest and sportiest of the open cockpit Waco biplanes was the Taperwing. These gave the already well regarded company an entirely new image, even though only relatively few were built—probably less than sixty.

The Museum's Waco 9 has a non-traditional Waco paint job, but one that was used on the aircraft during its active career and is thus retained.

adapted for use on the basic airframes. Prices were kept relatively low, in the $8,000–$10,000 range, fully competitive with anyone else's offerings. To recognize the extent of success, the firm formally changed its name from Advance Aircraft to Waco Aircraft in 1929.

Waco responded to the effects of the Depression much as many of the manufacturers of luxury automobiles did during the period, introducing somewhat smaller models with smaller engines, so that both initial and operating costs could be lowered without too much sacrifice in performance. During this period the cabin monoplane had come into vogue, as exemplified by the Curtiss Robin, Fairchild FC-2W, and others, and Waco, by 1931, was ready to adjust. With clever economy, it expanded the fuselage of one of its smaller types to make room for four passengers, and enclosed the area with a handsome cabin. There were other cabin biplanes on the market, but none were as pretty. It was one of those very rare instances in which improvisation with an existing design was better than starting over from scratch.

The new four-place cabin Waco was not only stunning-looking; it was stunningly priced at under $6,000. Once again Waco had measured the market perfectly and come up with a solution.

New improvements followed rapidly, as Waco worked every possible variation on a theme into the new cabin line. Each year successively more advanced and better-looking cabin biplanes rolled off the Waco line. Zack Moseley, the creator of "Smiling Jack," the freely adapted comic-strip version of Roscoe Turner, often has his hero flying Waco cabin jobs.

The firm used the same strategy it had done in the past, employing all available types of engines to tailor the aircraft to the individual customer's demands. And underneath the striking lines of the latest product off the line, one could always find the basic construction philosophy of quality and economy that extended straight back to the original Waco 9.

The war brought undreamed prosperity to Waco. The open cockpit biplane trainers, so often confused with Stearman trainers, were manufactured in great quantites for numerous civilian contract pilot training schools. Oddly

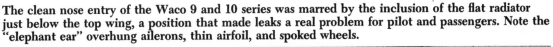

The clean nose entry of the Waco 9 and 10 series was marred by the inclusion of the flat radiator just below the top wing, a position that made leaks a real problem for pilot and passengers. Note the "elephant ear" overhung ailerons, thin airfoil, and spoked wheels.

The Waco Model ARE was perhaps the closest competition the Beechcraft had in the pretty biplane sweepstakes. There were some European civil aircraft that approached the two American classics in beauty, but none were produced in any quantity, and none had the utility of their U.S. counterparts.

The Museum's aircraft after arrival at Andrews Air Force Base. Note that the company employed a strut bracing instead of the traditional biplane wire bracing. The U1C model will be "brought back" to original by incorporation of wheel pants and bumped rocker box cowling.

The Wacos were work planes. This aircraft ended its career flying a pipeline to check for damage, spills, and so on.

Two views of the Waco at Silver Hill. The ubiquitous Martin Kitten, which seems somehow to get into every photograph, is at left, above sister ship Waco 9; to the right are arrayed a Boeing-Stearman N2S-5, Hawker Hurricane, and Curtiss Junior.

enough, however, the firm took an unknowing step in the wrong direction when it undertook the mass manufacture of troop gliders from 1942 on. Although Waco prospered with its CG-4 design, which was built under license by no less than fifteen other manufacturers, it lost its driving edge in the aircraft market. At the end of the war, it had under development only one type, the all-metal, pusher propeller, strut-braced "Aristocraft," a radical airplane that clearly failed to meet the performance challenge of either the Bonanza or the Ryan Navion. Without any subsidiary line to back up production, the Waco Aircraft Company went out of business, to the distress of its fans everywhere.

The name lives on, however, in the many biplanes that are restored and flown around the country, and in the two wonderful examples at the Garber Facility.

The first is a genuine Waco 9, handsomely done in red and black—an airplane that has already done a tour of duty in the old Exhibition Flight Gallery at the Museum and now sits comfortably amongst the equally distinguished company in Building 24. Its "Millerized" OX-5 engine is cool, awaiting only fuel and oil and a strong right arm to start it. (OX-5 engines were not noted for their reliability. Over the barnstorming years certain conversions came about that improved them, and an OX-5 to which the Miller rocker arm conversion had been applied was a highly desirable item. It was not unlike sending your 1949 Mercury coupe to George Barris's shop for customization.)

The Waco 9 started life in May 1927 with the manufacturer's serial number 389; it apparently had only one accident, when pilot Ford Bott piled it up on July 29, 1928, cracking the spars in the right upper and lower wings, tearing up the landing gear, and doing some injury to the fuselage but none to the pilot or passenger. Subsequently, it moved through a series of owners, sometimes staying out of license for long periods, but always somehow getting the reprieve that many other aircraft of its period did not. In September 1960, it was sold to Marion L. McClure, of Bloomington, Illinois, who flew it for a number of years until the airport he operated from made it illegal to fly airplanes without tail wheels or brakes from the field. This bureaucratic idiocy coincided with a mutual desire by Clayton J. Brukner, the original sparkplug of the Waco firm, and the National Air and Space Museum to have a "Nine" in the collection. Brukner generously made the necessary arrangements with both McClure and the Museum, and the lovely, unrestored Waco entered history.

The Waco 9's stablemate is a beautiful Waco U1C, the first of the really cosmetic Waco cabin planes. The transformation from open cockpit to cabin plane previously mentioned had, in truth, been quite austere, and it wasn't until the 1933 U1C emerged that Waco took the time to do a little stretching and a little fairing to make the basically handsome aircraft actually quite dashing. The Waco firm went all the way, installing wonderfully comfortable seats, excellent insulation, and oversize windows for improved visibility. Powered by a seven-cylinder Continental R-670 engine, the U1C was capable of a top speed of 140 mph, and could cruise for almost four hours at 125 mph. The Waco was a working airplane, but it was also a preeminent toy, and models were sold both to oil companies and to playboys.

Unlike most of the aircraft of the time, the Waco was dressed up at the factory with things that normally cost extra, including such eye catchers as wheel pants or the sexy close-fitting cowl, which had sporty, streamlined bumps over the rocker arm fittings. If you wanted to doll it up with further extras, such exotic items as Edo floats, metal propeller, or a variety of radio equipment were also available.

The first owner of the Waco was Frank K. Jackson, then of Oakland, California, who purchased serial number 3715 in March 1933. The last owner was John A. Masek, of Casper, Wyoming, who owned four aircraft for patrolling oil pipelines, and who used the Waco for that purpose. It was flown to Andrews Air Force Base on December 5, 1979, and then turned over to the Museum, filling a long-felt need. It is at Silver Hill now, but you can almost sense its readiness to take off again to follow some pipeline through the Wyoming countryside, or, if need be, to take Smiling Jack up for one last border patrol.

9

The Villains of Silver Hill

I t usually takes a great deal before pilots come to absolutely hate an aircraft they fly, particularly if they are able to log a reasonable amount of time in it. The sleek but heavy Republic F-84, the fat and ugly Fairchild C-119, or the fatter and uglier Curtiss SB2C-4, all have hordes of detractors among people who have not flown them, but still retain a loyal following among the pilots who have.

There is something about familiarity, even with airplanes that don't have the best performance, or even the best manners, that allows pilots to become tolerant and finally affectionate toward their wayward mounts. You compensate for the bad factors and take advantage of the good, ultimately gaining a perverse pride in being able to make an airplane that is generally regarded by others as a monster fly well.

But there were a few aircraft whose characteristics were so bad, for whatever reason, that no pilots enjoyed flying them. They were either so demanding, so dangerous, or so treacherous that there was no way to live long enough to become familiar with them and learn to love them. Silver Hill has its share of these.

Nazi Desperation Weapons

Gathered at Silver Hill is a collection of German warbirds large enough to warm the heart of any Oberst equivalents to the colonels of the Confederate Air Force. Some, like the Junkers Ju 388, are obviously efficient aircraft from a sound lineage, fully equivalent to Allied counterparts. Others are like the Horten flying-wing design, the Gotha Go 229 pre-production prototype, which promised good performance but was not completed by the end of the war.

But some are villains, pure and simple, menacing in appearance, apparently illogical in design, black-hearted, and for the most part lethal in operation not to the Allies but to the Germans themselves. We'll look at three of these, the volatile, explosive, egg-shaped Messerschmitt Me 163 Komet; the tiny, aptly named Bachem Ba 349 Natter (Viper); and the Heinkel He 162 Volksjaeger. Then there will be just time for a brief look at two Japanese equivalents, the Ohka kamikaze rocket plane and the Nakajima Ki-115 throw-away fighter.

All of these aircraft were tiny, the largest, the Messerschmitt, spanning under 31 feet, and the smallest, the Natter, less than 12 feet. Placed next to even the smallest current jet fighter today, the Northrop F-5E, they seem almost toylike.

Yet during the closing days of the war, when the Allies first became aware of their existence, they loomed large on the aviation horizon, out of all proportion to their real or potential importance.

Although they were all vastly different designs, stemming from totally different sources, they had one sad common thread: each was intended to make up for its home country's lack of materials, and lack of time, with the lives of its pilots. All were pilot-killers, for they attempted to achieve performance standards beyond that of conventional aircraft, with engines that were not yet developed or with tactics that stipulated death.

Oddly enough, two of the lot were reported to be pleasant to fly. These were the Messerschmitt Me 163 and the Natter; but while pleasant to fly, they had engines with notoriously dangerous characteristics, and landings were either difficult in the case of the Me 163, or in the case of the Natter, not even intended.

Let's take a look at them individually.

The Messerschmitt Me 163 Komet

If you judge only by performance, the Messerschmitt Me 163 had almost everything going for it. It was the fastest fighter to see combat in World War II, with a level top speed capability of 596 mph, a service ceiling of 54,000 feet, an initial climb rate of 16,000 feet per minute (remember that the Mustang's initial climb rate was about 3,500 feet per minute), absolutely lovely flight characteristics, and a heavy armament of two 30mm cannon. An early version of the aircraft had exceeded 630 mph in 1941, so the Komet, as it was called officially, was a magnificent advance in technology.

In other areas, unfortunately for the Germans, and particularly for the poor pilots who volunteered to fly the airplane, there were some terrible deficiencies that could be made up only in blood. These produced operational difficulties that reflected the almost inevitable result of pushing too far forward in some areas of technology while not being able to bring other necessary areas along as rapidly.

Most of the problems stemmed from the volatile nature of the fuels used in the Walter rocket engine that was the heart of the aircraft, but others stemmed from the general conditions of the time, which included material shortages, continual bombing, lack of time to train, and so on.

The Me 163 was a classic engineering case study of trade-offs. The whole process of designing a fighter aircraft is one of bargaining and suboptimizing, trading off the things you can dispense with, or cannot avoid, against the things you want. If speed is your goal more than anything else, then you require streamlining and high power. Against these considerations, though, there are the needs for pilot's vision, armament, bomb gear, etc., that interfere with streamlining, and fuel-consumption factors that offset the quest for highest power. If you want maneuverability, you want a reasonable wing area and wing loading; but this runs counter to the requirements for speed, and for carrying a decent load of fuel and equipment.

So it went with the Messerschmitt Me 163, the joint product of two individual lines of development and the endless series of compromises needed to create a useful interceptor.

The airframe was developed originally by Dr. Alexander Lippisch, and the radical rocket plant by Dr. Helmut Walter, who had been an engineer employed by the German Army to develop antiaircraft aiming devices. A contract had been placed with the German Aviation Experimental Establishment for the development of a small liquid-fuel rocket to be used in test flying, and the success of this and other Walter engines led inevitably to the idea of its use in a combat aircraft.

Because the early development state of the engine produced only a relatively low thrust, it was apparent that a small, very well streamlined aircraft would have to be used. Dr. Lippisch's airframes immediately came to mind, and it was proposed that one of his flying-

The Messerschmitt Me 163B
Komet—an operational
rocket fighter with a speed in
excess of 600 mph. The tailless flying wing derived from
the designs of Dr. Alexander
Lippisch, who had created
over ninety different flying-
wing types, and saw thirty of
them actually fly. This is a
captured specimen.
(USAF Photo)

The Komet did not have an auspicious career, due to troubles with the engine, training, and the vast
Allied air superiority. It was a formidable threat, however, for if the Germans had been able to employ the aircraft in great numbers (and they were relatively inexpensive to build), losses might have
become prohibitive. This is gun-camera film from an Allied fighter. The Me 163 was very vulnerable
after it had exhausted its fuel and had to land. (USAF Photo)

wing–type aircraft be built to handle the rocket motor. Lippisch, quite coincidentally, had had a long interest in rocket aircraft himself.

The result was the DFS 194 (from the German acronym for German Research Institute for Sailplanes), which was designed to take the Walter rocket engine of about 600 pounds of thrust, roughly the same amount produced by the modern Williams jet engine that powers the Air Launched Cruise Missile.

The DFS 194 attained about 340 mph in 1940, and exhibited generally excellent characteristics. The Messerschmitt company was called in to provide the necessary secure design and production facilities, and this led to the slightly larger Messerschmitt Me 163, a much more sophisticated aircraft than the DFS 194. The integration of the Lippisch team into Messerschmitt's production effort served to prove that personalities can be as volatile as rocket fuel, and often quite as explosive.

The terrible engineering logic of design requirements reflected the personal difficulties. The Walter engine, even after development, was going to be able to develop about 3,750 pounds of thrust, consuming fuel at a prodigious rate. This meant that at least 336 gallons of the two necessary volatile fuels had to be carried. In addition there was the usual cockpit equipment, oxygen, radios, armament, and so on that had to be installed. To achieve the desired performance, the overall size of the aircraft must be very small, with a wingspan of 30 feet 7 inches and a length of 18 feet 8 inches. With all the fuel and equipment to be squeezed into the tiny fuselage, there was no longer any room for a landing gear, so the aircraft had to take off on a jettisonable trolley and land on a skid.

Similarly, the small size of the aircraft reduced the number of guns it could carry. As 20mm cannon had been found not to be very effective against the big Allied bombers, two 30mm Mk 108 cannon were installed. These had an enormous punch but a relatively low rate of fire. As a result, at the tremendous closure rates of as much as 750 mph in a head-on attack (and 450 in a tail attack), the German pilot could expect to get off only a few rounds.

Perhaps even more detrimental to the employment of the aircraft was its short duration—the pilot could expect to attain only seven to twelve minutes of flying time, depending upon how expertly he husbanded the fuel by cutting off the engine and gliding. With the existing German radar network, it was difficult to muster the attacking Me 163s in exactly the right position to make an effective attack.

And the very nature of the fuels used by the Me 163 posed overwhelming physical and psychological problems. The engine obtained its thrust by combining two fuels in its rocket chamber, where they spontaneously ignited to create a sustained burning, building up pressure rapidly to create the thrust. One fuel was called *C-Stoff*, a mixture of alcohol, hydrazine hydrate, and water; the other was called *T-Stoff*, and consisted of hydrogen peroxide.

Handled correctly, which meant an absolute exclusion of one from the other until their introduction in the rocket chamber, and with good equipment, the fuels worked perfectly to provide a very powerful thrust effect. But they were potentially fatal if any mistake were made, if any seal failed, or if any rupture of lines occurred. The fuel was extraordinarily corrosive, and could consume a human body, bones, teeth, and all, in minutes. The engines were still in their early stages, and even while being used operationally had a tendency to "flame out" under certain negative conditions. If the pilot was unable to restart the engine in flight—a task in itself not without hazard—he had to attempt to land with a load of fuel aboard. Overweight, and thus needing to fly faster than usual into the minuscule fields the Germans had to use, the chances were that he would hit hard and explode.

Still, with all of this, the Germans had no problem obtaining pilots to man the units equipping the aircraft. The first operational sorties of the Messerschmitt Me 163Bs, the only production version of the aircraft, took place in early May 1944. It was not effective, nor were most of the sorties that took place on a sporadic basis over the next ten months. The Luftwaffe encountered fuel shortages, handling problems, and pilot-training difficulties that kept Me 163 activity at a low level.

The Allies, through their extensive intelligence reports on the aircraft, were naturally concerned and apprehensive that the rocket fighter might suddenly be put into operation in large quantities. The assumption was made that the best way to combat it was to destroy the fuel supplies on the ground, and this was accomplished with major attacks on the I. G. Farben plants where hydrazine hydrate was produced. In the air, the Komets flew the same gauntlet of .50 caliber bullets that other attacking German fighters did, but they flew it faster, and were a much smaller target.

Allied fighters could not engage a Komet during its climb, or during a diving attack; but they were able to bounce it on the glide back to home base. The usual Me 163 defense was to dive, and with its high Mach capability it was often able to get away. But the pilot was still faced with the problem of finding somewhere to land as soon as the excess speed from the dive had bled off. The nervous state of a pilot who had survived a rocket takeoff, an attack through a bomber stream of B-17s, a dogfight with eager young Yank pilots, and a screaming power-off dive to a fog-ridden countryside, only to contemplate landing his heavy glider on a short field on a tiny skid with practically nonexistent shock-absorbing capabilities, must have been something to behold. Added to all this was the possibility that he had some residual fuel lurking around, ready to blow him to kingdom come. One wonders how on earth the Luftwaffe was able to find volunteers.

The limited range of the Me 163 had forced the Germans to a plan of ringing Germany with Komet bases, about 60 miles apart, so that aircraft could take off from one base, make an attack, then glide down to land at another for refueling and rearming. In the end, the necessary ring of bases had not been completed, and bomber streams could negate the effectiveness of Me 163 opposition simply by flying a dogleg around known bases, keeping out of range of the attackers.

All in all, the Me 163 proved to be far more dangerous to the Germans than it did to the Allies. It was yet another diversion of resources into an unfulfilled project. After six years of effort and millions of marks, the Me 163 faded into oblivion having accounted for perhaps sixteen victories against Allied aircraft, and killing at least that many Germans in training or in combat.

The Museum's aircraft is one of several that was brought to this country for testing after the war. Even though pilots could no doubt have been found to try it, the Army Air Forces decided, quite logically, that it was just too dangerous to fly under power. Some flights were made by towing the Me 163 to altitude, just as the Germans had done early in the test program, to determine its gliding qualities; but in general there was no great enthusiasm for the aircraft in the United States.

The Japanese, who in late 1944 needed an interceptor even more desperately than did the Germans, obtained the manufacturing rights to the Messerschmitt Me 163B and its

At Silver Hill, the Me 163 is an interesting example of mismatched technology. The engine and airframe were far ahead of their time; the cannons, fuel, and systems were primitive in comparison, and greatly compromised the aircraft's utility.

Walter engine. A sample of the aircraft and its engine complete with blueprints was sent to Japan by submarine, but the sub was sunk en route. Nonetheless, the Japanese asked the Mitsubishi firm to create a rocket-powered interceptor based on the available information. The Japanese also built a glider version, to train pilots. The powered prototype crashed on its first flight on July 7, 1945, when its engine failed. The effort went on, but mercifully for the men who would have had to fly them, and especially for the U.S. crews who would have met them in combat, the war ended before any more could be flown.

The Viperous Natter

The Natter surely lived up to its name. A tiny, ugly aircraft, built of non-strategic materials, it was perhaps the least attractive of all Luftwaffe fighters, yet had performance and handling qualities that were better than most. If only it had not been semi-suicidal . . .

There is a tendency on the part of governments to take either past deficiencies or current emergencies out of the hides of their servicemen. In 1944, the Nazis had an ample supply of both deficiencies and emergencies, having failed to develop an effective defensive fighter force, and being systematically pounded into the dust by the combined Allied air offensive. *Something* had to be done to off-set the aerial strength of the Allies, and it had to be done inexpensively and in short order. While there were some technological possibilities at hand, their use was possible only at the sacrifice of the men who would test them and fly them operationally.

With Mustangs camping over Luftwaffe airfields like Southern Highway Patrol cars hiding behind billboards, waiting with relish for the few remaining German fighters to leave their flak-guarded sanctuaries and struggle into the air, and with German territory much diminished by the inexorable pressures from east and west, it became necessary to develop point-defense weapons, which would be

What an ugly airplane. Would you believe that this crude plywood rocket plane was a delight to fly, and was capable of speeds of 495 mph? Those white dots are rockets—24 R4Ms, the deadliest air-to-air weapon that Germany had devised. (USAF Photo)

The equipment to launch the Natter was quite as primitive as the aircraft itself. This was from a country that was defending itself against the United States, Britain, France, Russia, and the rest of the world. Pathetic. (USAF Photo)

launched vertically, and then guided by their human "autopilot" to carry out a one-way attack on the bomber fleets. The rocket engine offered the possibility of a vertical ascent with little chance of interference by Allied fighters. Once at altitude, new rocket weapons promised a fair chance at a kill on the one pass that the limited fuel duration allowed.

It only remained necessary to find pilots brave enough to fly these Roman candles into combat, becoming in essence the guidance system of a missile—the human mind replacing the computers that were not yet available.

In typically efficient German fashion, a competition was held to determine who would build these last-ditch weapons, and three major and one minor company responded. Against competition from Messerschmitt, Junkers and Heinkel, the tiny Bachem Company won, with a semi-expendable vertically launched fighter that was called the Bachem Ba 349—the Natter.

Despite its crude appearance—more like a SAM from Vietnam days than a fighter—the Natter was carefully thought out so that it would be easy to build at small subcontractors, easy to assemble, and easy to recover. Mainte-

The finish on the airplane is better than one might expect for one that required only 1,000 man-hours to complete. The Stub wooden wings were easy to build and quite strong. Note the simple ring sight—shades of World War I. (USAF Photo)

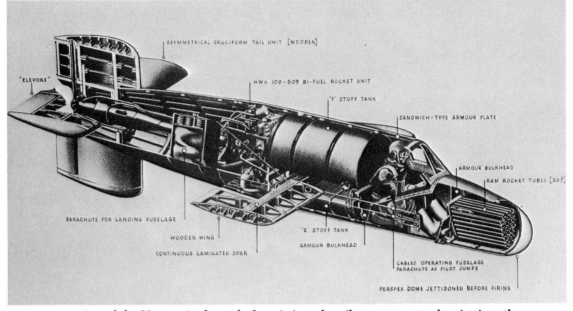

A cut-away view of the Natter. At the end of a mission, the pilot was supposed to jettison the nose-section, and then the rest of the aircraft would be decelerated behind him by means of a parachute, leaving him suspended in space, ready to use his own chute. The engine also was parachuted to the ground for reuse. (USAF Photo)

nance wasn't really a consideration, for these were Kleenex fighters; one blow and they were thrown away.

A tubular fuselage, built of plywood, and split by a slab plywood wing, was divided into three component parts. The first contained the armament, a veritable flak battery of twenty-four 73mm unguided rockets; the second contained the pilot and his primitive instrumentation and controls; the third contained the rocket engine.

Takeoff was by means of a vertical track, and the little 11-foot 9-inch-span plane was lifted by the power of its own 3,750-pound thrust Walter rocket engine, and four Schmidding solid-fuel rockets of 2,640 pounds each, in exactly the same manner that the Saturn boosters would later lift the Space Shuttle. The solid-fuel rockets burned for ten seconds to accelerate the Natter, then dropped away.

With an impressive total thrust of 14,000 pounds, the little Viper would be hurtled into the air, climbing initially on autopilot, for the pilot would be severely bothered by the acceleration G forces. Initial climb rate was better than 36,000 feet per minute, and the Bachem had an operational ceiling of 40,000 feet, where it could cruise for five minutes before making an attack.

Unlike the Me 163, the Natter had no landing problems at all, for it simply didn't land. After an attack, in which the pilot just jettisoned a nose cap over the armament, lined up, fired his rockets, evaded the gunfire of the formation, and then glided away, he would jettison the entire forward section of the cockpit, leaving him sitting out in front as in a Breezy. An automatic sequence then streamed a parachute from the rear of the aircraft, which decelerated the engine section away, literally ejecting itself from the pilot. As a final step in what must have been a nerve-wracking process, the pilot actuated his own parachute for a carefree drop through Mustang-ridden skies. The engine descended under its own parachute, and was recovered also.

Presumably the pilot would hitch a ride back to his base, have a snort of three fingers of *C-Stoff* with a *T-Stoff* chaser, and emerge ready for another sortie.

While the Bachem's propulsion system was under development, and while the manufacturer was setting up the essential subcontracting system that would feed components to final assembly areas, extensive flight testing of an unpowered version took place during October 1944. The engineless, ballasted Natter was towed to about 18,000 feet by a Heinkel He

111, and then released. Given the appalling looks of the aircraft, the crude sub-assemblies from which it was made, and the overall ominous atmosphere of the program, the little Viper glider flew like a champion. The test pilot called it superior to any German single-seat fighter in its handling characteristics, and in a glide he achieved speeds up to 435 mph.

The next step in the program was a series of unmanned vertical launches, and these worked fairly well, given that the booster rockets were themselves a developmental item.

The first manned flight, however, was a tragedy. The aircraft, piloted by *Leutnant* Lother Seibert, started off normally, but at about 500-feet altitude the canopy was seen to come off; the airplane went inverted, still continuing its climb, and then dove into the ground, killing Seibert. It was presumed that the pilot had been incapacitated when the canopy flew off.

Undeterred, the testing program went on, and there were reportedly at least seven additional successful manned flights. Both the Luftwaffe and the SS, which had obtained control of the vengeance and wonder weapons programs, placed production orders for the Natter, which was going to stud the approach route to Germany. But time ran out as Allied armies completed the land battles, and the Natter was not employed in combat, to the immense relief of its potential pilots.

The Natter was launched straight up, with rocket boost and a launching stand, just like the Space Shuttle. One wonders what survivors of this program would think about Cape Canaveral–type procedures and equipment. (USAF Photo)

The disassembled Natter, showing the pilot's compartment and the utterly crude but effective control system. (USAF Photo)

The Heinkel He 162— The People's Fighter

The Volksjaeger got its start as the Natter did, in desperation and wild hope. The success of the Messerschmitt Me 262 had finally convinced everyone that the only hope the Germans had of obtaining any kind of parity in the air was by use of jet aircraft in quantity. Because strategic materials were increasingly scarce, and because manpower was equally short, the idea of a lightweight single-engine jet fighter evolved, to be manufactured of such materials as were available and in such quantity that repairs and maintenance would not be necessary. It was a curious return to the very idea with which Germany had started World War II, and which had proved to be so falacious.

The Nazification of German industrial management had become almost absolute by 1944, under Albert Speer, the sauve and articulate spokesman of Nüremberg, who somehow managed to make the whole shabby Nazi apparatus plausible, and Dr. Otto Sauer, a draco-nian super-X–type manager who made Peter the Great seem like Peter Drucker. A proposal went out to German manufacturers for a Volksjaeger, a People's Fighter, whose performance would exceed that of contemporary Allied fighters, but would be powered by only one jet engine and be built largely of non-strategic materials. Other stipulations included the use of 30mm cannon, a flight duration of at least thirty minutes, and relatively good short-field takeoff and landing performance.

The Commanding General of Fighters, *Generalleutnant* Adolf Galland, and Willy Messerschmitt immediately rebelled against the suggestion that resources should be devoted to anything other than Messerschmitt Me 262 production. The Me 262, after years of labor, was finally coming into operational use and proving increasingly successful. Conventional engineers agreed with the well-respected Galland, but they were no match for

The Heinkel He 162 Volksjaeger at a display of captured equipment at what is now Wright-Patterson Air Force Base. Behind the He 162 is a huge Junkers Ju 290, which was flown non-stop across the ocean with a booby-trap bomb in its wing. The bomb did not go off and was discovered after landing. (USAF Photo)

The Heinkel HF-280 was a very advanced aircraft for its day, and if it had had room for more internal fuel might well have been put into production instead of the Messerschmitt Me 262.

the true believers, the fanatics, the rarefied group of Nazis who in late 1944 could still pretend to believe that there was a chance to win the war. Not only would Volksjaegers darken Nazi skies—production of 4,000 aircraft per month was planned—but there would also be the necessary pilots and maintenance men to use them.

The pilots would come, to Goering's intoxicated delight, from the ranks of the Hitler Jugend. Young boys, just turned sixteen, would be given primary training on gliders, and then turned loose in the Heinkel He 162 to pick up their operational experience in the best school possible—flying in the Mustang- and Thunderbolt-strewn skies of Germany. It was worse than insanity, it was an obscenity. Maintenance was not to be a factor, for after five hours' flying the plane would be replaced; so, too, would the pilots come and go.

But such was the discipline of the Germans that they damn near pulled it off. If there had been some lull in the war, some diplomatic miracle or simple exhaustion of the Allied

A Heinkel He 162 under test at Edwards Air Force Base. Famous aerobatic pilot Bob Hoover tested these aircraft, and this might well be him at the controls. (USAF Photo)

The design and construction of the Volksjaeger in just ninety days was extraordinary, but even more so was the remarkable mass production effort that was put into effect in the very last months of the war. He 162 production was scheduled to reach 4,000 per month by March 1945. These fuselage assemblies were built in a salt mine; one hopes that the inspecting Allied soldiers were aware that the He 162 had an ejection seat. (USAF Photo)

armies that gave Germany a six-month breathing space, the Heinkel He 162 would have been produced in vast numbers.

Somehow all the best of German ability was assembled for this futile last-ditch effort. The initial contract for the Heinkel He 162 was signed on September 24, 1944. On December 6, the strange-looking little fighter, with its short wingspan and bulky BMW jet engine perched on top of its fuselage like a lengthy carbuncle, made its first flight.

Simultaneously with the design effort, a massive program of development and production was put into effect. The fuselages were built of light metal and were to be furnished by the Junkers and Heinkel plants, the wings and other associated wooden parts were to be built by smaller subcontractors. The entire program was orchestrated under what today would be called a systems management concept, with final assembly taking place in three factories. The Heinkel plant at Marienehe and the Junkers plant at Berburg would each produce 1,000 aircraft a month, while a modern plant at Nordhausen would produce 2,000.

The flight testing was not without incident; the prototype broke up during its first demonstration flight, killing its pilot, when the bonding of the wooden wing failed. Yet such was the determination of the people backing the program that the accident had no effect whatever upon development or production.

The actual fact was that the Heinkel He 162, no matter how simple in comparison to other jet fighters, was *still* itself a jet fighter, with all of the complexity inherent in the new area of

The Museum's airplane at three stages in its career. The first photo shows it during the Air Force test program; the second shows it in storage at Park Ridge; the third shows it at Silver Hill today.

aerodynamics, the problems associated with the high speeds, and such standard testing problems as harmonization of controls, testing of armament packages, and so on. There was a continuous stream of essential changes, ranging from the addition of anhedral wingtips for stability to the enlargement of the tail surfaces, or from the substitution of 20mm cannon for 30mm cannon that shook the nose apart to the provision of new wing fillets to smooth out airflow over the empennage. Despite all of this, and despite the virtually continuous bombing and strafing of the transportation network that supported the Volksjaeger's subcontracting system, the production program moved forward at a tremendous pace.

Test pilots soon discovered that the new Heinkel fighter was not going to be suitable for children to learn on, or suitable in fact for anyone but an accomplished pilot. It had an excellent performance, but it was tricky to fly and the thought of a fuzzy-faced sixteen-year-old, no matter how rabid a Nazi, transitioning directly from primary gliders was impossible.

There was, however, another source of pilots in Germany at this time. As it became more and more impossible to operate transports and bombers because of the fuel shortage, whole squadrons of pilots became available for retraining into the jet fighter program.

If there had been some sort of unforeseen lull in the war, if, for example, the Russians and the Western Allies had both overreached their supply lines, and for six months rested and regrouped, the Heinkel He 162 might have become a disturbing element in the German skies. Given such a breathing space, it might have been possible to retrain the veteran pilots on the He 162, and with fifteen or twenty hours' experience, these pilots would have been able to give a good account of themselves.

For a long time it was thought that the little Heinkel jet did not engage in combat, but there are recent findings among the personal logs of German pilots that at least a small number of dogfights occurred. Some Allied accounts note that the He 162 could engage a Mustang with some success, and one German Volksjaeger pilot is supposed to have scored nine kills in the airplane.

Fortunately for the allies, and for the Germans too, the lull did not occur, and most of the completed He 162s were captured on abandoned German airfields.

England, the United States, and presumably Russia flight-tested the aircraft after the war. Test pilots found it to be spirited and challenging, but there was no thought of development. It was a dying effort of a dying country, and the example at Silver Hill is more of a monument to folly than to aircraft design.

The Japanese Villains

Americans brought up on World War II motion pictures are convinced that all Japanese pilots wore funny goggles, and that their aircraft had slanted windscreens. In a dive, of course, they gave off an unusual hissing sound.

Nothing could be further from the truth, for most Japanese aircraft possessed elegant lines and remarkable beauty, by-products of their designers' quest for range and maneuverability. Even the villainous aircraft we shall consider here do not have the inherent thuglike looks of the Natter.

The fact that the Japanese turned to kamikaze aircraft like the Ohka and the Ki-115 is somewhat more logical than similar German efforts, far more in keeping with the Western concept of Oriental mentality in the 1940s. The war had turned very much against Japan, and America's technological and quantitative superiority grew every day. There was literally only one way to redress the balance, and that was through the sacrifice of young pilots, who would fly their bomb-laden aircraft to its target and their death.

The ideal kamikaze aircraft, then, was one that was cheap and easy to produce, could carry an adequate bombload, and had a reasonable chance of reaching its target. The Japanese, with the Ohka and the Ki-115, succeeded on every count except the last.

An Ohka 22 en route to the United States along with other captured Japanese equipment. (U.S. Navy)

The Ohka or Baka?*

The Ohka, or Cherry blossom, bloomed from the very heart of a Japanese fightingman. Ensign Mitsuo Ohta, a patriot who could clearly perceive the deteriorating war situation, conceived the idea of a radical new suicide weapon, one whose small size and great speed would permit it to penetrate the U.S. aerial screens and score effective hits on naval targets. Ohta, who was a transport pilot and not an engineer, was able to obtain sufficient professional help with his concept to receive approval from the Navy, which turned to the Yokosuka Naval Depot for professional engineering help.

Ohta had envisaged a small, low-wing rocket plane, which would be carried to the combat zone by a mother plane, and then dive toward its target under rocket power. The entire nose of the plane would be a warhead; there were to be no provisions for escape. It was literally a suicide weapon, unlike the German manned V-1 test counterparts, which offered, theoretically at least, a slim chance for survival.

* Baka was a pejorative name meaning "Fool," applied somewhat callously at the end of the war to the weapon that seemed to make so little sense to Americans.

Under the professional development of the Yokosuka engineers, the Ohka received the experimental designation MXY7 Ohka, Navy Suicide Attacker, and was entered into full-scale production before testing had been completed.

Fortunately for the Japanese, testing revealed that the little aircraft was not unpleasant to fly, and could achieve a speed of over 400 mph under power.

The first production series, the Model 11, had a 1,646-pound warhead and three rockets that delivered about 1,760 pounds of thrust for a period of eight to ten seconds.

The wings and tail surfaces were made of molded plywood, and were fabric-covered for a smooth finish. The all-aluminum fuselage was of typical aircraft semi-monocoque construction, and contained the 2,645-pound warhead. There was a simple cockpit with a bubble-type canopy; three rocket engines were fitted in the rear, with provisions for two additional engines, one on each wing.

The austere cockpit contained only four instruments—a compass, an airspeed indicator that read from 100 to 680 mph, an altimeter, and an inclinometer, a primitive type of turn

An Ohka 22; this version featured a jet engine for power. Note the Japanese copy of a Me 163 in the background. (S. P. Johnston)

The simple, almost primitive cockpit of the Ohka. It was literally a flying bomb. (USAF Photo)

indicator. The poor pilot aimed himself at the target by means of a ring sight reminiscent of World War I.

The wheezing Betty bombers could lug the Ohka along at about 175 mph, absolute sitting ducks for any passing Hellcat. If all went well, however, the Betty would sneak to within about 50 miles of the target and jettison the Ohka with its brave pilot. It would assume a glide angle of about 5 degrees nose-down, and begin a 230-mph drop toward the target. About 3 miles out, the rocket engines were switched on and the little aircraft would accelerate to nearly 500 mph, rendering it, at last, relatively safe from Allied fighters. The final portion of the trip, the dive into the target against the avalanche of antiaircraft shells, was at an angle of 50 degrees, and at airspeeds that approached 600 mph.

Despite the colossal losses inflicted upon the Ohkas, primarily while they were still connected to the parental Betty, they were a weapon that appealed to the Japanese psyche, and further developments, including jet-powered versions, were under way when the war ended.

More than 750 were built, but most were lost in transit or destroyed on the ground. The best records indicate that no more than sixty Ohkas ever actually made an attack, and the rumors of the cowardly kamikaze Ohka pilot with a fifty-mission crush to his hat are absolutely unfounded.

This is how it was supposed to be done, illustrated with U.S. Navy models. The Betty mother plane drops the Ohka, and peels away; the Ohka then dives to its doom—and presumably that of a U.S. ship.

The Museum's Ohka, hanging in Building 10. What a futile way to fight a war!

The Nakajima Ki-115 looked more like an advanced trainer than a flying bomb. It was very crudely made, and the young pilots were intended to have only the minimum training necessary for them to somehow evade the hordes of Allied fighters and fly straight into the side of a ship. (Edgar Diegen via Dick Seely)

The Japanese Saber

Aesthetically far less appealing, the Nakajima Ki-115 Tsurugi (saber) was an equally desperate attempt by the Japanese to solve the fuel, pilot, and material shortage problems by the use of a suicide weapon. Instead of being carried by a Betty, it would simply be a one way, relatively low-speed fighter, equipped to take off and fly a comparatively short distance from mainland Japan to strike the enemy.

Of fairly conventional appearance, the Ki-115 had some features not obvious at first glance. Built from composite materials—fabric-covered wooden tail surfaces, a fuselage of steel, a cowling of tin—and fitted with a jettisonable non-retractable landing gear, the Ki-115 could carry a 1,754-pound bomb semi-recessed in its center section. Reconditioned engines, Nakajima Ha-35s of 1,150 horsepower, were the standard powerplants, although the airplane was designed to use any engine from 800 to 1,350 horsepower.

The first flight tests of the Ki-115 began in March 1945, when the U.S. Navy was knocking at Japan's door. But despite the urgent need for

the aircraft, results were disappointing: it was difficult to taxi, and visibility was very poor. Redesign was necessary, yet the aircraft was put into production, with some 105 being built by the end of the war. None, so far as is known, were employed in combat.

It's rather interesting to speculate on what the modern generation of Japanese youngsters would think of a demand by their government to enter combat with such a pathetic weapon. Surely they are no less brave today than they were in 1944, but they've been conditioned by more than a generation of transistor, Toyota, and tofu prosperity. Somehow it is hard to imagine the studious young computer engineer one meets here in the United States wrapping a Hinomaru marked scarf about his head and embracing the fatal choice offered the cream of Japanese youth in 1944. One certainly hopes that this generation is smarter—but that it nevertheless respects the bravery of the youth of another time and another culture.

Many things about the Tsurugi were hasty improvisations; the landing gear was originally without shock absorbers, because the Japanese thought it wouldn't be landing after a mission. The pilots quickly found out that no shocks made the airplane almost impossible to taxi, and even suicide pilots had to taxi out to take off. (Edgar Diegen via Richard Seely)

Construction was composite, with steel and tin used in the fuselage, aluminum and wood in the wings. (Edgar Diegen)

The fact that the Japanese were serious about the Tsurugi is evident from this line-up of aircraft awaiting completion at war's end. A poor photograph, but indicative of the extent of effort involved. (Richard Seely)

10

Ghost Airplanes and Airmen

So far we've covered only about a fifth of the airplanes at the Garber Facility. There are another 120 or so types, each with their own histories, each backed by the stories of the men and women who designed, built, and flew them.

Just a sampling from the alphabetical listing evokes a whole series of provocative ideas. What of the Japanese Aichi B7A1 Grace, that lovely gull-winged torpedo bomber, a 360-mph winner that clearly demonstrated how competitive the Japanese aircraft industry had become by 1944? Or the Bell P-63, that mid-engine, laminar-flow wing pinball machine that was unloved by the United States but highly favored by the Russians? Or the Heinkel He 219A night fighter, the "Owl," which had to be manufactured almost surreptitiously because Heinkel was no longer in favor, but which had some remarkable features and performance? Or two other exotic Japanese types, the Nakajima Kikka, the first Japanese jet fighter, which looked like a three-quarter scale Messerschmitt Me 262, and the plane intended to bomb the Panama Canal, the Aichi M6A Seiran?

The first American heavy bomber, one that started a dynasty, the Martin GMB (Glenn Martin Bomber)—an airplane that shaped American airpower for more than a decade.

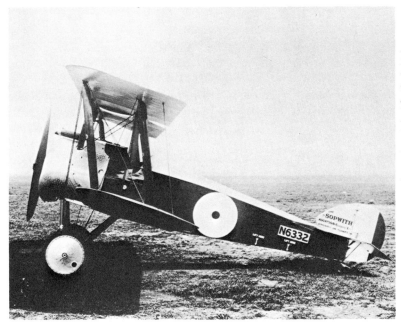

A famous aircraft long before Snoopy, the Sopwith Camel shot down more German airplanes than any other Allied aircraft during World War I. It probably killed more Allied pilots than the Germans did, too, for it was "a fierce little rasper" that could snap into a spin on takeoff. Some sources say that students transitioning to Camels had a 30 percent loss rate.

Equally famous, equally deadly to friend and foe alike, the Fokker Dr I triplane suffered from structural difficulties that caused many crashes. Still it was regarded as the most maneuverable fighter of World War I, able to "climb like a lift."

The German Gotha received a fame and a notoriety far beyond its actual value in combat. It was successful over England where the Zeppelins were not.

The list could go on and on. What tales could be told about Reginald Denny's remarkable target plane, the TDD-2, or Northrop N-1M of the three flying wings, of the Lippisch DM.1, and the Horten brothers' Gotha Go 229. There are ancient gliders like the Martin or the Montgomery, or classics like the Franklin PS-2 Eaglet, Frank Hawks's old mount, the Bowlus–duPont Falcon, or powered versions like the Nelson Dragonfly. For the automotive-minded, there are those valiant attempts at "plane-cars" like the Fulton Airphibian, the Waterman Whatsit, and their near cousins the Stout Skycar and the Stearman-Hammond Model Y. If you are looking for fighting machines, the Junkers Ju 388, the Messerschmitt Me 410, the North American F-100D, or the Arado Ar 196A, a survivor of the German cruiser *Prinz Eugen*, should suit.

And should you be into kinky airplanes, there's the sadistic Crosley-Mignet Flying Flea, the most innocuous-looking man-killer in history; the Avro Canada VZ-9V flying saucer; the (Alister)* Crowley Hydro Air Vehicle; or the Princeton Air Scooter.

Behind each of these aircraft was a team of

* Just kidding, folks.

men and women; they were all designed, financed, marketed, built, and flown by people to whom they were the most important thing in the world at the time. I like to think that the shades of these creative people came back to visit their children, their products, and that if a Karilian image could be obtained, it would show a vast gathering of energetic, industrious, innovative presences.

And beyond all of the aircraft at Silver Hill, there are many more that should be there. For our purposes here, these could be divided into two classes: those that do exist in the world today and conceivably could be obtained; and those that no longer exist but should be represented, if only by their ghosts.

Available, Somewhere—and Wanted

There are certain choice aircraft, real pioneers or classics, which would be right at home at Silver Hill, but are jealously guarded by their present proud possessors. We'd like to have a Seversky P-35, and there is a definite possibility, since the Air Force Museum has two, and we are on excellent terms with that wonderful institution. We need a Sopwith Camel; there are at least seven original Camels

The English Handley Page design was adopted for manufacture in America. More than 100 were built, but only a handful were actually assembled and flown.

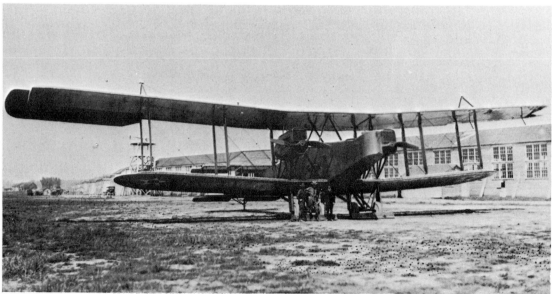

Not a famous airplane in its own right, but important for its technological contribution, is the Boeing B-9. Boeing expected to win big contracts with its cantilever monoplane, retractable gear airplane, which was faster than current fighters; but only seven of the aircraft were ordered. (USAF Photo)

This Boeing P-12 is remembered by its pilots as being the most enjoyable airplane ever flown. Only the Sopwith Pup of World War I and the P-12 have almost universal approval as a pilot's airplane. (Robert Cavanagh)

Repressed by the Versailles Treaty, German aircraft manufacturers resorted to subterfuge and to building in other countries. This Dornier "Wal" is similar to many used for record-setting flights all through the 1920s and early 1930s.

This is the airplane that beat Boeing out of a contract. The Martin B-10, shown here during its airmail service, was an outstanding military aircraft, the joint product of research at Wright Field and the Martin Company.

The Gee Bee Super Sportster racers set an image of the golden age of flight that time will never dim. Small, hot, and dangerous, they captured the soul of the American airplane-racing fan.

Today's Gee Bees are mostly ex-North American P-51 Mustangs, but few are so finely tuned as *Jeannie*, in which Skip Holm won the Unlimited Class at the 1981 Reno National Championship Air Races. (Birch Matthews)

in the world, and perhaps someday one will be loaned or donated.

A Gloster Meteor would neatly round out our collection of early jet aircraft, and there are almost forty of these in existence, some in private hands. It would also be great to have a Hawker Typhoon or Tempest to bridge the gap between the Spitfire and the Meteor.

There are others, too, like the Curtiss P-6E, or the Curtiss P-36, each of which only one known example exists in the world, and which we are not likely to get.

There is a need for a better collection of contemporary aircraft. These, we hope, will come in time, when we have the proper space at an airfield to receive and exhibit them. Our own proud Boeing 707, the most important jet prototype in existence, should be brought back from its desert storage to a place of pride in the nation's capital, and it should have as stablemates a Boeing B-47, B-52, and KC-135, for these aircraft formed the foundation of America's jet age.

Similarly, a Concorde is a clear requirement, and one that in all probability will be fulfilled in the next few years. A 747 is also needed, as is the Space Shuttle *Enterprise*. A host of other aircraft, representative of today's modern business jets, should be brought in— Citations, Gulfstreams, Falcons, and so on. In time, no doubt, these needs will be met.

Not Available—But Badly Wanted

Many an illustrious type, manufactured by the dozens or even the hundreds, are no longer available anywhere, thanks to the ravages of the salvage yard and the inattention of their owners to the future. Other aircraft were one of a kind, and perished in an accident, or were left to molder anonymously at some airfield until a public-spirited citizens' group swept them off to the trash bin. We'd like to have some of these, too, and as they are completely unavailable, we can desire as much as we wish, without any regard for movement, for storage, or for cost, as they are only dreams.

What would be nice to have? Well, certainly a Martin GMB bomber from World War I. This important airplane has completely disappeared from the scene, which is especially sad as the Museum once had one in its collection. It was returned, for some obscure reason to Army storage and was reportedly destroyed in a flood at Bolling Field. A Keystone bomber, one of those wonderful assemblages of wings, struts, and engines, would serve as a stepping stone from the Martin to, say, the Boeing B-9, an equally unavailable type.

And as there are no storage or maintenance problems with wishes, we should just as well have a Dornier DO-X, that giant twelve-engine monstrosity that had so many good ideas

What a combination of lithe, lean record-setters and the ponderous Dornier DO-X, the largest plane ever built at the time. The planes in the foreground are, respectively, a Bellanca C.F., the Liberty, Wiley Post's Lockheed Vega *Winnie Mae*, and Russ Boardman's Bellanca C.F. Note that the twelve engines of the DO-X have been removed.

The Seversky P-35A (actually in this case a Swedish EP-106) is an aircraft the Museum would like to have to round out its collection.

The *Los Angeles* had a long and useful service career and was ultimately dismantled. It is shown here nearly dismantling itself; the dirigible ultimately rose to an absolutely vertical position, then settled back down. (USAF Photo)

and such marginal performance. Similarly, a dirigible, the *Graf Zeppelin* or the *Los Angeles* or the R-34 or the R-100, all airships of good memory, would be welcome. (Spare us the *Hindenburg*, the *Roma*, the *Akron*, the *Macon*, or the *Shenandoah*, please.)

Small airplanes of the untouchable past would be desirable, too. A Gee Bee Super Sportster, the R-1 if possible, would be a must, as would the Verville Sperry R-3. There are lots of Fokker Dr. Is in replica form about, but none of the genuine article; as long as we're dreaming, we may as well select Manfred von Richthofen's own 425/17, in which he was shot down on April 21, 1918.

Again, this list could go on and on, for everyone would have favorite additions. Why not add your own?

And in many ways, Silver Hill, the Garber Facility, does make the list possible, for if these particular dreams cannot be fulfilled, their counterparts can. Although the actual airplanes cannot be represented there, their cousins or their descendants can evoke nearly the same dreams as the originals might have done. Silver Hill provides a spiritual home for all of these aircraft, and for the ideas and the talents of the people who created them. The people who work at Silver Hill are the inheritors and the preservers of every pioneer whose product is already there, or will be there, or should be there. It is a true Valhalla for aviation.

Afterword

by PAUL E. GARBER,
Historian Emeritus, NASM

When I learned that our Museum's facility for the preservation and restoration of flightcraft was to be identified henceforth with my name, I was surprised. Why me? I thought of other persons who might have been so honored, those in high places whose administration, planning, and decisions had been of critical value in the advancement of our Institution. But as my thoughts whirled from person to person, my informant interrupted me to say, "Yes, it's you."

It is understandable that I should think of other names associated with the Smithsonian. First and foremost is that of our founder, James Smithson, who, beset by loneliness and resentment, planned a generous bequest to America whereby he predicted ". . . my name shall live in memory of man." True—his name graces our entire establishment. Other people have been generous in their donations with the understanding that their names would identify their buildings. They planned it that way. I didn't. Thus I was the more surprised when I was told about the Paul E. Garber Facility.

I cherished the honor although difficult to understand. It's like a beautiful airplane: as you admire its form and flight, you don't take out a computer to try to calculate its wing loading and power loading, nor to analyze its capacity or aerodynamic features. Whether it is in the air, at an airport, in a museum or restoration facility, you just admire it. So it is with this honor that I have received. I accept it in humble gratitude.

As with the airplane, I think of the ways in which my efforts have advanced or made better known the story of flight, mankind's most efficient means of transportation. Airplanes are more than things. They are the embodiment of human minds and skills; and as I study the history of flight, I revere the people who have brought it to its present marvelous advancement.

In one way I can concede that my name does have a place in the history of the aircraft shops at the Smithsonian. I began my career here in a shop. I have always enjoyed working with my hands. I admire mechanisms. I save tools the way some zealots save stamps—I think of tools as an extension of a person's mind and hands. Starting here on June 1, 1920, I was entitled "Preparator," one who repairs and prepares Museum material. The unit I worked with then was the Division of Mechanical Technology in the Department of Arts and Industries of the National Museum. My shop was on the top floor of the northeast pavilion of the Arts and Industries Building. When I applied for the job, the incumbent was Luther Reed, who had been one of the principal mechanics and carpenters for Dr. Samuel Pierpont Langley. Langley was the third secretary of the Smithsonian, from 1887 to 1906, and was a renowned astronomer and aviation pioneer. Reed had worked on the Aerodrome models, and the full-size aircraft, as well as the engines for each. He launched the famous model flight of May 6, 1896, which covered a distance of about 3,000 feet, surpassing the best efforts of

Paul Garber, Historian Emeritus of the National Air and Space Museum, explains some details of his first love, the Wright Flyer, to visiting members of the Civil Air Patrol.

any other experiments with models by about ten times. I had first met Mr. Reed as a boy when I came to his shop with two school chums who had access behind the scenes, being sons of a regent of the Smithsonian. Later, I went there because of his always friendly welcome. I enjoyed hearing his recollections of Dr. Langley and the aerodromes.

In Luther Reed's day, there was no Social Security. A person who had no savings or independent income had to keep working in order to live. Soon after Luther Reed worked his last day, I started. It was an honor to use tools he had handled. I worked on all forms of mechanical devices. Occasionally when I was making a repair to one of the Langley Aerodromes, I would go over to Langley's old shop, which was then just about as he had left it. There was a better lathe there than the one I used, which was my own, rotated by foot power. Also there was a rich supply of the same tubing and hardware and wood that re-

mained from Langley's time. Thus my repairs were the more authentic.

That shop was in a two-story building on the south side of the "castle." Two of Langley's other mechanics, Mr. Cole and Mr. Kramer, still worked there, making and repairing instruments for the Astrophysical Observatory, which Langley had started and his successor, Dr. Abbot, continued. There I also met Mr. Charles Manly, who had been engineering assistant to Dr. Langley. Manly identified engine castings and other equipment for my accessioning for Museum records. In later years I tried to have the shop preserved as a Langley Memorial, but I had no support from those who made the decisions. Turned down on that, I did rescue as much as I could that remained.

Thus, through me, work on aircraft at the Smithsonian is perpetuated from Langley's Aerodrome shop to my mechanical-technology shop to the current shop in our facility. It is a historic sequence.

On the day when I was to receive this honor, June 3, 1980, I was thinking of the many Museum associates who deserved to share the occasion with me. I didn't have much time to prepare a formal acceptance speech. The morning, when I had hoped to do so, was taken over by a persistent writer who wanted a Museum story for her paper. Finally, when she left, I went down to the basement and into my car where there is no telephone. I began listing names that might precede the word "Facility" and soon had several dozen. I wondered how I could arrange them most creditably, and finally decided that alphabetical order would be impartial. In a short time I filled all twenty-six slots. Ever since then I keep recalling names I could have added—this facility is by no means a one-man project.

I have special admiration for the crew. Everyone is a superb craftsman. (We also have an excellent craftswoman.) Some are artists, too. Look at the beauty of the "paint job" on our aircraft, the fidelity with which original colors are reproduced, insignia are copied, and precise lettering and numbering, the accurate placement of decorative or identifying details. Beneath those exteriors every unit of the structure is authentic to the day of its first flight. In the hands of our artisans, the historic and technically significant aircraft and spacecraft become alive again.

Years ago, when we were discussing the restoration of a "basket case," one of the crew asked: "Paul, how far do we go with this restoration?" I replied: "Make it so I could fly it and you'd go for the ride." That was the precept when I was in the Postal Air Mail Service. Of course we don't fly our Museum aircraft, but our crew knows every detail of what is necessary for airworthiness, and how to do the work. There are none better in the world. Among the many reasons why I am proud to be associated with our facility, the principal one is my esteem for the men and women who work there.

My elevation in this world of flight is due to two fortunate circumstances. First is my interest in aviation, which began in 1909. This interest has advanced because aviation itself has advanced tremendously; my career has been lifted by the wings of aeronautical progress.

Second is my association with a marvelous Institution which, also during my time, has progressed from a few hundred employees, several buildings and some exhibits to several thousand employees, ten buildings on the Mall, plus three uptown, the Zoo, and more. The exhibits in our National Air and Space Museum alone have attracted more than 50 million visitors since it was opened. Again, my advancement has been lifted by associated progress.

At our facility this same relationship and personal advancement applies. The Act of Congress which in 1946 gave aeronautics a separate status in the Smithsonian authorized us to make recommendations to Congress for a suitable site and building. But first we had to preserve what we were acquiring. Our collection has increased greatly due to accessions of aircraft related to World War II. The Air Force had brought their significant aircraft to Park Ridge, Illinois, the site of O'Hare Inter-

Even though his greatest fondness is for aircraft, Garber understands very well the accomplishments of the space age.

Paul Garber in communion with his greatest coup, the *Spirit of St. Louis*. Garber initiated the request from the Smithsonian for the airplane before Lindbergh had landed in Paris.

national Airport; the Navy's aircraft were mostly in Norfolk, Virginia. But the Korean War had started, and space was needed in both locations. I had to find some place for our "treasures." No warehouses were available anywhere, yet even outdoor storage was better in the Washington area than in sub-zero Chicago or near-ocean Norfolk.

After much searching I finally found the 21 acres that we now occupy at Silver Hill. I was grateful to the Park and Planning Commission when they showed it to me on the map and agreed to lend it. When I first went there and walked around, the tree-filled "wilderness" was just about as the Indians had known it, and my only companions were the bull frogs and mocking birds. The way we scrounged for free help and the cooperation of Smithsonian personnel is a classic in procurement, saddened by the lasting injury to one of our crew, whose unique ingenuity and capabilities could not be replaced. During this difficult period, an assis-

tant curator was recalled to active duty in the Navy, and two other employees were "riffed." I was working from 8 to 10—that's A.M. to P.M.

During the intervening thirty years, and with gratitude to many persons, we have become the world's outstanding facility for the preservation, restoration, and preparation for display of the finest collection of aircraft.

I have many cherished recollections of flightcraft and their pilots and designers as I walk through the Museum and the facility. Mentally nodding in recognition of these memories, I feel the same reverence as in a genuflection. Let's choose one at random. My first visit to the Smithsonian was in about 1912: I entered the Arts and Industries Building. The North Hall was filled with mahogany cases containing the memorabilia of famous Americans. Nearly every center diaphragm was topped by a jeweled sword. I was drawn to the chess set of General McClellan because my Civil War grandfather was an expert player and I had inherited his interest. I went from case to case, and then to the center of the building, where in a pool on a hemispheric pedestal was the plaster cast of the statue of Freedom, which in bronze adorns the pinnacle of the Capitol. As I turned to the right, I gasped. There was suspended the very plane which I had seen flown by Orville Wright for military demonstrations at Fort Myer, Virginia. It was about as high from the floor as when it had flown over my head on the drill field.

In the Museum, I relished the view of it from all angles, and then hurried up the steps to the balcony so that I could see it at wing level. On the other side of the balcony some visitors were strolling along. They were arguing about which way it flew, the elevator being in front and propellers in the rear, which was opposite to the usual locations. They decided it went "that-a-way." I called across the hall to correct them. They asked how I knew. I told them I had seen it fly.

From then on during my many boyhood visits, that airplane was my principal magnet. No visit was complete without a loving look and a thrilling recollection. When I began my career at the Smithsonian, my next stop, after leaving the official who among other duties was in charge of personnel, was to head straight for the Wright Military Flyer. As I thanked it for stimulating my employment, I again saw some visitors discussing which way it flew.

So one of my first jobs after I had completed my initial assignment was to make a mannekin to put in the pilot's seat so visitors could *see* which way it flew. I made a wooden frame and padded it for the contours of a seated person, got a plaster head and hands from the sculptor

Paul Garber and the Wright Flyer. The mannikin of Wilbur on the wing of the Flyer is dressed in clothing Garber himself used to wear.

A quiet day in the Museum. Paul still walks through the galleries, stopping to chat with delighted passers-by.

in the Department of Archaeology, dressed the figure with parts of my World War I uniform and my spare shoes, topped him off with a football helmet which is what pilots wore in those days, and then, rigging up some pulleys and lines, hoisted him and myself to the level of the airplane. I swung us over to the two seats, which were not much more than boards on the entering edge of the lower wing. After I finally got him seated comfortably with his feet on the crossbar, hands on the control levers, and head posed at an alert angle, I took a few minutes for retrospection. I thought: "Orville sat there, and Lieutenant Lahm sat there. When Orville pulled this lever, the airplane climbed, and when he pulled or pushed those other levers, the aircraft was balanced or turned." I mentally recalled the flight I had seen, and having soloed myself about a year before that, made a few comparisons between the Jenny and this Flyer. Then I awoke from my daydreaming and decided I should get back to my shop.

As I reached out for the pulley line and board so that I could let myself down to the floor, a little child called out: "Oh, look, Mamma. That other dummy's moving!" And I'd best move on with this Afterword.

Going back again to that alphabetical list of associates recited at the name-changing celebration in 1980, I had no difficulty in selecting a person for the first letter. Dr. Charles Greely Abbot had been the key figure in arranging with Orville Wright for the return of the "Kitty Hawk Flyer" to America. Dr. Abbot also had recognized the terminology of genius in a letter received from a Massachusetts scientist who believed that he could develop a means for raising instruments or even men to higher elevations than could be attained by balloons. Dr. Abbot recommended financial support for the writer, Dr. Robert Hutchings Goddard. With Smithsonian sponsorship, the first successful launching of a liquid-fuel rocket was accomplished.

The Albatros D Va, a German fighter from World War I, was saved from destruction by Paul's efforts. He found that it was dilapidated and slated for use as a toy in a children's park. With his usual tenacity, he ferreted out the owner and wheedled him into donating it to the Museum. Today, it is one of two remaining Albatros fighters in the world.

Garber uses three pencils to illustrate the three axes of flight. The Wright brothers' realization that control had to be effected in all three axes made their eventual success certain.

Nor did I have any hesitancy in naming a person for the second letter—Walter Boyne. Through his ability to work with other efficient personnel, his knowledge of the history of flight and the mechanics of aviation and space technology, and the same inherent drive and ingenuity that earned his promotion in the Air Force from private to colonel and the accumulation of several thousand hours as a pilot, Walter Boyne embodied the ability to initiate and advance many improvements in our facility. He was closely associated with the decision to change its name, and has honored me further by asking me to write this Afterword. I know that all of you will enjoy his book and benefit from reading it.

Index